Scenic Crossroads
The History of
Wayne

By Richard K. Cacioppo, J.D.

Tercentennial of Settlement, Sesquicentennial of Township
Dual Anniversary Edition
Dream City Publishing Company
Wayne, New Jersey

township of wayne

475 Valley Road
Wayne, New Jersey 07470-3586
Internet: www.WayneTownship.com
(973) 694-1800
FAX: (973) 694-8136

Office of the Mayor
David Waks

November 25, 1998

Dear Members of the Wayne Lions Club:

It is with pleasure that I write to you, and to the author Richard Cacioppo, to express my congratulations and profound thanks for providing us with "Scenic Crossroads--The History of Wayne."

We have a lot to be proud of. Our residents have made significant contributions to our community and to our Nation over the past three centuries. We are a good community in which to live and to raise our children, and one principal reason for that is the rich tradition of volunteerism in Wayne Township. We are fortunate to be the home of fine organizations like the Wayne Lions Club.

The Wayne Lions Club has served Wayne Township and other communities for four decades. The Lions have helped many people in time of need, with free eye examinations, eye glasses, food and other assistance, scholarships for worthy students, and other fund raising events to support charities and civic organizations such as the Foundation for the Handicapped, our five Volunteer Fire Companies, our Volunteer First Aid Squad, and of course, our Public Library.

It is my pleasure to thank the Wayne Lions Club for yet another service to the Township, the presentation of this fine publication. I am sure that we will read and re-read our story for many years to come. Thank you all so very much.

With best wishes,

Sincerely

DAVID WAKS
Mayor

DW/bt

AN EQUAL OPPORTUNITY EMPLOYER

Cover: The Schuyler-Colfax House, circa 1696

Contents

Preface and Reader's Guide

One hundred and fifty years ago Wayne Township was formed. It was ironically incorporated on the 150th anniversary of its settlement. (While founder Arent Schuyler is believed to have built his still-standing residence in 1696, records uncovered set the date he became an official resident as 1698).

The primary purposes of writing and publishing this work are to Recognize, Reconstruct, Revisit, Celebrate and Preserve the roots of one of New Jersey's most historic communities, Wayne Township. We trust that along the way the reader will be both educated and entertained. Never before has there been such a comprehensive look back at the region that has been called Wayne for the last 150 years. For some, this book will be a startling revelation. Even many longtime residents do not realize just how historic their community is. For whatever reasons, Wayne is rarely mentioned in the same breath with Princeton, Mount Holly, Morristown, Burlington and an assortment of other widely recognized historic communities of similar size. This book is intended to demonstrate just how historic Wayne (and the other names the present Township area has been known as) is.

While this presentation contains more information about local history than ever before published in a single volume, it is not meant to be an encyclopedia. For this reason, we have included a *Worth Reading* segment for those who are inspired to learn more about the Township. It is strongly recommended that the books, articles and other references mentioned in these segments be purchased or borrowed and read, as we have only been able to touch the tip of the proverbial iceberg. Others have labored long and hard to dig out and preserve Wayne's truly amazing and diverse history, and their efforts are certainly worth exploring.

Despite the fact that this work is filled with thousands of facts and hundreds of anecdotes, historic maps, photographs and drawings, many never before published, it is presented in a manner that is reader-friendly. It can be used for someone looking for just a good read, or as the perfect starting point for the serious researcher. It can be read cover-to-cover as a story, or by opening virtually any page in between for tens of short essays and nearly 300 informative, captioned illustrations.

Any story can be told in numerous ways. This is particularly true with a community history. An author of a historical work must choose among various alternative methods. In our approach to this story, we have elected to emphasize physical structures, landscapes and major events, with less stress on genealogies and government. Wayne is more a confederation of several individual communities or regions than the traditional New Jersey town. It is roughly divided into the following geographical regions: Pompton Falls, Old Wayne, Mountain View, Upper Preakness Valley, Lower Preakness Valley, Pines Lake, Packanack Lake, and even (north) Singac.

For those who want a teaser, we suggest you refer to the *Historical Spotter's Guide* on the back page. It provides a thumbnail reference of a number of the most historically significant remnants. Some are easy to find, and still much the way they looked during their heyday. Others will take a true *Historical Detective* to find.

The individual chapters are intended to give the reader a general feel for the development of each major area and era in Wayne's history during each phase of their development, before and after the Township was formed in 1847. In almost every chapter are various *Historical Highlights*. These are more in depth looks at the thirty or so people, places, things and events that we felt deserved special attention. At the end of the book are two supplements that are designed for the reader who seeks even more detailed information. The *Place and Name Word Guide* at the end of the book contains the etymology, alternatives and various different spellings of the names used over the last 300 years of regions, major streets, rivers, mountains and other popular things and places.

Every effort has been made to be accurate in our portrayal. However, since this is the first book written

about the full 300 year history of what we now call Wayne, much of the source material was available in a puzzle we had to piece together. Whenever documentary evidence could be obtained to confirm a fact, it was. Things that could be double or triple checked were. However, often the information reported on came from individual sources, be they single works, documents, personal interviews or maps. The author was forced to accept much of the information derived from these sources as accurate. Most of it probably was, but some may not have been. When we came upon information that seemed to be true, and was par ticularly interesting, but its authenticity could not be satisfactorily confirmed, we indicated the source was a rumor or recollection.

No community history going back over four centuries can be anywhere near complete. Without a doubt, unknowingly and unintentionally, we have failed to mention countless persons, places, things and events of some significance in the long history of Wayne. While we apologize for the oversight, in most cases the omissions could not be avoided. However, we are confident the great majority of readers of this book will find what we have uncovered and written about good reading.

Acknowledgements

Any undertaking such as this requires the assistance and cooperation of literally hundreds of participants. From Wayne to Trenton to Washington, D.C. hundreds of helpful individuals, entities and agencies contributed to The History of Wayne. The author gratefully acknowledges the following for their help and contributions:

Wayne Historical Commission, Wayne Public Library, Wayne Township Clerk, Chuck Snyder of the Wayne Department of Parks and Recreation, Acting Director Andy Slik of the Passaic County Historical Society, Passaic County Register Jerry DeStafano and his staff, Passaic County Bridge Engineer Aura Mayer, National Archives and Records Administration, United States Library of Congress, Brian Carey and the National Park Service of the United States Department of Interior, Richard Weingraff, unofficial historian of the United States Department of Transportation Federal Highway Administration, National Cartographic Information Center, United States Board on Geographic Names, Federal Highway Administration of United States Department of Transportation, The Smithsonian Institution's National Museum of American History's Division of Roads, National Trust For Historic Preservation, New Jersey State Archives, New Jersey State Library, New Jersey Historic Preservation Office, New Jersey Geological Survey, New Jersey Department of Transportation, New Jersey Historical Society, Paris Cuniglio New Jersey Department of Environmental Protection, Newark Public Library, Pat Riley, Historian of the Aviation Hall of Fame and Museum of New Jersey, Special Collections and University Archives of Rutgers University's Alexander Library, National Railroad Historic Reference Center, Thomas Taber, Curt Carlough and Tim Stuy, President of the New Jersey Midland Railroad Historical Society, Erie-Lackawanna Historical Society, Montclair Public Library, Montclair Historical Society, Cedar Grove Public Library, Caldwell Public Library, Essex Fells Public Library, Roseland Public Library, Verona Public Library, Little Falls Public Library, Pequannock Public Library, Pompton Lakes Einstein Public Library, Bergen County Historical Society, President Bob Barth, Frank Mentone and the New Jersey Canal Society, William Paterson University's Office of Public Information, Packanack Lake Country Club and Community Association, Pines Lake Association, Gregory Schwalenberg, Curator of the Babe Ruth Museum and Hall of Fame, Bill Roady, Howie Ungermach, Richard Wild, Mr. and Mrs. George Kuehm, Joe Hanan, Lynn Dunkerly, Bernie and Ellen Rosen, Anna Mae Conlon, Richard Wild, Donald Kuser and Dave Chernick.

Special recognition is due to the following:

Cele Paccioretti, Curator of the Wayne Museum, who so generously and patiently assisted the author on a score of occasions, without whom this book would not have been possible. Dr. William Brubaker, President of the Wayne Township Historical Commission, who not only answered many questions, but took his precious time to duplicate tens of photos used in this publication, Marcia Sills, probably the single most knowledgeable person on Wayne's history, who filled in most of the cracks.   Bob Craig of the New Jersey Trust for Historic Preservation, who provided invaluable background information and research guidance. George Sellmer, Editor of The Highlander, official publication of the New Jersey Highlands Historical Society, who took a personal interest providing the author with countless facts about the Morris Canal and Pompton Feeder. Mark Schiffer, Director, Passaic County Board of Social Services for use of his wonderful historic post card collection. Donald E. Bender and the New Jersey Missile Site Survey provided photographs and consultation about the Nike sites in Wayne. Harold "Timer" Peer, who contributed numerous pictures and facts and provided invaluable insight into the archeology of Wayne. Joan Springwaldt for some of the photographs and information about Al Henn's Tavern. Helen and C.W. Dittig, for the photographs and information about the Van Ammens' farm and C.W.'s great map of old State Route 23. Harry Sylvester, a member of the Lions Club took some of the color photographs that help punctuate the book. Ken Rosellini, a young lawyer of immense talent, for his skillful legal research and patient proof-reading, along with brother Ron who not only helped solicit sponsors, but assisted in a myriad of research, photo taking and overall assistance. Their father Mario, played an enormous part in bringing in the Lions Club and helping us proofread the manuscript.

The foregoing individuals and organizations strongly contributed to the research, writing and proofreading of this book, however, it would have never been published without the assistance of a whole new group of dedicated people. The Wayne Lions Club jumped aboard this project and made it come to final fruition. Their special committee headed by Robert Kievit and ably assisted by Robert Jelderks and Edward Lenczak picked up the slack when business sponsors were few and far between and made things happen. This book was too long and too good a project not to eventually be published. Two very special people stepped in when it appeared it might take far longer than anyone realized to published this book---Charles Tumminello and Joseph Hallock. Mr. Tumminello, owner and President of Mark Lithography, our magnificent printer, and also a Lion, took on this job as a pet project. He and his company guaranteed a princely job for a pauperly price, and went well above and beyond the call of duty.

Mr. Hallock, a long time Lion and outstanding lawyer, deserves extra, extra special acknowledgement and thanks. He not only guaranteed the necessary funds for printing, but spent many long hours working closely with the author in proofreading the manuscript, over and over again, a job that took a great amount of time, skill and enormous patience. The author, publisher, Lions Club, the citizens of Wayne and certainly every reader who will enjoy this book, hopefully for generations, owes Mr. Hallock a particularly special "thank you."

And then there are our co-sponsors. A book of this undertaking is not only a time-consuming, but enormously expensive undertaking. Therefore a very special gratitude is owed the business and personal co-sponsors whose ads and messages are scattered throughout the book, not only by the author and publisher, but by every reader who enjoys the work.   We ask that you return the favor by patronizing those businesses and thank those individuals and families whose ads and messages appear in this book.

Words and Phrases......
An Explanation

A few clarifications are in order before delving into the following pages:

First and foremost should be an explanation of exactly what geographic area we are alluding to which we almost uniformly refer to as Wayne. 1997 has been the sesquicentennial of Wayne Township, formed 150 years ago in 1847. Yet this book is published both in commemoration of this anniversary, as well as the tercentennial of the settling of this same basic area before it attained its present moniker. As will be discussed below, before Wayne was Wayne the present Township boundaries were part of three larger townships. There has always been a great deal of confusion as to the boundaries of present day Wayne. Even many historians have referred to portions of the area squarely within Wayne Township proper as Pompton, Pompton Plains, Pequannock and even Totowa. For example, the Historic American Building Survey (HABS), which the National Parks Service administered beginning in 1939 as part of President Franklin D. Roosevelt's Works Project Administration (WPA), lists Wayne's oldest home (see cover) as being in Pompton. Without question, the most famous of all Wayne landmarks is George Washington's 1780 headquarters, the Dey mansion. Its location is frequently listed as part of present-day Totowa. While it may not always be technically accurate, for the sake of consistency all references to Wayne are to that area within the present Township boundaries.

There are numerous places and things within the Township that are frequently referred to by other than their technical or legal names. The best example is that of the Pompton, Pequannock and Ramapo Rivers. Throughout history their names have often been used interchangeably. The same is sometimes true of the mountains within the Township. Preakness Mountain and Second Watchung Mountain are occasionally interchanged in referring to one or the other. For the most part, we refer to the present technical and legal term for the place or thing. Other times we elected to refer to a name which when the reference was made was accurate, if for a short period of time. For example, Valley Road was once called Parsonage Road. Another example is the western portion of Alps Road was originally called Prospect Road.

Other times, in the case of street names, what was technically a correct name in one community was legally named something else in another town. It really depended on where the map or document referring to the particular byway was created. In Wayne one of the earliest names of present-day Terhune Drive (Route 202) was The Road to The Ponds. A map made in The Ponds (Oakland/Franklin Lakes) probably referred to the very same route as The Road to Wayne (actually The Road to Pompton, which was the name generally given to northwestern Wayne, Pompton Lakes, Pompton Plains and Pequannock). In this work we have attempted to generally use the most popular, present-day name used by Wayne residents.

Another confusing aspect of place and thing names was the spelling. Many names, particularly those of Dutch or Indian derivation, have been spelled in many different ways. Pequannock, Passaic and Preakness are the best examples of such diversity. This can be explained in a number of ways. One is that something was lost in the translation from the native Indian or Dutch language to English. Another is that the translator was not necessarily well schooled in either his or her native or second language. A corruption of Dutch, Indian or some other foreign tongue is more often the rule than the exception. And speaking of the term Indian, it is no longer politically correct. With all due respect to those who prefer themselves to be called Native Americans, we use the long popular term "Indian." (To be technical, the Lenni Lenape were neither Indians nor Native Americans, as their ancestors were believed to have traveled here from Asia {and probably Africa before that}).

Many of the foregoing mistakes, misunderstandings and multi- and misinterpretations were eliminated

when the places and things began to receive official recognition. Early in the 18th century road commissions were established, and later in that century the present day system of municipalities was adopted. So called *official recognition* certainly helped unify and more accurately identify the names of places and things, but since Wayne was primarily rural well into the 20th century, there were far less places and things officially recognized than older urban areas like its neighbor Paterson. Nevertheless, here again we attempted to use the most widely used present name or term.

Rather than take up space discussing the derivations and translations, and some cases history, of many names of significance in Wayne over the last three centuries (or more), we've elected to include the *Place and Name Word Guide* in the back of the book. There the reader will find the etymology of some of the most popular words and phrases along with some different ways each has been spelled over the years.

Worth Reading

The following books are among those used to research Scenic Crossroads-The History of Wayne and are suggested for any readers who seek more detailed information of the general subjects included in this work.

The Archaeology of Wayne by Edward J. Lenik (1985)
A History of Little Falls, Centennial Edition by Robert R. Beckwith (1968)
A Wondrously Beautiful Valley by Robert M. Brubaker, Anne Brubaker Burns and Gratia Mahony (1976)
From Indian Trails to Iron Horse by Wheaton J. Lane (1939)
The Glory of Montclair, Past and Present by Richard K. Cacioppo (1995)
The Indians of New Jersey by M.R. Harrington (1938)
Historic American Buildings Survey of New Jersey by William B. Bassett (1977)
Historic American Building Survey, National Park Service, U.S. Department of Interior
Historic American Engineering Survey, National Park Service, U.S. Department of Interior
Historic Pequannock Township by Emil R. Salvini (1987)
Historic Tour of Wayne Township (1987) by Barbara Luisia Olsen
History of the Explosives Industry in America by Arthur Pine Van Gelder and Hugo Schlatter (1926)
The History of Bergen and Passaic Counties by William Nelson (1884)
Land Use In Early New Jersey, A Historical Geography by Peter O. Wacker and Paul G.E. Clemens (1995)
The Morris Canal, A Photographic History by James Lee, 1994 Reprint
The National Gazetteer of the United States of America, New Jersey, 1983 prepared by U.S. Board on
         Geographic Names
North Jersey Country Club, Celebrating 100 Years by William L. Quirin (1995)
Passaic River and Its Environs by W. Wooward Clayton, assisted by William Nelson (1891)
The Passaic Valley, New Jersey, In Three Centuries by John Whitehead (1901)
Paterson & Passaic County, An Illustrated History by J. Palmer Murphy and Margaret Murphy (1987)
Paterson State College, A History 1855-1966, Kenneth B. White (1966)
Preakness and the Preakness Reformed Church. Volume 1 by George W. Labaw (1902); Volume 2 by
         Albert A. Smith (1990)
Reminiscences by Julius Howard Pratt (1910)
The Singack and Mead's Basin Brickyards in Wayne Township by Charles S. Jackson (1978)
New Jersey, A Guide to Its Past and Present by the Work Projects Administration (1939)
         reprinted as The WPA Guide to 1930's New Jersey by Rutgers University Press (1986)
The Van Riper-Hopper House by Charles S. Jackson (1973)
This is New Jersey by John T. Cunningham, 1997
Under the Sign of the Eagle by William Berce (1964)

Introduction
Why Wayne?

This 1960 photograph taken above the southwestern portion of the Township shows Wayne's proximity to the isle of Manhattan in the distance and helps explain its historical importance. The intersection of U.S. 46 and Riverview Drive and the old Totowa Drive-In can be seen in the lower right hand portion of the photo.

The all-too-typical response I received from research assistants as close as right here in Wayne to as far away as the Library of Congress in Washington, D.C. when I indicated I was writing a book on Wayne was, "Why Wayne?" The project started after it became apparent that despite what appeared on the surface to be a community with at least a modicum of interesting history, there was virtually no comprehensive work ever penned. At least none in a single volume.

In 1902 Pastor George Warne Labaw wrote a history of his church and the nearby area entitled *Preakness and the Preakness Reformed Church.* It included a very interesting study of the early settlement of the area, particularly the Preakness Valley, but most of the book was devoted to the genealogy of families of the area's earliest European inhabitants, and the church itself. His work was updated 88 years later by one of his successors on the pulpit, the late Albert A. Smith.

Reverend Smith included a short segment entitled *The Local Scene* at the beginning of each chapter, but most of the book was largely dedicated to the history of the parsonages between Reverend Labaw's and his own.

In 1964, what is largely recognized by local historians as the classic history book on Wayne was written by William Berce as part of Wayne's participation of the 300th anniversary of the State of New Jersey. *Under the Sign of the Eagle* was obviously exhaustively researched and is an extremely well written account of the settlement of the Wayne area, and particularly its role in the Revolutionary War. However, other than a few short essays on a number of selected more modern topics, Mr. Berce's book barely touches the 19th, much less the 20th century. In fact, in his Preface the author acknowledges that his story represents "the first phase" of the Township's history, as he suggests the second "or modern" phase be a "project for a future date."

In 1976, the Township's Bicentennial Committee published a booklet written by Dr. Robert M. Brubaker, presently chairperson of the Wayne Historical Commission, Anne Brubaker Burns and Gratia Mahony. It provided a historical glimpse of Wayne in the 17th through 20th centuries.

We've taken the liberty of borrowing the title of that work, *A Wondrously Beautiful Valley*, for the heading of our first chapter on the geology of the Township.

These works were supplemented by a series of short books, reports and articles on more specific subjects written by other local historians and experts. Probably the two most prolific writers on local history have been Charles S. Jackson and Edward J. Lenik. Mr. Jackson nicely covered the Township's brick industry in his 1978 short book which he called *The Singack and Mead's Basin Brickyards*. Mr. Lenik, a noted local archaeologist, has arguably done more digging into Wayne's past than any other individual. As head of the the Township's Archaeological Research Laboratory and Member of the Wayne Historical Commission, he has written countless in depth articles and reports on a wide variety of topics. They range from the Pompton Furnace to his findings relating to the first true inhabitants of the region, the Indians. Unfortunately, only his 1985 book *The Archaeology of Wayne* has been published and made available to the general public. It provides great insight in the so-called *Original People*.

After reading through each of these books and articles, and the magnificent, largely undiscovered historical treasures stored in the research department of the Wayne Township Museum in the Van Riper-Hopper House on Berdan Avenue in Upper Preakness Valley, it was evident that Wayne in fact had a very intriguing and exciting history that needed to be told. More important it had a history that should be shared with all members of the general public who might even have the slightest interest. Here are some of the answers to Why Wayne?:

Wayne has a long, exciting and significant history.

Wayne includes some of the most beautiful landscape found anywhere.

Wayne topography and resources were vital to America's fight for independence.

Wayne has played host to numerous historical luminaries such as the Marquis de La Fayette, Benedict Arnold, Alexander Hamilton, and of course George Washington.

Wayne was perhaps the most important stopping point along the legendary Morris Canal.

Wayne was one of the favorite hunting and fishing areas for the Lenni-Lenape Indians, and their predecessors, perhaps going back as far as 10,000 years ago.

Wayne was the eastern gateway to the New Jersey Highlands and its iron mines, forges, furnaces and bloomeries used to build the infrastructure of America's earliest and greatest cities.

Wayne was the site of the broadcast of the Voice of America during World War II.

Wayne was one of the favorite hangouts of the great Babe Ruth.

Wayne's Preakness Valley was the namesake of the winner of the first running of the oldest of thoroughbred horse racing's Triple Crown, as well as the stakes race itself.

Wayne was home of one of New Jersey's first three and busiest airports.

Wayne's still standing oldest home was built in the same century when European explorers first set foot on New Jersey soil.

Wayne at the turn of this century was considered one of the New York metropolitan area's, as well as the State of New Jersey's, premiere vacation destinations.

Three important rivers, two major railroad lines, portions of the state's major Indian trail, two of the longest and most important New Jersey turnpikes, as well as the legendary Revolutionary Highway and Cannonball Run all passed through Wayne.

Wayne is filled with scores of Dutch farmhouses, Colonial and Victorian buildings, steel and stone bridges, numerous waterfalls, picturesque lagoons and swamps, remnants of the last Ice Age, Indians caves and trails, a 300+ year old iron mine, miles of beautiful, wooded trails, one magnificent bird sanctuary and almost too many lakes, streams, ponds, and brooks to count.

That's Why Wayne!

Richard K. Cacioppo
Wayne Township, New Jersey
September 4, 1997

Chapter One
A Wondrously Beautiful Valley

In many communities the land is simply incidental to the history and being of the town. In Wayne it is, and always has been of paramount importance. It was the nature of the topography that drew Arent Schuyler of New York here in the 17th century on his way to meet with the Indian tribal chiefs on Minisink Island in the Delaware to help quell rumors of possible uprisings incited by the French. It was the beauty of the land which convinced him to make it his home. It was the richness of the land which helped him make his fortune.

Virtually every major event during Wayne's recorded history can be attributed in some respect to the configuration and topography of the land which the Township is situated upon.

New Jersey is divided into four major geological subdivisions, all running in a southwest to northeast direction. The Coastal Plain stretches out over three-fifths of the state, its western boundary running between Trenton and Staten Island. All of south Jersey is included in it, as well as the famous Pine Barrens. Another fifth of the state is a narrow plain of wide valleys and low-rounded hills known as the Piedmont. The Palisades of the Hudson (nee North) River mark its eastern boundary. Included in it are the marshes of the Hackensack and Passaic Rivers. The third belt, the Highlands, includes the Appalachian Mountains. This area ranges from ten to twenty five miles wide, with an average elevation of about 1,000 feet above sea level. Finally, the Appalachian Valley lies on the extreme northwestern portion of the state. It is subdivided between the broad Kittatinny and Upper Delaware Valleys, separated by Kittatinny Mountain which rises to the highest point in New Jersey, over 1800 feet at High Point along State Route 23 near where New York, Pennsylvania and New Jersey meet.

Wayne lies on the Piedmont, on the border of the Highlands. When Schuyler first passed through it along a major branch of the Minisink Trail, he was

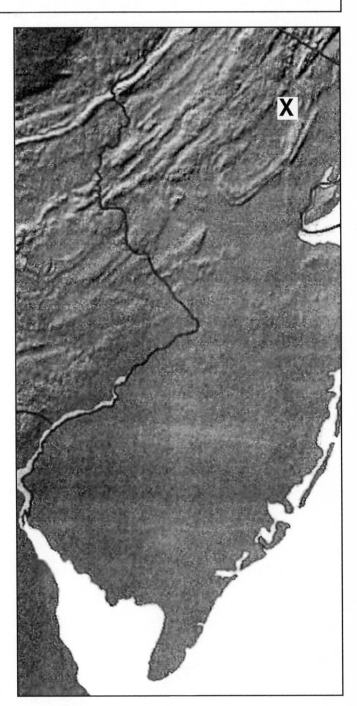

Wayne is located where the Piedmont Plain meets the New Jersey Highlands, explaining why it has such a varied landscape. 200 million year old mountains, carved by the massive glaciers tens of thousands of years ago, have resulted in the land evolving into the way it is today.

Ancient Lake Passaic covered much of the area to the southwest of Wayne 15,000 years ago. The Township was once lakefront property.

apparently inspired by both its beauty and the potential riches it appeared to hold. When he returned to New York he described Pompton as a "wondrously beautiful valley," fed by crystal-clear brooks and wide streams, sheltered pasture land, Indian orchards and cultivated fields for the raising of corn, tobacco, beans and squash. He noticed the presence of heavy stone implements used by the Indians, leading him to believe that there might have been local deposits of valuable minerals.

The "crystal-clear brooks and wide streams" of course included the three major rivers that bordered Wayne on the west and south. The Pequannock flowed from present day Sussex County where it met with the Wanaque in Pompton Plains just west of northern Wayne, before joining the Ramapo flowing down from Rockland County, New York and becoming the Pompton River, just north of Cross Pompton Plains Road. A few miles downstream at The Forks, now known as Two Bridges, the Pompton flows into the state's largest and greatest river, the Passaic. The Passaic begins near Mendham in Morris County, flows south and then north in a snake pattern until it rounds Paterson and then continues southeast until it enters Newark Bay. It is more than 90 miles long, despite the fact its mouth is located only about 25 miles from its terminus. Flowing into these rivers are many small to medium-sized streams, including the most noteworthy and important ones, the Singac and the Naachtpunkt which become one in Lower Preakness Valley near the Dey Mansion.

The middle of the three Watchung Mountain Ranges, Second Watchung Mountain helps form Wayne's eastern border. It seems to merge with Preakness Mountain in the extreme northeast portion of the Township just below High Mountain. Preakness Mountain runs northwest, separating Wayne from portions of North Haledon and Franklin Lakes. High Mountain which rises to 885 feet, is not only the highest point in Wayne, but in the three Watchung ranges. Sea weary sailors who arrived in America when transatlantic passages became routine, after a hard and rough journey were thrilled to see the first land color breaking the monotony of the deep ocean swell. What they saw was

The dam at Pompton Falls was built as early as 1726 to harness the hydro-electric power of the Ramapo River for the ironworks. However, the Indians, who called the cascade "Awarigh," hunted and fished here for thousands of years.

the crest of High Mountain. In virtually the center of Wayne is but another small mountain, the upside down "U" shaped Packanack Mountain, which with the mountains to the east form the Upper and Lower Preakness Valley.

What is geologically known as the Triassic Subdivision of the Piedmont Province was not always so mountainous. In fact, 300 million years ago Wayne was flat and swampy, mostly underwater and had a tropical climate. A sudden upheaval of the earth's crust caused the sedimentary rock to fold and distort, forming the Appalachians and the Wayne-area mountains. During the Triassic Period, a great basin was formed and over the course of several million years it was filled with sand and mud carried in by the rivers. Volcanic eruptions caused lava to flow over this concoction of muck, which hardened to form rock known as basalt. The process repeated itself numerous times, resulting in horizontal layers of sandstone, shale and basalt. During the Jurassic Period, 136-190 million years ago earthquakes occurred fracturing the rock and causing numerous faults in the landscape.

This active geologic phenomena has resulted in the land of northern New Jersey becoming rich in ores and minerals. In nearby Franklin, hundreds of different minerals have been mined, including one variety never found anywhere else on earth. Iron and copper filled the hills and mountains giving rise to the state's rise to prominence as the source of raw materials which allowed America to become the major industrial power it became in the 19th century.

Gradually the earth cooled significantly, leading to four known Pleistocene or Ice Ages. At least three directly affected the Wayne area, the last and probably most significant was called the *Wisconsin*. The massive Wisconsin Glacier rolled further south than any of the other three. It advanced south from Labrador and the Hudson Bay areas of Canada. The southern fringe of the great mass of ice came to rest about twenty miles south of Wayne along a line stretching from Perth Amboy as far west as Belvedere in Warren County alongside the Delaware River. This line is referred to as a terminal moraine. To this day ample evidence of the glacier is visible, including silt, fine soil, gravel and an uneven land surface.

About 15,000 years ago the Wisconsin Glacier began to melt. A huge lake was formed that stretched about 30 miles long by 20 miles wide, with an average depth of more than 200 feet. It followed the western slope of Second Watchung Mountain from Lower Preakness Valley south to near the point of the terminal moraine, west to Far Hills and north to a point above Morristown, and back to the original point. For several thousand years Lake Passaic was the largest lake in New Jersey.

The massive inland lake seemed to disappear in what amounted to a geologic moment. A large rock mass at what later was known as the Little Falls of the Passaic on the present border of Wayne and Little Falls had served as a giant plug in the lake. It suddenly gave way, causing the lake to drain and creating the second greatest waterfalls in the eastern United States, the Great Falls of the Passaic (aka the Totowa Falls). A smaller but similar lake formed and also disappeared

Pompton Lake borders Wayne and Pompton Lakes. It was enlarged, if not formed, when the original ironworks were built early in the 18th century.

several miles to the east. Neither lake ever fully dried up. The remnants of the smaller lake are now known as the Hackensack Highlands. The bed of Lake Passaic remains as the Great Swamp southwest of Wayne in Morris County, along with the Great Piece Meadows, Little Piece Meadows and Hetfield Swamps near where the Rockaway and Whippany Rivers flow into the Passaic west of Caldwell. In Wayne there are sporadic vestiges of the once-great lake as well, the largest being found mid-Township along the Pompton River. The marshes where the WABC and Voice of America tower once stood were part of the northern portion of the glacial body of water. So are the other small swamps found here and there in the Township.

Most of Wayne's streams and bodies of water trace their existence to the melting of the Wisconsin. However, the three largest lakes within the Township do not. At least not directly. A 1901 description of Wayne in a book entitled The Passaic Valley, New Jersey, In Three Centuries, written by John Whitehead describes the Township in part as follows:

> "It contains 17,107 acres, 96 of which
> are covered by water, 9,488 are cleared
> and 7,523 are still forest land."

It is obvious that this description does not include Pines Lake, Packanack Lake or even Lionshead Lake, the first two alone are each more than 96 acres. The reason, as discussed in a later chapter is that these were

man-made creations.

The geologic and climactic changes over thousands of millenniums have resulted in Wayne becoming a diverse and beautiful area. Few realize the beauty, much of it hidden out of sight of travelers along today's main streets and superhighways. For example, the first mile or so of the Pompton River after it is formed by the confluence of the Ramapo and Pequannock actually encompasses many miles of waterfront, streams, coves and small ponds. Few visit here, as the river is virtually hidden from the main streams of travel, and rarely navigated any more. Yet encompassed in this relatively small piece of Wayne are beautiful meadows, swamps and lagoons where relaxed waterfowl and a great variety of other animal life coexist in the bucolic landscape.

Wayne has never been extensively mined, other than for several stone quarries and the 1695 Iron Mine in the Glens area of Pines Lake featured below. That is except for the iron-rich clay that gave rise to the major brick industry that emerged here from the mid 19th to early 20th century. The clays found along the former northern shore line of Lake Passaic around Meads Basin (Mountain View) were the result of the combination of rock debris, crushed into a fine flour-like substance, and brought here by the Wisconsin Glacier. The clay at Singac was 10 to 15 feet below the surface.

Along the Passaic, just below where the river dropped hundreds of feet over a half mile cascade as it left Wayne at Little Falls, beautiful brownstone was quarried for decades. This stone was used to build and decorate many elaborate public and private buildings throughout the northeast, including the present Trinity Church at Wall Street and Broadway in Manhattan, built in the late 1840's. This stone was also used to build the two massive stone aqueducts in which the famous Morris Canal entered and left Wayne over the Pompton and Passaic Rivers.

In addition to the mountains and waters of the area, the beauty of the area that so astounded Arent Schuyler was of course also owed in large part to the colorful (most of the year) vegetation. It developed the way the Dutch explorer saw it in 1695 over fifteen millenniums following the retreat of the glacier, and gradual global warming. Spruce forest developed between

15,000 and 10,000 B.C., and later changed to pine and deciduous hardwoods. Gradually black, white and red oaks filled the woodlands, while typical trees found in the swamps included pine oak, red maple, ash, elm, silver maple, yellow birch, basswood, tulip, willow, sycamore and box elder. Higher elevations gave rise to chestnut, oak, sugar maple and hemlock. The Indians were proficient at growing corn, beans, squash, pumpkin, goosefoot, sunflower and a wide variety of herbs, and some fruit to supplement their diet of natural berries and nuts found throughout the area.

Where there is such lush vegetation, there is almost always a large animal population, and Wayne was no exception.   Nearly 400 species of wildlife have been identified here. They include 14 varieties of frog, 14 of salamanders, 8 of turtles, 2 of lizards, 15 of snakes, 268 of birds and 52 of mammals. The latter category included white-tailed bear, elk, black bear, turkey, raccoon, fox, mink, possum, weasel, beaver, rabbit, squirrel and ruffled grouse. Evidence has been found that wooly mammoths, collared lemming and caribou once roamed here, along with mastodon, ground sloths, giant moose, musk-ox, tapir, snowshoe hare, porcupine and other species of land animals.

There have been 87 species of fish reported to be in and bordering Wayne, including Atlantic salmon, trout, bass, carp, eel, suckers, catfish, sunfish, pickerel, herring and freshwater mussels.

It is no wonder that Schuyler fell in love with Pompton, but also why he was far from the first human to enjoy and profit by the land.

The Erie Railroad entered Wayne in the early 1870's, crossing the Passaic River at Singac, which referred to both sides of the river in earlier times. To the right (west), the Newark and Pompton Turnpike had been in existence since 1806. It was formerly part of the Wayne branch of the Minisink Trail, and one of the earlier Colonial roads in the Township.

Chapter Two
The Forgotten People

Perhaps the most visible evidence of the multi-millennium occupation of New Jersey by the Indians is the large boulders which can be seen in the Passaic River, just above the twin spans of Two Bridges. It is believed that the so-called natives may have erected a rope bridge between these rocks which served as a major crossing, connecting the Wayne branch of the Minisink Trail with the main branch in Morris County.

Call it white or European arrogance. Our school teachers really misinformed most of us in even hinting Columbus or Erickson discovered the New World. Or that John Cabot discovered North America. Or that Henry Hudson's men were the first humans to set foot on the shores of New Jersey. As a point of fact, archaeological findings lead to the conclusion that the land we now call New Jersey was inhabited by intelligent human beings 9500 years before Columbus even set sail from Spain.

Excavations and studies by the Wayne Archaeological Research Laboratory have confirmed findings made at the turn of the century by pioneer archaeologist Max Schrabish of Paterson that the Indians not only traveled through Wayne, but spent a considerable amount of time fishing and hunting here. In fact, more than forty prehistoric sites have been discovered here since Schrabish's explorations in 1900. Several of these sites appear to be full villages, although the Lenni-Lenape were migratory and if any area was con-

sidered their actual home, it would probably have been tiny Minisink Island. Located in the middle of the Delaware River just south of Milford, Pennsylvania, about a mile south of where State Route 206 leaves New Jersey, the island was the beginning and ending locations of the continuous voyage between the Delaware (nee South) and Hudson (nee North) Rivers. Tribesmen traveled only on foot or by canoes cut from fallen tree trunks. They favored the area in which the Shrewsbury and Navesink Rivers empty into the Atlantic, between Sandy Hook and Long Branch.

They called themselves the Lenni-Lenape, but the white men referred to them as the Delawares because of where Minisink Island was located. There were three sub-tribes, the *Minsi* ("People of the stony country"), the *Unami* ("People down the river") and the *Unalachtigo* ("People who live near the Ocean"). Each had its own totem, which were the wolf, turtle and turkey, respectively. These three divisions were in turn subdivided into a series of even smaller sub-tribes.

Stony country meant the mountains, and it was mainly the Minsi who frequented Wayne. There is a great amount of misinformation published on exactly where the Minisink Trail, the main route of these Indians between the Atlantic and Minisink Island, crossed. Other than the places George Washington allegedly slept, few so-called historical facts have proven to be as generally inaccurate. In truth, the main branch of the Minisink Trail ran from the mouth of the Navesink River east until the point where the Raritan narrowed near New Brunswick, north to about the present State Route 10, and east until the south bank of Lake Hopatcong. From there it roughly followed the path of present day U.S. 206 to the Delaware.

The Van Duyne House, now located on the grounds of the Wayne Museum on Berdan Avenue in Pancake Hollow, was located here on Fairfield Avenue and present Route 23 from about 1750 to 1974.

The house had to be either demolished or moved in the mid-1970's when the State of New Jersey improved Route 23. The stairs of this footbridge over the state road are on the original site. Archeological excavations have uncovered evidence of Indian cultures here, going back thousands of years.

A major offshoot of the main trail passed through Wayne. It was a continuation of the route that crossed First Watchung Mountain at the Great Notch, continued to Little Falls and north to Two Bridges and then alongside the east bank of the Pompton and then Ramapo Rivers until the Pompton Falls, and then northwest along Hamburg Turnpike (State Route 23). This is borne out by the findings of numerous artifacts along the east bank of the Pompton and Ramapo Rivers. On the river bank directly west of present day Sheffield Park along Farmingdale Road, about a half mile south of Pompton Plains Cross Road, diggings have found ample evidence that a transitory village existed here in the late Woodland period between 1000 and 1600 A.D.

Just to the north another base camp seems to have existed along the riverbank just in back of present day George Kuehm Farm (Farmview) on Black Oak Ridge Road. The site overlapped the Kuehm place along with that of the adjoining former Graham Farm which was situated between Farmview and the former Sheffield Dairy Farm complex, highlighted below. Mr. Kuehm's family has owned what is the last major farm in Wayne since 1894. He possesses a collection of more than 100 Indian arrow heads and other artifacts that he has been collecting in the area since his childhood. This location being just below the confluence of Pequannock and Ramapo Rivers, and near the Morris Canal Pompton Feeder Dam, was probably near a major crossing spot of the Pompton River. It is believed that Indians occupied this site as long as 4,000 years ago.

Perhaps the most intensively explored archeological site in Wayne was the former location of the Van Duyne farmhouse, that was moved to Berdan Avenue north of the Van Riper-Hopper House, which houses the Wayne Museum. The original house site is on the spot on the south side of Fairfield Road on the west side of State Route 23. The location is now occupied by the stairs of a pedestrian overpass. Three boulders protruding out of the Passaic River just north of the Fairfield Road portion of Two Bridges are believed to be the remnants of an ancient Indian rope bridge. This leads to the conclusion that the Van Duyne Farm may have been a major junction of Indians traveling north and south along the Wayne branch of the Minisink Trail and those roaming east and west along the road that crossed the river. Hundreds of artifacts found indicate that as many as 15 different prehistoric cultures might have visited this location, some as far back as 6,800 B.C., during the Early Archaic period.

Other important sites found include a rock shelter found by Schrabish and explored by Edward Lenik,

longtime head of the Township's Archaeological Research Laboratory. It is located in the Clove, just above where Singac Brook crosses Valley Road extension in the northern portion of Wayne.

Although the Minsi were considered the most belligerent of the three sub-tribes of the Lenni-Lenape, themselves believed to be a branch of the Algonquins, for the most part these people were peaceful and welcomed the white man. When Henry Hudson's party first set foot on Sandy Hook in 1609, they were greeted by Indians that were clearly friendly. Although they numbered probably no more than 10,000 in the entire state at this time, they made life for the explorers, then traders and finally colonists much more bearable. They found the best routes through and around the mountains and across the rivers and streams. They located the best farmland. They taught the newcomers how to grow corn and other crops, and how to find and hunt wild game. They pointed out a green compound found in the rock which Dutch miners optimistically believed might be gold. While it only turned out to be copper, millions of tons of valuable ore was mined and shipped back to Europe, or utilized in America.

Many of today's major highways and byways were once Indian trails. In addition to the Minisink, the main trail in the northern portion of the state, there were at least six other major routes the immediate predecessors of the white man followed. The most prominent of these was the Assanpink or Lower Trail which connected the area around Elizabeth with the Falls of the Delaware near Trenton. It connected with another trail paralleling the Hudson. The Lower Trail broke off near New Brunswick and led to Burlington by way of Crosswicks. This became what was probably the most famous road in the state well into the 20th century, the Kings Highway, later part of the cross county Lincoln Highway, and now State Route 27. The Old York Road connected Lambertsville with Newark Bay, and was used by a tribe of Pennsylvania Indians. The Burlington Path connected Burlington with Shrewsbury and Middleton by way of Freehold. There were also two additional roads, both simply referred to as Branches of the Minisink. One left the main trail at Lake Hopatcong and led through the Great Meadows and Hackettstown to the Delaware River. The second

broke off at Metuchen and led by way of Bound Brook and Somerville to the Forks of the Delaware. There were of course hundreds, if not thousands of progressively smaller trails which connected the larger ones with waterways, temporary villages and other stopping, fishing and hunting places. In Wayne one such path is believed to be the path of present-day LeGrand Terrace off Parish Drive in Mountain View. Another was probably a trail that began near the Dey Mansion, leading south down Riverview Road into Little Falls, up Cedar Grove and Little Falls Road into Cedar Grove and along Grove Avenue into Verona where it meets Bloomfield Avenue, also rumored to be a sub-trail of the Minisink.

These trails were anything but wide passageways. The main branch of the Minisink was probably not much more than a well-beaten dirt path, no more than two to three feet wide.

The Indians never considered themselves owners of the land, but did believe they inherited the exclusive right to possess it. It was sacred to them. Despite their long inhabitation, it remained virtually untouched and pristine. Wood was only cut when it was absolutely necessary. Dead, fallen trees were always preferred to be used as firewood or for canoes. Their homes were temporary structures usually built in round and oval shapes. Generally the villages consisted of a collection of single family huts, however, there was an occasional long house shared by several families at a time. They wore scanty clothing, usually tailored from the skin of deer, elk, bear, wolf or raccoon. Men wore small loin cloths, with a blanket thrown over their shoulders. Leggings and moccasins completed their wearing apparel, except for necklaces and armbands of sharks' teeth, shells, wooden and stone beads and pendants. Women wore short skirts, with a loose tunic fastened on one shoulder.

There is much dispute among historians as to when the Lenni Lenape came to New Jersey. They called themselves The Original People and believed they were the ancestors of an ancient tribe which began in Southern Canada. However there is evidence that perhaps as recently as a few centuries before the Europeans arrived the Lenape themselves immigrated here. Under this theory, these Indians came from Asia,

crossing a land bridge over the Aleutian Island area of the Bering Sea to Alaska and then slowly making their way southeast. It is known that that land bridge existed during the Ice Age when the oceans were far more shallow than they were when the earth cooled, therefore, those who crossed over from Asia may be predecessors, or possibly ancestors of the Delawares.

The archaeological evidence found in Wayne clearly indicates that if it was not the Lenni Lenape who lived here thousands of years ago, it must have been some other Indians. Perhaps they may have crossed here from the east, maybe across Atlantis, the so-called lost continent. Given recent findings in northeast Africa that point to the Great Rift Valley in Ethiopia probably being the first place on earth man ever lived, absent new evidence, it must be concluded that that continent was the Indian's, as well as the white man's original home.

Today the Indians are a largely forgotten people. There are no villages, enclaves, and maybe not one pure bred Lenni Lenape left in the State of New Jersey. They seemed to have disappeared almost as fast as did the dinosaurs 65 million years ago.

The Lenni-Lenape traveled on foot and by canoes made from dug out tree trunks (top). They lived in either natural rock shelters for a day or two, or in temporary villages for longer stays. Several of the rock shelters and temporary villages have been found in Wayne. The photos above and lower left are typical Indian huts and "long houses," while the photo below is of a typical cooking area. These are from the very authentic recreated Indian village at Waterloo Village in Sussex County.

Harold "Timer" Peer stands by only a small part of his massive Indian artifact collection which he has been assembling for over a half century. Most of his artifacts, some believed to be as old as 8,000 years, were dug up on his Fairfield Road property in Mountain View. A self-proclaimed "amateur archaeologist," Mr. Peer is an ancestor of many of Wayne's "Jersey Dutch" founders. In addition to his Indian finds, in digging a 12' hole in his yard, he has also found silt from what he concludes was Lake Passaic which emptied out 12,000-15,000 years ago into the Passaic River. Fairfield Road is believed to have been a major Indian trail and perhaps the site of several Indian villages over the centuries.

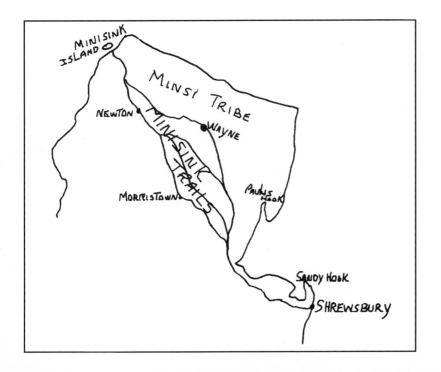

The area that is now Wayne Township is believed to have been along one of the major trails the Lenni Lenape traversed between their main village on Minisink Island in the Delaware River and their favorite fishing grounds near Shrewsbury and the ocean.

Chapter Three
A Changing of the Gods

This small section of the main house, which is located at 231 Parish Drive at Maple Avenue (constructed in the second decade of this century by LeGrand Parish), was originally the Mead Homestead, built in 1780. The first Mead homestead was reportedly made out of sod.

Imagine 100 centuries from now, in the year 11,998, New Jersey being invaded by a race of people with a different color skin from another part of the globe which they never knew existed. Further imagine barely two hundred years later those of us living here being banished and forced to leave the land of our ancestors for over 10,000 years. As impossible as this scenario may seem, this was basically what the Europeans did to the Indians. Fluted projectile points have been found locally that are believed to go back to the Paleo Indian Period between 10,000 and 8,000 B.C. The findings suggest the existence of a culture of people capable of making sophisticated tools such as drills, knives and scrapers; of people who hunted mastodon, mammoth, caribou and other animals.

In 1609, explorer Henry Hudson, an Englishman employed by Holland, sent a party of white men ashore at Sandy Hook. Sandy Hook is a small peninsula jutting out into the Atlantic that was formed by the Wisconsin Glacier only 12,000-15,000 years ago.

Hudson's men were greeted by a number of scantily clad, dark-skinned savages, whose ancestors possibly arrived within two millenniums after the peninsula itself was created. To them, New Jersey was their own Garden of Eden. Virtually every description of that biblical haven fits early 17th century New Jersey. It was deeply wooded, crisscrossed by so many waterways that it was often referred to as the Venice of America. The streams, rivers, lakes and ponds were pure and refreshing, stocked with hundreds of varieties of fish. Other than along the marshy Coastal plain, the land was deeply forested, filled with colorful vege-

number of trading posts established, primarily along the rivers and the coast lines. But

In 1947 this iron mine was discovered in the Glen section of Pines Lake in back of a residence located on Brook Terrace Schuyler family records indicate that Arent dug it in 1695, over 300 years ago.

tation and the abundance of animals. The sky was often a deep blue, embellished with an occasional white puffy cumulus cloud.

Soon afterwards a trading post was established at Bergen.   Later to be known as Paulus Hook, a town was laid out in 1660. Today that town is called Jersey City. By 1666 the settlement had two neighbors, Elizabethtown (Eliza-beth) and New Ark on the Passaik (Newark). After years of Dutch control, England grew jealous and greedy, and in an almost bloodless takeover, assumed ownership and control of New Netherlands in 1664, including New Amsterdam and Albania.   New Amsterdam became New York, and Albania became Nova Caesarea, or New Jersey. It was named in honor of the Isle of Jersey where the Duke of York's good friend Philip Carteret had shielded his royal friend from puritanical England. It seemed that the Duke wrongly interpreted a mistakenly-placed line on a map to be a river, and assumed Albania was an island.

Both the English and the Dutch took advantage of the Indians from the start. Initially the natives were extremely valuable. They were encouraged to go into the wild and bring back animal furs to the growing

as the trading posts gradually gave way to settlements, the Indians began to be viewed more as a detriment than a benefit to further development.   To the Lenni Lenape, land was not something one owned. Possessed, passed through, yes.   But owned, no. They believed they had inherited the right of possession and passage, and if the white man wanted any rights to this land, he would have to deal with the Indian chiefs.   Unfortunately the *red man* was no match for his pale face counterpart when it came to

Bicycling over the driftway (Pompton Feeder of the Morris Canal) at the turn of the century (above) on the original Colfax Bridge which connected the Schuyler-Colfax House with family property across the waterway (see below, r.). The bridge was removed when the canal was abandoned and replaced with a concrete structure (below l.) which currently carries Dawes Highway over the river.

The original bridge (above) was removed, along with hundreds of other structures that spanned or were associated with the Morris Canal when it was formally abandoned by the State of New Jersey. Condition had absol-utely nothing to do with any of the demolitions. Oppon-ents of the action called this mass destruction a case of "Official Vandalism." Remnants of its moorings remain behind the Schuyler-Colfax House.

shrewd bargaining. For a few beads of wampum, a couple of pouches of gunpowder, a few axes, a little fire water, and maybe a blanket or two, large parcels of land were deeded to the Europeans by the Indians. They took solace in believing their trading partners would keep their promises that the Indians would forever have the right to hunt and fish on any land involved in the transactions. It was a promise that was not kept very long. No known deal ever favored the Lenni Lenape. And the worst thing of all was that with each land deal they were conned into entering, they lost another foothold on their entire existence. Since there were probably no more than 10,000 Indians in all of New Jersey in the 17th century, they undoubtedly had no conception of the great number of Europeans that were about to immigrate here and overwhelm the Original People.

The sale of the land, disease, liquor and this massive immigration of outsiders was a death knoll to a people who had lived here long before the Egyptians built their pyramids in the desert, before the Chinese discovered silk in Asia and before their South American counterparts first grew cotton in the foothills of the Andes. Amazingly and tragically, by 1758 their population had dwindled to but a few hundred in the entire state.   In that year a 3,000 acre parcel in Burlington County was secured and reportedly served as the first reservation in the United States. It was called Brotherton, now Indian Mills. Ironically, what virtually amounted to a prison camp was located on the southern end of the very same U.S. 206 which led to Minisink Island. All of the Indians were rounded up and sent there as virtual inmates. At first it appeared that this was a sort of Utopia for the natives. Private homes were constructed for them, along with a general store, a meeting house, and even a saw mill. In addition, they were allowed to continue to keep their rights to unrestricted hunting and fishing. Another short-lived promise.

The reservation did not last long. Within four years the Indians were forced to ask the state legislature for financial assistance to pay bills for provisions, for clothing and for nails. Things went from bad to worse, and in 1801 all of the Indians moved out when Brotherton was sold for between $2.00 and $5.00 an

acre, just enough to pay for passageway to New York, Oklahoma, Wisconsin and other points where they were sent.

Even today their heritage is disrespected. Recently the author decided to explore Minisink Island, trying to approach it off the still-existing Old Mine Road. (This historic highway was the first long road (100+ miles) in the United States that might have been built by Dutch copper miners as early as 1637. It stretched along the route of present day U.S. 209 to Esopus (Kingston), New York).   About a half mile south of U.S. 206, the dirt path leading to the eastern bank of the Delaware River across from the Island was entered with hopes of at least catching a glimpse, if not actually visiting the most historic Indian location in the entire state.   The attempt ended upon the discovery of a prominent sign in large, bold letters:

"NO TRESPASSING. THIS IS PRIVATE PROPERTY. IF YOU ENTER YOU WILL BE ARRESTED."

Religion has often guided the expansion of cultures into different parts of the world. Religious intolerance led many a group asunder. Few of New Jersey's Indians were Christianized, thus they never were assimilated into the new cultures that replaced theirs.

The Dutch Reformed Church was the leading force in the establishment of many new settlements. In the general Wayne area, the first such church was established just to the north of the eventual Township boundary in The Ponds, now Oakland/Franklin Lakes. Before 1695 there was not only no church here, but no settlement. All of that began to change with the coming of Arent Schuyler.

In 1694 the thirty two year old New Yorker was given a confidential assignment to investigate rumors that the French were inciting the Minisink Indians against the English, and report his findings to the governor. His trip took him through what was called Pompton, probably along the Wayne branch of the Minisink Trail. It was on this first trip that he discovered his "wondrous valley." It must have been love at first sight, as he almost immediately formed a company with Major Anthony Brockholst to purchase the

land. Brockholst was a long-time supporter of Schuyler, and since 1677 Commander-in-Chief and Lieutenant-Governor of the Province of New York. He often served as Acting Governor as well whenever the Governor was absent. For a time he was even the Mayor of New York. The two enlisted the backing of Colonel Nicholas Bayard and his son, Samuel, wealthy New York merchants, to become co-investors in the venture. Soon well-to-do farmers Samuel Berry, Hendrick and David Mandeville, George Ryerson and an affluent weaver, John Mead, joined together to form an investment group to purchase Pompton.

Arent was selected to conduct all details of purchasing the land rights the Indians claimed. Brockholst and the Bayards, with their status and political contacts, were picked to simultaneously obtain the rights owned by the East New Jersey Proprietors. New Jersey had been divided into an eastern and western province, and the eastern province was controlled by its headquarters in Perth Amboy.

Given the fact that the main Indian trail was on the east side of the Pequannock and Ramapo Rivers, and it appeared the land there was better suited for farming, Schuyler recommended that his partners purchase the land on this side of the rivers. They all agreed to that course of action.

On June 6, 1695 an agreement was entered into on Minisink Island in which the Indians gave away their land in Wayne for "a certain quantity of wampum and of goods and merchandise to the value of $250 English pounds." Wampum was white, blue and purple beads cut from the insides of the periwinkle, conch and clam shells, cut, bored, polished and strung upon dried animal sinews. The deed outlined the land boundaries as:

"Beginning at the mouth of a small creek, in the Indian language called Sinkaak {Singac Brook}, which said small creek is a branch that falls into Pequannoc Creek {Passaic River}, and lies opposite the great hill, call by the Indians Meelonagkas {North Caldwell}, extending from said mouth of Sinkaak Creek northward along the said small creek as far until it meets the Indian path that goes toward Pompton, called the Minisink Path, and so along said Path toward Pompton Creek {Pompton/Ramapo Rivers} and then running again northward, along the east side of said creek, taking in a stroke of land on said east

Built in 1810, this was the residence of George Washington Colfax. The house originially was located next door to the Schuyler-Colfax House on Hamburg Turnpike, the present site of a Chevrolet Dealership. The house was later moved around the corner on Dawes Highway where it sat until very recently, when it was razed. By then it bore little resemblance to its original design.

side, till it meets with the falls {Pompton Falls}, in the Indian language called Awarigh, and from said falls westward, comprehending all the low land, then to the hill, called by the Indians Hackaeckonck, and then southward along the foot of the hills to the great hill called by the Indians Simpeck {Old Mine Mountain} and from said hill Simpeck, eastward to Pequannoc Creek, and then all along down said creek, till it comes to the first station {just below Two Bridges on Fairfield Road}, called the mouth of the Sinkaak Creek before mentioned, as may more fully appear by

Colfax "Milk House," in 1936 on Hamburg Turnpike.

a map or card made by the description of the said natives annexed to the said deed."

This purchase included about 2/3's of the area that is now Wayne.

Five months after the Indians gave up their claim to the area, the East New Jersey Proprietors issued a land patent to the Schuyler-Brockholst group on November 11, 1695. It actually included three patents, the Lower (2750 acres) and Upper (1260 acres) Pacquanac Patents and the Pompton Patent (1250 acres).

The Lower Patent ran north from Singac Brook to what is now Ryerson Avenue in Old Wayne. It was three miles long and one and a half miles wide. The Upper Patent ran from the northern border of the Lower Patent to a point equal to where the Pequannock and Ramapo Rivers meet to form the Pompton. The Pompton Patent covered the northern portion of what is now the western portion of Wayne from the northern border of the Upper Patent to the foot of the hills.

Schuyler and Brockholst were the first of the group to settle in their newly purchased land at a time fixed between 1696 and 1698, 300 years ago. Schuyler built the original section of what is now called the Schuyler-Colfax House on Hamburg Turnpike in 1696. Brockholst's house is believed to have been built a short distance away in the vicinity of the Pompton Falls. Both officially became residents in 1698.

Samuel Berry settled on a hill called *Sleckbergh*, just north of Mountain View. He died in 1701.

George Ryerson settled on the west side of what was

to become the Newark and Pompton Turnpike (in 1806) in Old Wayne.

John Mead decided to live on a site that was once an Indian orchard on the east side of present day State Route 23 in Mountain View. He and his sons named their settlement Meads Basin.

In 1966 a battle erupted over the planned removal of the remnants of an old cemetery at the end of Courter Avenue, south of Fairfield Road in Mountain View. Members of the legendary Ryerson family were reported to have been buried here. An old monument was found in pieces. This artist's sketch appears in a local newspaper depicting what it was originally believed to have looked like. It is believed some of the remains and headstones were moved to the graveyard next to Preakness Reformed Church on Church Lane.

In the vicinity of what is now Laguna Beach, just to the north of Mountain View, Hendrick and David Mandeville built their home.

The Bayards apparently opted to remain simply as investors, and elected to maintain their residences in New York.

Unlike many other New Jersey communities, Wayne never developed around a single village square or main street.

In fact, the first church congregation organized exclusively for Wayne residents was not until more than 100 years after the foregoing settlings.

300 years later after Schuyler built his home, Wayne remains divided into several communities, Pompton Falls, Old Wayne, Mountain View, Upper Preakness and Lower Preakness, along with Packanack, Pines, and Lions Head Lakes.

The Founder of Wayne

Wayne was discovered and founded by an extraordinary individual. Arent Schuyler was a multi-dimensional frontiersman, being a trader, guide, Indian scout, military hero, statesman, farmer, miner, merchant and builder. He was born on June 25, 1662 in the upstate New York colony of Beverwyck, the child of Dutch immigrants Margarita Van Slichtenshorst and Philip Pieterse Schuyler. Beverwyck was formerly known as Fort Orange, later to be called Albany. The settlement predated Manhattan by a year.

By all accounts the Schuylers were among the most affluent of all residents of Beverwyck, and young Arent enjoyed the privilege of an elementary school education, rare in the 17th century. He was trained to be a businessman, and since his village was the center of important Indian commerce, he quickly learned how to understand and communicate with the natives. He commenced his adult life as a trader, but soon found himself involved in defending the region from threats of the French who seemed hell bent in coming down from Canada and seizing all English possessions.

While still a relatively young man, Arent met and soon became a close friend of another outstanding New Yorker. Anthony Brockholst was a trusted soldier in the employ of the British crown, and would rise to become a Major in the army, Commander-in-Chief and Lieutenant-Governor, and for a time acting Governor of the Province of New York, with a stint as Mayor of New York thrown in for good measure. The two would become partners in one of the first real estate syndicates in New Jersey.

Schuyler's prowess on the trails and in a number of skirmishes with the French and hostile Indians did not go unnoticed by the powers that be in Manhattan, nor with the friendly Indians, and he was highly respected by both. So much so that he was commissioned by the authorities to explore "the rivers of New Jersey."

In 1692 Brockholst apparently convinced his friend to move to Manhattan. Soon afterwards he was assigned to travel to the Counsel Fires on Minisink Island in the upper Delaware River to look into rumors of attempts by the French to incite the Lenni Lenape. The Minisink Trail was an important commercial route and trading with the Indians was vital to the existence and expansion of the British interests here. An example of the riches the Indians brought to the new immigrants is demonstrated by a story told by an early traveler. He reported meeting a party of 700 Indian braves, "carrying over 70,000 pelts."

After accomplishing his assignment with great success, Arent was given additional assignments, many again taking him through the area the Indians called Pompton. He could not help but fall in love with the land. It was not only beautiful, but he saw tremendous

potential here for farming and mining.

Schuyler's reputation with both the Indians and government officials served him well and played a great role in allowing him the opportunity to purchase the valley between the Passaic River and the northern hills on the east side of the Pompton-Ramapo Rivers. When the feat was accomplished he chose a plot of land to build his home and carry out his plans that could not have been better-situated. Located on the east bank of the Ramapo River driftway, a half mile from the falls, the site of what remains Wayne's oldest house was surrounded by rich farmland, heavily-forested woodlands, and was close to what Schuyler suspected were mineral and ore rich mountains. It was also right along the Wayne branch of Minisink Trail where it met Old Pumpton Road.

The year 1696 was undoubtedly a year of great joy, as well as great sadness for Arent Schuyler. He had moved onto the land he had grown to love, while losing another great love. His first wife, Jenneke, died just as he was establishing his long-awaited homestead in his Wondrously Beautiful Valley.

While what is now known as the Schuyler-Colfax House remained in the family for almost 300 years, Arent only remained in the house for fourteen years. In 1710 he picked up and moved again with his second wife, Swantie Dyckhuyse. This time he purchased a large parcel of land in what was then known as the Township of New Barbados (Hackensack), marshy land on the east bank of the lower Passaic River, from Harrison to beyond the Belleville Turnpike. It is now in the community of Belleville.

Schuyler had little success attempting to cultivate the swampy property and grew so frustrated that he was reportedly negotiating to sell it and pick up stakes once again in 1719 when he simply got lucky. One of his slaves by the name of Jack made a discovery while plowing the fields that would insure Arent would die a rich man. Jack came rushing into the house with a large green-colored stone. Schuyler sent samples of the find to both New York and even London for analysis and was elated to learn it contained 80% pure copper. As could be expected, a copper mine almost a stone's throw from Newark and not much further away from Manhattan proved to be a highly profitable ven-

ture. But once again Arent's life took another pa doxical twist as Swantie died at about the same tim

In 1724 Schuyler married Maria Walter (Wallen), built a beautiful house with imported Holland brick was surrounded by lush parks, filled with deer. By time of his death in 1730, Arent's concern had ship 1,386 tons of ore to the Bristol Copper & Brass Wo in England. John Schuyler inherited his father's tune, and in 1753 made some historical news of own. After water began seeping into the still prod tive mine, he employed a young English engineer the name of Josiah Hornblower, later to become a tinguished patriot. Hornblower brought with him w was reported to be the first steam engine ever ship to America.

Arent Schuyler probably lived in this smaller, northern wing of the Schuyler-Colfax House, nearly eight decades before a Colfax moved in.

Historical Highlight
Schuyler-Colfax House

Located at Hamburg Turnpike, a few hundred yards east of Terhune Drive, this is probably the first home built in Wayne, and certainly the oldest in existence, by far. In terms of age, the second oldest is believed to be the Dey Mansion, forty years newer.

Residents of and visitors to Wayne have the opportunity to step back to the 17th century and experience a small piece of life as it then existed. Located at 2343 Hamburg Turnpike is an old home that can easily be missed in passing by the Old Barn Restaurant or Chevrolet dealership. Perhaps only those who have noticed and taken the time to read the blue steel historical marker erected in the front yard have any idea of the significance of the so-called Schuyler-Colfax House. Family records indicate the first (northern-most) section of the house was built in 1696, only 87 years after Henry Hudson's crew became the first known white men to set foot in New Jersey. It is thus not only the oldest building in Wayne, but one of the oldest in all of New Jersey.

Arent Schuyler's stay here was limited as he obviously had mercury in his blood. He did not seem able to stay in one place very long. However, his descendants lived in the homestead for nearly two centuries. When Dr. Jane Colfax sold the abode to the Township just a few years ago and retired to North Carolina, only then was the line of Schuyler-Colfax lineage broken.

The house does not appear to be the typical Dutch stone farmhouse. It never was. It was not constructed of locally-quarried brownstone like so many of those surviving old homes built in the century after it was. But the venerable old estate was certainly as well built as any of them. It was expanded to 13 rooms, three attics and has eight large fireplaces. The outside walls are 18" thick and the walls are composed of imported

Holland brick, cut stone and hand-hewn timbers connected to uprights by carefully fitted wooden pegs.

There was obviously no Hamburg Turnpike at the turn of the 18th century. What became the Old Pumpton Road was probably situated further east of the front entrance to the home, closer to the foothills of the mountains. Running behind the property, down a short slope, is the Ramapo River driftway. A wooden bridge was constructed over the waterway, probably by the Morris Canal and Banking Company in the early 19th century. It began on the southwest portion of the property and ended at what is now Stiles Park in Pompton Plains.

While part of the massive abandonment and destruction process in dismantling the canal took that bridge with it, the eastern base can be seen on the hillside during the winter months when the brush is thin. A replacement bridge was constructed just down river at Dawes Highway.

The Wayne Historical Commission has patiently restored the home over the last three years. Most of the work was done by elderly, dedicated lovers of communi-

This smaller wing of the house was the portion built by Arent Schuyler.

The view from the driftway of the Ramapo River of the backyard of the house. A bridge built by the Morris Canal and Banking Company once crossed the waterway from the southeast corner of the property.

ty history. It is open on a regular basis for inspection and enjoyment.

Historical Highlight
Pompton Ironworks and Furnace

Photography was in its infancy when this image was captured of the Pompton Furnace in 1854. The furnace, however, was celebrating its 128th year at the foot of Pompton Lake.

Who exactly built and operated the first furnace, which probably was just a bloomary (a small furnace) has evaded later historians, but it is probable it was either a Brockholst or a Schuyler. The first known ironmaster was Casparus Schuyler, the grandson of Arent. What was probably during his ownership, the works reportedly supplied ball and shot for the French and Indian Wars. It also supplied firebacks (the back wall of fireplaces) and utensils for local residents.

In 1774 Casperus sold his interest to Gabriel Ogden, who would later acquire interest in many other similar and even larger facilities. During the Revolutionary War as many as 7,000 cannonballs, ranging from 4 to 18 pounds, as well as 18 tons of grape shot were shipped from Pompton to the Continental Army per orders from General Henry Knox. The biggest problem with most ironworks was finding sufficient manpower, and the Pompton Ironworks was no exception. Among George Washington's papers was a note lamenting that he had no way of transporting the ammunition produced at the furnace.

Because of its strategic location, direct routes between Morristown and the Hudson, and the flatlands and the highlands, the Pompton Ironworks were always very important to the American cause.

The next owner of the complex was another descendant of one of the original Wayne settlers. Martin Ryerson purchased the entire facility and soon added many others to his arsenal of properties. He was succeeded following his death in 1839 by son Peter, who took over when the Pompton Feeder Canal was being

In its heyday the main portion of the furnace and ironworks was situated on the west bank of the Ramapo River at the falls. Today, that means it would be technically part of Pompton Lakes rather than Wayne. However, during a great portion of Wayne's history, the Ironworks dominated the community, at least the northwestern portions of it. In addition, it was so large an enterprise, that locations on both sides of the river were integral to the operation of the entire complex. Finally, even though the exact location of the original furnace has not been confirmed, there is much speculation and evidence that it was built on the east bank of the river. The east bank is in fact in Wayne.

The Pompton Ironworks was one of the first in the state, dating back to 1726. The falls were well known and often the site of Indian hunting and fishing expeditions. When the Schuyler-Brockholst partnership made their land purchases three decades before the ironworks began, Major Anthony Brockholst built his home nearby the falls, along with a mill on the site.

built. Despite what should have been, and was, an influx of new business, Peter was unable to keep his

As the 20th century began, the ironworks had been supplanted by the steel works. While most of the complex was situated on the Pompton Lakes side of the river, there were still many vital facilities in Wayne Township proper.

Pompton Iron and Steel Company by 1875 before being renamed Horner & Ludlum, and by 1898 the Ludlum Steel & Spring Company. On October 9, 1903 a great flood signaled the beginning of the end of a long era. A record rainfall hit the area and all the rivers swelled well beyond their capacity. The dam at the falls gave way as did the Hamburg Turnpike bridge. Much of the company's river-front property was also washed away in a flash along with the coal docks for the Pompton Feeder Canal.

As with many architectural or business dinosaurs, a natural disaster often became the last straw in a slowly deteriorating situation. This was clearly the case with the once vital Pompton Ironworks. Closing in on its bicentennial year, the complex, its belching smoke polluting the air and waste thrown into the river, was barely being tolerated by the locals, and only those who depended on its existence for their livelihood. No one was about to spend millions of dollars rebuilding the facility. The flood only accelerated the pace of its inevitable demise. It was time for another industry to support those in need of work.

operation afloat and lost ownership.

By 1863 a steelworks was built to produce railway car springs and cast steel. It was later called the

The corner of Terhune Drive and Hamburg Turnpike today bears little resemblance to the important junction it was for over two centuries when the Ironworks, and later Steelworks were operating.

This lithograph depicts how the ironworks looked in 1864 when it was undoubtedly contributing to the war effort of the Union Army. Now a relatively quiet area, the Pompton Falls was nerve center of the entire valley for most of two centuries.

Ten years after the colonists declared their independence from the so-called Mother Country, what is now known as the Van Riper-Hopper House (l.) was built in 1786. It has survived more than two centuries and now houses the Wayne Museum on Berdan Avenue. It is open to the public.

The Murrays

Tom, Pat, Muriel, Lynn and her husband Bill Eberding

Celebrate
The Founding of
Wayne

Chapter Four
From Falls to Falls

The Van Riper-Hopper House on Berdan Avenue, shown here in 1936, was built in 1786. Along with the neighboring Berdan homesteads, it was part of an almost self-contained village of its own. It now houses the Wayne Museum.

The portion of what would later become Wayne Township adjoins the Ramapo and Pompton Rivers, running from Pompton Falls, past the Morris Canal Feeder Falls and eventually making a short jag to the east to the Little Falls of the Passaic. It is not generally known that Wayne actually shares a portion of the actual Little Falls with its southern neighbor by that same name (and Totowa). The Township's southern boundary extends from Two Bridges right down the center of the Passaic River to that point where the Morris Canal Aqueduct once crossed over the river (now the New Jersey Water District's pipe line bridge). The original falls were far more impressive than they now are, running from what has been called the Beatty Dam since the mid-19th century for about a half mile

downriver. The Beatty Carpet Company modified (some say massacred) the once-magnificent natural landmark by blasting out the original cascade to allow a greater drop, and thus provide greater hydroelectric power. Today, about the only place to view what remains of the Little Falls is right behind the former mill buildings, converted recently into condominiums.

The western settlements, from north to south, are unofficially known as Pompton Falls, Old Wayne, Mountain View, Two Bridges and Singac. The latter designation on the south side of the Passaic River is in Little Falls, but in olden days, at least before the Township was formed in 1847, both sides of the river were considered Singac. This section is named after the important brook by that same name which extends

from north of the Valley Road extension before emptying into the Passaic under Fairfield Road, equidistant between Two Bridges and State Route 46.

As colonization spread rapidly during the 18th century, most immigrants were either Dutch or English, with a smattering of others. The English traveled in and around the mountains, while the Dutch stayed close to the rivers, preferring the relatively-flat, but slightly sloping river banks to set up their farms. They found New Jersey's riverbanks very similar to the landscape in their native land, where they remain world-famous for getting the most out of the land. Most of the original settlers in the Schuyler-Brockholst group were Hollanders, or at least of Dutch ancestry. Schuyler, Ryerson and Mead were pure Dutch. The Mandevilles and Bayards came from Holland, but their ancestors originally immigrated there from France and were French Huguenots. The Berrys were believed to be of English extraction, as was Brockholst, a Roman Catholic from Lancashire (although the name indicates at least some of his ancestors may have been of German descent).

The fact that the prime attraction of northern New Jersey was originally its rich farmlands, it is no wonder that the Dutch lowlanders led the settlement of this portion of the state. With the exception of a small band of Hollanders who were more interested in golden ore than golden wheat, and began mining operations on both sides of the Delaware River Valley, most were farmers. As time went on, these farmers created their

own culture. While the Jersey Dutch were certainly more Dutch than the Pennsylvania Dutch, who are actually German, by 1700 most who lived here by then were no longer purebreds. Families had gradually intermarried with Swedes, Finns, Germans, French, Huguenots, English and even Indians by the advent of the 18th century. Even their language no longer was pure Dutch. The last names of most of these new colonists were also augmented. For example, De

The Colonists stored their fruits and vegetables in a "Root Cellar" such as this still existing one located on Alps Road, opposite Maple Avenue (mound to the left of well).

Reimer became Doremus, and des Marest became Demarest (see *Place and Name Guide*). And a Doremus was not necessarily related to another Doremus as one Doremus may have originally been a De Reimer, while another could have been a DuRemus. Eventually even first names were loosely translated into English. Jan or anything close to it became John. Genealogists therefore had a really awesome task when tracing family histories.

In 1702 New Jersey again became one as East and West New Jersey were united under a royal governor.

Located at 378 Fairfield Road is the 1760 Demarest House. It was taken apart and reconstructed in 1850 to allow the resident ghosts to escape.

The settlement of Wayne was the second in what would not become Passaic County until 1837. Twelve years before the three Wayne patents were issued, a group of fourteen led by Hartmann Michielson, a trader, purchased approximately 10,000 acres of land covering parts of what is now Clifton, Passaic and Paterson. In 1684 their purchases was formally recognized with the issuance of the Acquackanonk Patent. This became a very important settlement in the history of the entire state, if not the nation, mainly because it included those sections of the Passaic River where it became navigable to Manhattan.

While the three major settlements within the Acquackanonk Patent developed into something relatively rare in New Jersey, municipalities operated as cities, those within the Schuyler-Brockholst patents never did. This was probably because they included better farming lands and more rugged topography, thanks to the fact Pompton was the gateway to the New Jersey Highlands, where the land suddenly begins to change from relatively flat to steeply mountainous. The original Wayne families, being well-healed, appear to have been fiercely independent because they were obviously self-sufficient. They built their homes and farms far apart from each other. Each such homestead provided the occupants with virtually everything they needed to survive. They planted and grew crops, fished the streams and rivers, and found more than sufficient wild game in the woods. Livestock was brought

Virtually the entire state was rural and the government played a minor role in most New Jerseyan's lives during the 18th century.

The rich farmlands, lush fishing and hunting grounds, and mineral and ore-packed mountains were obviously quite alluring to the newcomers seeking to make their fortunes in the New World, or at least provide the basic necessities of life for their families. However, the first step was improving transportation. The heavily-wooded forests, scores of waterways and numerous hills, valleys and mountains were major obstacles to exploration and development. The burden of early pioneers was eased thanks to the numerous existing paths cut through and used by the Indians. Since these paths were only wide enough for a man, and maybe a horse, much work had to be done to allow the movement of carts and wagons. The mattock and ax were requisite tools that had to be carried to clear away wild vines and stunted bushes that encumbered the paths. Trees had to be felled to fill in gullies, shore up the roads to support horses and heavier loads, and to allow easier stream crossing at convenient fords.

The Van Duyne house, originally located on Fairfield Road, as shown in top photo in 1936. It was moved (middle photo) to its present site (bottom photo) in Pancake Hollow in 1974. While the cornerstone says "1706", it is believed to have been built around 1750.

in for milk, butter and additional food. Many had functioning saw mills, grist mills and/or cider mills on the property, or close by. They did their own blacksmithing and carpentering until merchant stores became economically feasible. The women of the homestead weaved wool and thread from animals and plants raised on the property on small spinning wheels. They sewed the family's clothing, and cooked sumptuous meals in their large Dutch Ovens and hearths built with local brick and stone. They served the meals on home-made pottery. About the only help they ever received was from traveling woolers and cobblers. Woolers would travel around the countryside with their large looms loaded in their wagons. They would disassemble it, reassemble it in their customer's farmhouses, and weave larger blankets and rugs that were too big to make on the family equipment. The cobblers would make shoes, saddles and rigs out of the hides skinned from animals raised on the properties and wild animals shot in the woods.

There was more than adequate building material all around Wayne, clay to make bricks (and the pottery), a wide variety of both functional and decorative stones and rocks, and of course plenty of timber. The typical Dutch stone farmhouse was surprisingly not an exact design imported from Holland. Like diets, clothing, and even language, early New Jersey Dutch architecture was a hybrid, incorporating the knowledge the new immigrants brought with them from their native lands with what was most functional and available here.

The size and completeness of these large homesteads, along with the great variety of the topography, hills and mountains, valleys, meadows and swamps and scores of all types of moving and stationary bodies of water, all were obstacles in Wayne taking on the characteristics of most other New Jersey communities. The closeness of Manhattan, Elizabethtown, Newark and Paterson minimized the need for the community to covet merchants and develop a typical main street.

The original Wayne families soon expanded and

were joined by many others. Arent Schuyler's stay here was brief, moving to a large parcel of land near present day Belleville where he became even wealthier operating a huge copper mine. However, the handsome home he began to build less than ninety years after the first white men set foot on New Jersey soil stayed in the family for almost three hundred years. When Dr. Jane Colfax sold the historic homestead to the Township only two years ago and moved to North Carolina, it ended three centuries of occupancy by the Schuyler and Colfax families. Many of Arent's descendants became prominent members of the community, especially after the Schuyler family joined with the Colfax clan in 1783 as a result of the marriage of Hester Schuyler and Captain William Colfax, one of George Washington's top assistants.

The Schuyler-Colfax family long dominated the area generally known as Pompton Falls (aka Schuyler's Basin). Arent probably was more interested in mining than farming. This may explain why he reportedly dug an iron mine as early at 1695. The mine was rediscovered in 1947 and sealed for safety reasons. It is located in the Glen area of Pines Lake behind a residence located at 32 Brook Terrace, just east of Route 202. Surrounding the main homestead on what is now Hamburg Turnpike, less than a half mile from the falls, were acres of crops. Since the so-called driftway of the Ramapo River bordered the backyard of the Schuyler-Colfax home, a wooden bridge had to be erected to allow the family and employees access to their farmland across the waterway. The driftway is that portion of the river between the falls and where it joined with the Pequannock River near Cross Pompton Plains Road to form the Pompton River. This was used between the early 1830's and the early 20th century as the most northern portion of the Morris Canal Pompton Feeder, the legendary canal's main source of water in the eastern portion of the state. Casperus Schuyler was instrumental in building and operating the Pompton Furnace, which from 1726 to the early 20th century played a vital role in everything from the American Revolution to the building of the infrastructure of many northeastern industrial cities. The Schuyler-Colfax name was nationally prominent during the mid-19th century as the grandson of William

Colfax, Schuyler Colfax, served the country as Speaker of the House of Representatives and as Vice President under President Ulysses S. Grant. Unfortunately after one term as the nation's second in charge, he was not asked to remain on the ticket due to his involvement in a bribe-taking scandal. There are still numerous Schuyler and Colfax descendants living in and around Wayne today.

The Brockholst name disappeared from local logs with the death of Anthony's son Henry who inherited his father's wide range of properties, including Brockholst Mill built at Pompton Falls. However, the bloodline produced several influential Americans. Susannah, Anthony's great-granddaughter became the wife of Philip Livingston, famed governor of New Jersey during the American Revolution. Their daughter Catherine married John Jay, first Chief Justice of the United States. Brockholst Livingston, another product of this union, himself became an Associate Justice of the nation's highest court.

The Ryerson clan dominated the section of the community often referred to as Old Wayne. This is the area alongside the Newark and Pompton Turnpike between where it branches off from State Route 23 to the point where it crosses the Pompton River and enters Pequannock Township. The descendants of George Ryerson, most notably Martin and his son Peter, during the 19th century, owned and operated both the Pompton Ironworks and the larger and even more important Ringwood complex twenty miles up the mountain. One operated a sawmill in the vicinity of Tom's Lake in a hollow along a stream that later was dammed to form Packanack Lake, a mile or so to the south.

The Mead family developed what was to become the first semblance of a town center in what is now known as Mountain View. Known as Meads Basin, John Mead and his descendants helped develop this area into what eventually became the commerce center of Wayne where two major state highways, the Morris Canal and its Pompton Feeder and two major passenger and commercial railroad lines all converged and crossed one another.

The Berry and Mandeville clans were more instrumental in the development of neighboring Pequannock

Township than Wayne, but given the close proximity of the two communities, their influence was also felt here.

The Bayard family who never did move to New Jersey, appear to have had far less influence on the development of the original purchaser's holdings than their co-investors.

It was only natural that some of the larger parcels would be subdivided, some again and again. Also, many new families moved in. They included, among others, the Joneses, Roomes, DeMotts, Slingerlands, Van Gelders, Vanderbrooks, Jacobuses, and of course the Dey family. The Deys are deservedly associated with perhaps the most famous structure in Wayne, the Dey Mansion in Lower Preakness Valley. A branch of the family also settled several miles to the west on the border of present-day Lincoln Park. Derrick and Thomas Dey lived at Two Bridges on the banks of the Passaic and Pompton Rivers. As will be discussed later on, this was a key site in this area during the Revolutionary War.

The peninsula Willowbrook and Wayne Town Center shopping malls now occupy was originally a combination of marsh and farmland. The John Stagg family, who came here from Holland during the middle of the 17th century, appear to be the largest, and possibly earliest residents of this area.

Clearly most of the major activity in this western portion of Wayne, at least up to the time of the Revolutionary War, was centered in the Pompton Falls. As early as 1726 an iron bloomery was built, possibly on the Wayne side of the waterfalls, and ten years later the first house of worship was constructed at a convenient ford in the river just about where the Pequannock and Ramapo Rivers converge to form the Pompton River.

Two Bridges today where the Pompton River flows into the Passaic River. It was known as "The Forks" when the Colonial Army first marched over the original bridges. In Indian times a rope bridge may have spanned the large boulders just north of the left bridge shown in this recent photograph.

Packanack Mountain has a very unique shape as can be seen on this old 1877 topographical map of the Township (below). It is likely that it was sculptured during the last Ice Age about 15,000 years ago when walls of ice, some close to a mile high, slowly drifted down from eastern Canada. Packanack Lake was still half a century away when this map was drawn.

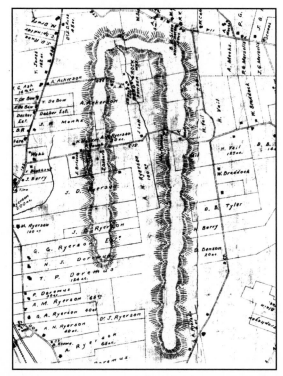

When the first local settlors moved in, the heartiest of them likely climbed to the summit of High Mountain at some point during their residency. The view 300 years ago was virtually the same as it is today, with some notable exceptions----there were no homes, bridges, major thoroughfares, nor cities like Newark, Paterson and New York, all of which are part of the breathtaking view today. With this 360 degree panorama, especially after a climb that ranges from moderate to extremely difficult (depending on the route), most observers would not be expected to look anywhere but out. However, for those truly interested in history, a trained eye can observe traces of history that occurred 15,000-20,000 years ago. The loose boulders were brought by the huge glaciers from parts north and northeast. Other remnants of the last Ice Age are exposed protruding rocks, some of which were polished and scarred with long track marks of the massive land icebergs.

Historical Highlight
The Mystery of
The Ancient Dutch Church
Where Was It?

ANCIENT DUTCH CHURCH.

This is the only known drawing of Wayne's first house of worship, built in 1736 and soon thereafter abandoned.

This 1936 photograph was claimed to show the site of ancient church on Maple Lane. It is actually on Shore Drive and has changed little over the last 62 years.

Perhaps the two major burning historical mysteries of Wayne related to the precise route of the hidden Cannonball Road and the exact location of the ancient Dutch church. Of the latter, this much has been known: In 1736 an octagonal church building was constructed in the Schuyler's Basin area of Wayne, on the east bank of the Pompton River, just below the confluence of the Ramapo and Pequannock Rivers.

Given the fact that by 1760 the church had relocated to the other side of the River in present day Pompton Plains, its short life here and the passage of more than two and a half centuries have dulled its memory.

In 1936, on the 200th anniversary of its founding, Reverend Eugene Keator of the Dutch Reformed Church of Pompton Plains researched the church's archives and wrote a commemorative book. In his work he theorized that the original location was along present day Maple Lane.

Among the evidence he relied upon was an 18th century map and an old description that it was located "along a public road near a convenient ford in the river." No one challenged his theory until 1975 when longtime Wayne resident Howard "Timer" Peer came up with some contradictory evidence.

Legend has it that two of the steps to the ancient church were imbedded in two stone pillars that marked the old gateway to the former Graham Farm. The farm, just north of the massive Sheffield Dairy Farm on the corner of Black Oak Ridge Road and lower Jackson

Avenue, now Pompton Plains Cross Road, was believed to encompass the land where the church was located. The stone steps were believed to have been retrieved from the nearby ruins of the historic structure.

An undated, but well-worn old photograph of the pillars, clearly shows the two steps. Time dulls history, and even the exact location of the gate grew into a matter of some controversy. In order to place the church where Reverend Keator placed it, the gateway would probably have to have been along Black Oak Ridge Road. A 1936 photograph of the alleged site on Maple Lane depicts a scene that has changed little over the last 62 years, with most of the old homes shown in the photograph still surviving. The problem is that the scene is not of Maple Lane, but Shore Road, just to the north, between South and North Roads. Perhaps it was then called Maple Lane in 1936 as it begins close to where present day Maple Lane ends, but this location is clearly not on the grounds of the Graham property.

If the ruins of the church were close by the stone pillars, then the stone pillars probably were not on Black Oak Ridge Road. And in the early 18th century, it is quite doubtful that routes of either Maple Lane or Shore Road were much more than dirt paths, certainly not considered much of a "public road," which Black Oak Ridge Road was. Therefore the question must be asked, "Where were the pillars located?"

Peer knew. He obtained a 1903 photograph from an old friend, Otto Klaner, who had a penchant for taking pictures around the turn of the century. The photo shows five young men walking along a snow-covered road that is not hard to identify as present day Pompton Plains Cross Road. Both the Graham and Sheffield farm buildings are visible in the distance. Lo and behold on the left side of the photograph are two stone pillars. Enlarging the photograph clearly shows these are the very same stone pillars found in the 1936 photograph; the decorative steps can clearly be seen. Peer relied on his own memory as well, and he remembers seeing those pillars just where they obviously were, not on Black Oak Ridge Road, but on what was for years known as lower Jackson Avenue.

Seeking some confirmation of his new theory that the ancient Dutch Church may have been located, not where Reverend Keator placed it, but at least a half mile or more to the south, he contacted Reverend George B. Scholten of the Pompton Plains church and asked him to revisit the issue of the location of the first structure by conducting some additional research of the church archives. Reverend Scholten responded by sketching a map of the area depicting the location exactly where Peer believed it to be.

Peer's theory is supported by another fact. Historical records show that present day Pompton Plains Cross Road was indeed a public highway as far back as the 18th, and possibly even 17th century. It appears it was the lower branch of the western extension of the Old Pumpton Road.

The mystery appears solved!

Another related, albeit less important mystery that exists is exactly what happened to the old steps, as they and the stone pillars they were embedded into are long gone. The former location is approximately now the site of a branch of the United States Post Office.

It was reported that in about 1950 several members of the Pompton Plains church requested that Mrs. Graham consider returning the old steps to their rightful owners, the church. And she did. But what happened to them?

The First Reformed Church of Pompton Plains is located along the old Newark and Pompton Turnpike, just south of where Jackson Avenue starts its journey to the east. The successor to the ancient Dutch church that is the subject of this Historical Highlight was constructed in 1771 and was improved over the years. In 1931 the entire sanctuary burned to the ground. It was rebuilt into the beautiful edifice it remains as today. Its grounds include several church buildings, various monuments, and the old graveyard. A visit to the site in search of the old steps, expected to be prominently placed somewhere on the grounds, initially proved frustrating. They were nowhere to be found, and no one seemed to know much about them.

One report stated they were originally placed in front of a passage way between the main church building

and an adjacent church house. That walkway is in the rear of the buildings and has been enclosed in recent years. A small yard between the buildings extends from the sidewalk along the old turnpike to the enclosed walkway. There is a small m o n u m e n t twenty or so feet into the yard surrounded by some heavy shrubbery which appears to continue right up to the enclosure. At first glance it appeared that someone, perhaps ten, twenty, thirty, forty, maybe even close to fifty years ago moved the steps, assuming they were even placed near the passageway.

However, the key to uncovering history, the very theme of this book, is persistence. A walk around the shrubbery resulted in paydirt! There, laying unceremoniously in a horizontal position were the ancient steps. No monument, no pedestal, no plaque, not even a little sign. They appear to be cut from the same type of brownstone that was mined along the Passaic River in Little Falls, and used in the construction of New York's Trinity Church and the impressive Morris Canal bridge that spanned the Passaic at the southernmost tip of Wayne.

Another mystery solved?

These stone pillars graced the entrance to the old Graham Farm, but exactly where they were located seemed to be a forgotten memory, leading to confusion as to the location of the site of the ancient church.

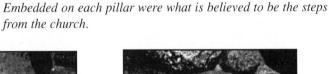

Embedded on each pillar were what is believed to be the steps from the church.

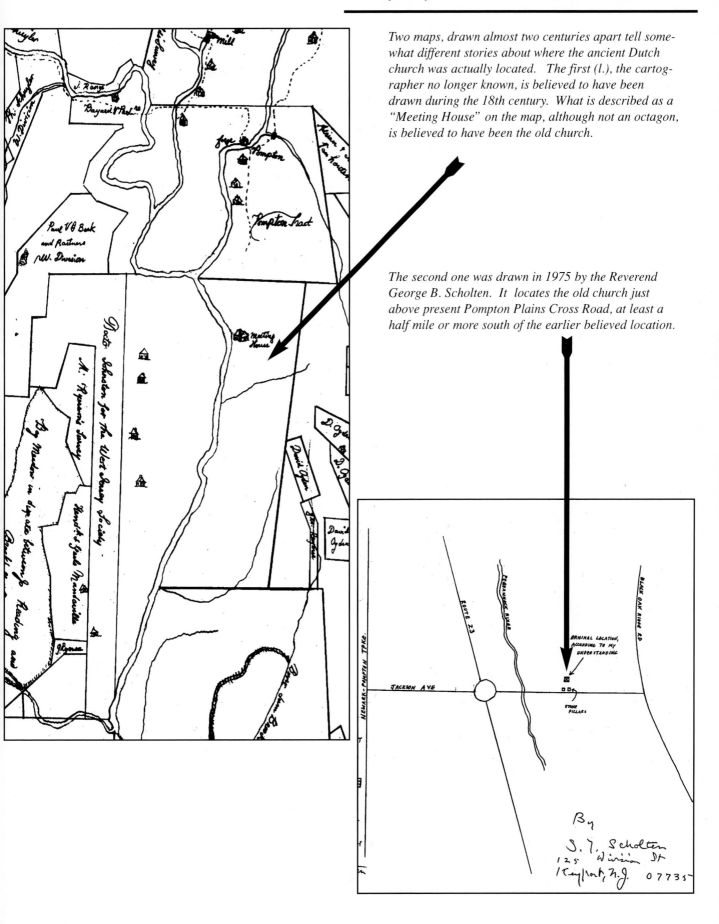

Two maps, drawn almost two centuries apart tell somewhat different stories about where the ancient Dutch church was actually located.   The first (l.), the cartographer no longer known, is believed to have been drawn during the 18th century. What is described as a "Meeting House" on the map, although not an octagon, is believed to have been the old church.

The second one was drawn in 1975 by the Reverend George B. Scholten. It locates the old church just above present Pompton Plains Cross Road, at least a half mile or more south of the earlier believed location.

Taken in 1903, this photograph along lower Jackson Avenue provided the evidence of exactly where the stone pillars were located, and possibly the church as well.

The same road today (lower, l.).

Hidden behind some shrubbery (arrow) in a small yard between the main church and a church building in Pompton Plains (above), the famous old church steps lay unceremoniously on both sides of a long-closed entrance to the walkway.

Chapter Five

Valley of the Deer ...or Quail

Overlooking the Preakness Valley atop Preakness Avenue was "Crows Nest." This Doremus house was allegedly burned down the day President Lincoln was assassinated.

Arent Schuyler's Wondrous Valley is joined by another valley which makes up almost 1/3rd of present day Wayne. The exact origin of the word Preakness is in dispute. However, one thing is certain, it was not the namesake of a famous horse or stakes race. Both that thoroughbred and the second jewel of horse racing's Triple Crown, the Preakness Stakes, were in fact named after the Valley where the winner of the first major stakes race at Pimlico Race Track in Baltimore, Maryland was raised. The Berdan family which dominated the early settlement of the so-called Upper Preakness Valley reported to Reverend Labaw for his fine early history of the valley and church, that the original Indian spelling P-r-a-q-u-a-l-e-s-s meant quail woods because the forests of this section were full of quail and partridge in early times. William Nelson, Recording Secretary of the New Jersey Historical Society in the late-19th century, and author of the classic History of Bergen and Passaic Counties, New Jersey formed a different opinion.
In his view, the original spelling was P-e-r-u-k-u-n-c-

e-s, which meant "a young buck." This interpretation might be supported by the fact that the Indians reputedly referred to Preakness Mountain as Mountain of the Deer. In that there has been as many as twenty different spellings of the word (see *Place and Name Word Guide*), one interpretation is probably as likely as another. What is undisputed however is that locally the word is not pronounced Preakness, as it is on national television every spring when the stakes race is run, but "prake-ness."

Sometimes called The Wayne Valley, the western portion of the Township that the investors of the three aforementioned patents first acquired in 1695, runs from the Pequannock-Ramapo-Pompton rivers east to the Packanack Mountain, and from the Passaic River north to the foothills of the Ramapo Mountains. On the other hand, the Preakness Valley, extends north to south from above so-called Pancake Hollow, where the Point View Reservoir was built in the 1960's, to the

many of the wealthy English merchants who bought into New Jersey, never visited the New World, much less the area west of the Hudson (North) River, the fact that Indians still roamed the land was insignificant. However, the Europeans who decided to move here, build homes and plant crops and raise their families, could not ignore the Original People. As a result, they had to actually purchase the land they wanted twice, once from the Indians, and a second time from the Proprietors who were deeded the land by the royal government.

The Jacob Berdan homestead, located just south of the Van Riper-Hopper house. It's foundation was buried under the Point View Reservoir in the early 1960's.

lower Singac Creek near the intersection of Riverview Drive and Totowa Road, and east to west from Packanack Mountain to Second Watchung, High and Preakness Mountains.

The Indians never considered it necessary to formally record land ownership, believing the land belonged to their gods, not man. Even if they had a different view of things, the fact that their writings were apparently limited to pictographs inside caves would have made any recording virtually ineffective. However, even though they did not claim ownership in the land, they certainly claimed the exclusive right to possess it. This was especially true after they realized the white men would gladly depart with quantities of wampum and other interesting goods as a purchase price. The royal government, on the other hand never bothered to negotiate with the so-called red men, whom they viewed with utter contempt as simply savages. If they decided to push aside Holland on a whim and claim all of New Netherlands and Albania (which the Indians called Scheyichli) with nary a shot having to be fired, they certainly were not about to make a deal with the Lenni Lenape. In that the royals themselves, as well as

One of the twelve original Proprietors who were granted title to all the land in East New Jersey was Thomas Hart. Hart acquired 4,481.81 acres, almost 1/3rd of present day Wayne Township. A Quaker, Hart was a merchant in Enfield, County of Middlesex, England who transferred the entire Preakness Valley to his sister, without ever visiting his property. She in turn gave up her interests to her grandson, Richard Ashfield. From that point on the valley was divided, and sub-divided among many new residents. A New York attorney, Rip Van Dam, was retained in 1714 to "legally look after the rights of Thomas Hart," and did his duty by confirming an earlier bargain made in 1707 by way of an Indian deed.

On September 3, 1714, three Indians of the Minsi sect of the Lenape tribe met with the white settlers of Lower Preakness to "formally relinquish forever all claims to the Valley of the Singack." They were Paejecop, Massatouwop and Matihback. Apparently government red tape is not something of recent vintage, as it took the Proprietors until 1753 before the Preakness Patent was formally "returned to the heirs or assigns of Richard Ashfield."

During the 18th century names like Doremus, Hopper, Van Houten, Van Riper, Ackermann, Neafic and Nafee, along with a few others began to show up in official records. Many others are now remembered on street signs, such as Terhune, Laauwe, Jacobus and MacDonald. In 1723 Cornelius Kip and Jonis

Doremus became partners in land holdings within the eastern valley. Each married a Berdan, the most prominent name in Upper Preakness. In 1715 Jacob D. and Garret Berdan purchased 362 acres of the Hart holdings, north of what is now Hamburg Turnpike between Singac Brook and the Pequannock Patents in what became known as Pancake Hollow. The purchase price was less than fifty cents per acre. The Berdans' farms were typical of the larger holdings in early Wayne....almost completely self-sufficient. On their property was a grist mill, a saw mill, a cider mill, a distillery, a blacksmith shop, and a number of slaves. There has also been reports of a school house being located here as well. Adjoining the Berdan farms was the Van Riper-Hopper House, now site of the Wayne Museum. A visit to the 1786 home, open for public tours, is a journey back into time.

The Berdan properties survived until the early 1960's when what was left was bulldozed. The old road and remaining foundations were flooded with the waters of what became Point View Reservoir.

In 1717 another legendary local name showed up on local records--"Doremus." Johannes Doremus became a landowner, accumulating significant holdings east of Valley Road on both sides of Preakness Avenue. One of the Doremus homes was atop the mountain. It was the so-called Crow's Nest and had to be rebuilt after a suspicious fire broke out in 1865, the very day President Lincoln was assassinated, allegedly following the murder of a physician who lived there. The Doremuses later sold a large portion of their holdings to Samuel Van Saun, who in turn sold a portion of his holdings to John Sanford, owner of the Preakness Race Track and the famous race horse. The same year Doremus came to town, David Danielson Hennion purchased a large tract of land in Lower Preakness for 130 pounds sterling. It included the entire north section of the lower valley between Singac Brook and the Pequannock Patents. Gerritt Gerritson, Jr. followed in 1719, and became another of the larger landowners.

Just after mid-century, in about 1759, came Edo Marselis, whose house at the northeast corner of Hamburg Turnpike and Berdan Avenue stood for 200 years until it was reportedly burned to the ground in a practice session by the local fire department. (Since it

was partially built of stone, any such fire would have needed some help with a bulldozer). Marselis deeded the land which the Preakness Reformed Church was first built on in 1798 along Church Lane. This house of worship was not only the moral center of the community for decades, if not centuries, but served as community center as well, at least until the municipal offices were established at Meads Basin (Mountain View).

A later colonist was James Hinchman who came here in 1825 from Vernon in Sussex County. He operated a large gravel pit above Hamburg Turnpike, on the Green Brook Farm, now the site of the North Jersey Country Club. One of his neighbors, or at least those of his descendants, was the family of Garrett Hobart, who owned the land where William Paterson University is located. Hobart was President William McKinley's first Vice President. He probably would have become President of the United States when McKinley was assassinated, but he also died in office as a result of natural causes.

By and large the most famous of all Preakness Valley, Upper or Lower, residents was Theunis Dey. Little did he and his father realize when they began building their very untypical residence, Bloomsburg or Bloomsbury in 1740, that it would be one of the most significant residences in the history of the country.

Dirck Jansen Dey came to America as a soldier with the Dutch West India Company in 1641. He lived on what was called the Old Company Bowerie (Dutch for Farm) on Manhattan Island. His grandson, also named Dirck, purchased 600 acres from the heirs of Thomas Hart in 1717. He may have lived in the area since 1691 since his widowed mother married George Ryerson, one of the original investors in the three western patents. Skilled as both an architect and builder, the second Dirck undertook the construction of an eight room Georgian Manor at the southern end of Lower Preakness Valley. His son Theunis, linked to the Schuyler family when he married Hester the granddaughter of Arent, eventually inherited the project and the house. His friendship with a fellow farmer from Mount Vernon, Virginia put Preakness on the national map for the first time.

Historical Highlight
Crown of the Valley

Atop Berdan Avenue is the Van Riper-Hopper House, home of the Wayne Museum. To the rear of this 1786 structure is an even older abode, the Van Duyne House, moved here in 1974. The property borders the beautiful Point View Reservoir.

Pancake Hollow is loosely that area from the upper extension of Valley Road to Pines Lake. Within it are Pines and Lionshead Lake, a number of small ponds and streams, as well as the largest body of water, 450 acres, in Wayne proper, the Point View Reservoir. The area that the lake covers has not always been underwater. In fact, prior to the early-1960's when the reservoir was constructed by the Passaic Valley Water Commission to help remedy a severe drought that New Jersey was experiencing, it held remnants of one of the Township's most historic areas. Here were the farms and homesteads of the Berdans, the Van Ripers and the Hoppers. All that remains of this historic region, other than scattered ruins buried under the water is the Van Riper-Hopper House, currently home of the Wayne Museum. It is truly not only a venerable landmark, but the magnificent lakeside setting it occupies along with the rescued and restored Van Duyne House can easily be called the crowning jewel of one of New Jersey's most beautiful communities.

The Preakness Van Ripers are descended from the family of Jurian Thomasse who settled in Bergantown (Jersey City) in 1663. Thomasse Van Riper, Jurian's son was one of the Acquackanonk Patentees. Thomasse's tenth child, Richard, purchased 145 acres bordering the Berdan Tract in Pancake Hollow in 1762 and developed the land into a highly profitable farm complex with numerous community services. Foundations of a grist mill, a saw mill, a cider mill, a distillery, a blacksmith ship, a tannery, and a smoke shop are now under water in the reservoir. The original homestead faced Hamburg Turnpike, later the site of the First Baptist Church.

Richard's first son Uriah Van Riper married neighbor Polly Berdan in 1786 and built a honeymoon cottage, that is now the center area of the home, just to the right of the museum entrance.

The Hopper family traces their ancestry to Andries Hoppen or Hoppe, who arrived in New Netherlands in 1651. One of Andries' direct descendants, Andrew married Mary Ann Van Riper in 1845. Their home became known at the time as The Hopper Place.

The home itself is consider a Dutch Colonial design, more of the type built in the 1740's than the 1780's. It was almost a victim of the building of the reservoir before the entire parcel of land was saved in 1960. Today it serves as the Wayne Museum. In the backyard is the Van Duyne House, where the Wayne Archaeological Research Laboratory operates.

The Wayne Historical Commission and companion Archaeological Research Laboratory have literally preserved the roots of this most historic community. Wayne Township's commitment to its historical roots is one that deserves great praise. In the midst of the Township's centennial celebration in 1947 an active archives was built. Out of it came one of the very few municipally-sponsored historical commissions. Unlike most other communities who rely on a volunteer historical society to preserve its historical roots, Wayne Township funds its own museum, run by the commission, made up of a wide variety of community-interested citizens. Each year the mayor appoints the commissioners, aiming to take advantage of the residents with a particular expertise in various areas. Among its possessions are not only the Van Riper-Hopper complex, but the Schuyler-Colfax house, and an impressive archive collection, including hundreds of photographs, early newspapers, and artifacts.

What was lost in history by the construction of the reservoir was made up for in beauty. It is an awe-inspiring setting, particularly at sunset. Adjacent to the Van Riper-Hopper House is the Point View Reservoir Bird Sanctuary, which not only includes the 450 acre lake, but 200 additional acres of mud flats where over sixty species of water bird have been identified by the New Jersey Audubon Society. A Herb Garden and picnic grounds add another desirous characteristic of a locale that typifies The Beauty of Wayne.

The inside of the Van Riper-Hopper House probably looks much the same as it did two hundred years ago.

Among the activities undertaken by the Commission are events where the members dress up in historic costumes (above) and numerous fairs and demonstrations where authentic dishes are recreated, many personally by the museum curator, Cele Paccioretti, (l., seated on left).

Historical Highlight
Was Wayne's Most Famous Resident........ A Horse?

The great "Preakness"

As idiotic as that may sound, it just may ring true. Unless, of course, that animals qualify and George Washington did not live here long enough to qualify for residency. Without a doubt, the name Preakness is on the lips and in the minds of millions of horse racing enthusiasts each Spring, although most mispronounce it. God forbid that it should be pronounced phonetically, but locals have long pronounced the word "prake-ness." At Pimlico Race Track in Baltimore, Maryland, the oldest of thoroughbred racing's Triple Crown stake races is held annually between the running of the other two, the Kentucky Derby and Belmont Stakes. The Preakness Stakes are internation-

ally famous. Many visiting Wayne for the first time and learning it includes a region by the same name as that renowned stakes race figure there must be some connection. A few local residents have been known to explain that there is. They say that great race horse by the name Preakness once roamed around on a pasture off Valley Road; that this horse won the first big race at Pimlico. They continue by claiming that in its honor the valley where he was bred was named after the three year old. 'Tain't so! As anyone with even a little knowledge of Wayne's history knows, the name Preakness was around years, decades, probably centuries before the nag. The race was named after the

horse. The horse was named after the horse farm where he was raised. The farm was named after the Valley. And the Valley was named after---a deer?

Well, since some say Preakness ran like a deer, it was probably apropos to give him that name, although it is more likely Milton Holbrook Sanford never thought about it that way. Who was Milton Holbrook Sanford? He was the owner of Preakness Farms, Preakness Horse Racing Track, and the Township's most famous resident.

Born in Medway, Massachusetts on August 20, 1812, Sanford was the son of Samuel Sanford, reportedly the owner of the first cotton thread mill in the United States. He was only 19 when his father

Built in about 1770, making it one of the oldest, if least known historic houses in Wayne, the Milton Sanford home was originally occupied by Eno Van Saun. The stucco structure is located at 1158 Preakness Avenue.

passed away and young Milton assumed control of the family business. It was apparent early on that he inherited his father's business prowess, and then some. Within two years, by his 21st birthday, Milton had increased the family fortune to more than $200,000.00. Although personally wiped out by the Financial Panic of 1837, the young businessman was somehow able to keep the family assets intact. He then figured out a revolutionary method of manufacturing jute and built his own small mill in Southboro, Massachusetts. Soon

he was considered one of the wealthiest New Englanders.

Sanford had a touch of the playboy in him and loved fast horses. He purchased a number of race horses and built his own racing stable. In doing so he helped form the American Jockey Club. As the country was in the midst of turmoil during the Civil War, Milton moved his offices to New York City. At about the same time he decided to establish a training farm for his equines. He set about looking for just the right location, somewhere preferably around Paterson, New Jersey where a race track had opened in 1864 that featured the Jersey Derby, America's first horse racing derby. He found it just over the hills in the Lower Preakness Valley. On November 18, 1865 Sanford became a Wayne resident at the age of 55.

The Van Saun family was well established in the Township, with large land holdings in the vicinity of Valley Road and Preakness Avenue. The Marquis de La Fayette had reportedly stayed in Samuel Van Saun's Dutch Colonial home on the west side of Laauwe Avenue while assisting the Colonial Army in 1780. Around the corner at 1158 Preakness Avenue, Enos Van Saun lived in what today is one of the oldest existing homes in all of Wayne, built in about 1770. The Berry family had even older local roots in that Samuel Berry was one of the partners in the Schuyler-Brockholst syndicate.

Sanford paid Enos Van Saun $12,000.00 for a tract of 64 acres, and another $1,500.00 to Henry K. Berry for a smaller parcel of six acres. He built three stables and forty two stalls, a blacksmith shop, a training ring and a 3/4 mile track. The track was located on the northeast corner of Valley Road and Preakness Avenue, now occupied by the shopping center where the A&P is situated. Like all elite racing stables, he needed a name and formal colors. The name he chose was Preakness Farms. The color dark blue.

In 1870 he found the type of horse all stable owners dream about, a four year old dark bay colt that stood sixteen hands high. Preakness was not born on Sandford's property, but at the Woodburn Stock Farm in Kentucky, the son of the great Lexington. The price: $4,000.00, a princely sum in the mid-19th century. In his maiden race, Preakness was entered in the Dinner Plate Stakes, at the inaugural meeting of the Maryland Jockey Club at the new Pimlico Race Track in Baltimore. The stakes were established as the country's second richest with an $18,000.00 purse. On October 25, 1870 the bay colt not only paid for himself, but made Milton Sanford a hefty profit as he finished ahead of the pack by a full length. Over the next five years the horse won 17 of of the 40 races he was entered into, and finished in the money 33 times, an amazing record. His victories included finishing in a dead heat in perhaps the most famous race in the county, the Saratoga Cup in 1875, his last race in America.

In 1873 Pimlico held the first stakes race in America for three year olds. In honor of Sandford's great horse, it was christened the Preakness Stakes. In appreciation, Milton donated the trophy his horse had won three years earlier in the Dinner Plate Stakes. That is the same trophy contested for today.

Preakness was shipped to England along with a string of other horses Sanford sent to compete there in the fall of 1875. Preakness raced four times, finishing first, second, third and fourth. The victory came in the last of the races, the Brighton Cup. His star had now risen in Great Britain, and Milton, always the businessman, offered it and his other thoroughbreds for sale at an auction. It was a tragic mistake.

The Duke of Hamilton purchased the great America champion and put him out to stud. Preakness was a high-spirited animal, and probably found being penned in a stall too confining for an animal who was used to running like a deer. Unfortunately the Duke was apparently even more emotional. After one encounter in the horse's stall, in a fit of anger the blueblood shot and killed the former most famous resident of Wayne. There was a silver lining to the horrific event. It caused a great outcry of animal lovers worldwide, and resulted in the formation of animal cruelty laws, and

reportedly, may have been the inspiration for England's version of the SPCA, *The Society for the Prevention of Cruelty to Animals.*

Eight years later, Milton Holbrook Sanford joined his prize colt in the hereafter, that is, of course if animals qualify.

The upper photo is the former site of the "Preakness Race Track," at the corner of Nellis Drive and Valley Road, used in the 1930's as a bicycle and motorcycle racing facility. Sandford's original "Preakness Track" was located on the northeast corner of Preakness Avenue and Valley Road. Here "Preakness Farms" was the breeding ground for great thoroughbreds. The latter appears on an 1878 map (lower photo).

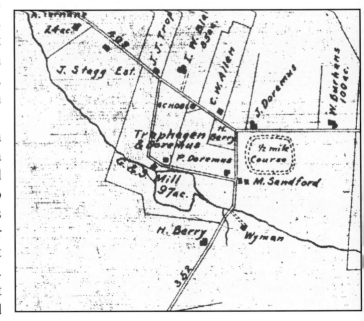

The Kievit Family
Bob, Laura, Bill & Brian

Congratulations to Wayne on its
300 year anniversary, and
Thank You Wayne Lions
for your dedication to our community!

---

*Best Wishes and Congratulations
To the Wayne Lions Club
In Providing Our Township
With This Outstanding Book.*

* * * * * *

*Charles and Patti Tahan
Claudine, Charles, Patti Ann and
Renee*

Kevin Decker, A.R.M.
Insurance Consultant

**Property Casualty
Non Profits
Public Entities
Manufacturers
Hospitals**

**Bus (732) 747-0800
Fax (732) 530-4220
Home (732) 530-5009**

High and Dry! *Debris from the Aquaduct, removed in 1924, which spanned the Pompton River, covers the site where the famous Morris Canal entered Wayne, just north of the Lincoln Park Bridge (r.). shown here in 1998. The photo shows the unpredictable river during a fairly dry period. The same could not be said many times over the years, such as April, 1984. The scene from the air (upper r.) during one of the more renowned floods shows a far more ferocious and problemsome river flooding Mountain View Boulevard. A close-up view (above) is graphic evidence of how bad things were for residents and businesspersons. Too bad , unlike horses, fish are not named, if so Wayne may have had a few famous ones swimming on its roads and in driveways.*

Chapter Six
1780, The Center of the World

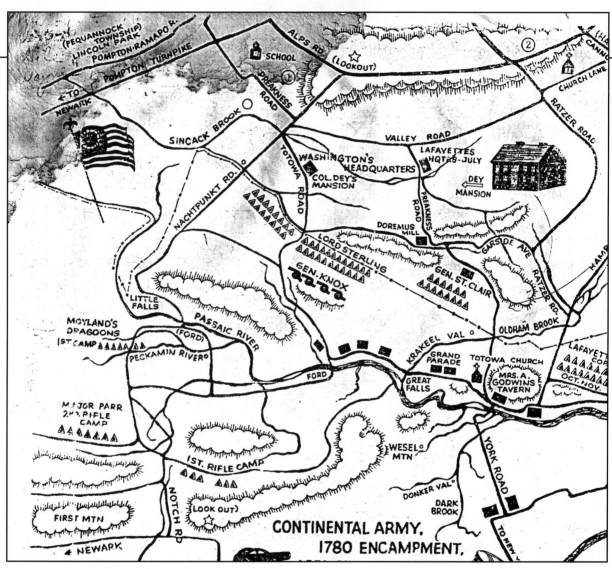

The labels on the map include:

(PEQUANNOCK TOWNSHIP) LINCOLN PARK · POMPTON-RAMAPO R. · POMPTON TURNPIKE · ALPS RD. · SCHOOL · (LOOKOUT) · CHURCH LANE · ② · CANN · RATZER ROAD · ← TO NEWARK · PREAKNESS ROAD · SINCACK BROOK · VALLEY ROAD · LAFAYETTES HQTRS-JULY · NACHTPUNKT RD. · TOTOWA ROAD · WASHINGTON'S HEADQUARTERS · COL. DEY'S MANSION · ← DEY MANSION · PREAKNESS ROAD · DOREMUS MILL · GARSIDE AVE · RATZER RD · HAMP · LORD STERLING · GEN. KNOX · GEN. ST. CLAIR · LITTLE FALLS · PASSAIC RIVER · OLDHAM BROOK · MOYLAND'S DRAGOONS 1ST CAMP · (FORD) · PECKAMIN RIVER · KRAKEEL VAL · GRAND PARADE · TOTOWA CHURCH · LAFAYET COR OCT. NOV. · FORD · GREAT FALLS · MRS. A. GODWINS TAVERN · MAJOR PARR 2ND RIFLE CAMP · WESEL MTN · YORK ROAD · 1ST. RIFLE CAMP · DONKER VAL · DARK BROOK · TO NEW · FIRST MTN · NOTCH RD · (LOOK OUT) · ← NEWARK · **CONTINENTAL ARMY, 1780 ENCAMPMENT,**

The Preakness Valley was ablaze, if not with gun and cannon fire, at least with the colorful uniforms of the many battalions and regiments of American soldiers from throughout the colonies in 1780.

If telecommunications were what they are today, the Lower Preakness Valley in 1780 would have been swarming with CNN and network camera derricks and microphones. Still photographers would have been taking pictures with close-up lenses of the scores of dignitaries who visited the Dey Mansion. Paparazzi would have been clamoring for just the right photo of Hamilton, and famous generals Henry Knox, Arthur St. Clair and Nathaniel Greene. The foreign press would have been pestering Frenchmen the Marquis de Lafayette, the Marquis de Chastellux and colorful Baron Von Steuben. Video magazines and print tabloids would have had their correspondents doing exposes on how New York born William Alexander used his wealth to buy himself a Scottish lordship to become Major-General Lord Sterling, or how "Mad" Anthony Wayne got his nickname. They would have had a literal field day when it was learned that frequent

The Marquis de Lafayette was reported to have stayed at the Samuel Van Saun house, still standing on Laauwe Avenue, just north of Preakness Avenue. Whether he actually lived within the main house, or in a tent on the grounds, remains a subject of some controversy. Nevertheless, this is the spot where the great Frenchman camped.

The house has been modified numerous times since then. To the right is how it looked in 1936, obviously given a Victorian touch in the 19th century. The other photos were taken recently, including one in 1997 (below, r.).

visitor Benedict Arnold became a turncoat. Court TV would have been closely following the rapid trial of Arnold's contact, British Major John Andre, and anti-death penalty advocates would have been picketing against the planned execution of the Englishman in full view of General Washington. The Today Show would have been doing side stories on Ringwood Ironmaster turned cartographer, Richard Erskine, Surveyor-General of the Continental Army. And certainly there would have been attempts to follow up the rumors of a romance between dashing young Connecticut-born Lieutenant William Colfax and local beauty Hester Schuyler. Lt. Colfax was a member and soon-to-be Commander of the elite corps of specially trained troops

responsible for guarding and protecting the larger-than-life presence of George Washington. Miss Schuyler was a relative of the host Dey family, and a descendant of Arent Schuyler, who lived in the second-most famous residence in all of Wayne, the almost 100 year old Schuyler house.

Then again, there may have just been a news black-out of the entire scenario, for security reasons of course. Virtually the entire Upper and Lower Preakness Valley was filled with soldiers in blue coats, brass buttons and long muskets. On both sides of Valley Road, extending from Singac Brook to where it

The Marquis de Lafayette

At The Forks, other members of the Dey clan also played host to the Army. On the Beavertown (Lincoln Park) side of the Pequannock (Pompton) River, on the Thomas Dey property stood a tannery which made shoes for the soldiers. Also located here was the army's post office, commissary and ammunition depot.

And finally, along High Mountain to the east and Pacquannock Mountain to the west, soldiers were erecting watch towers to warn the Americans of the site of any movement of British troops in their direction.

The warm summer breezes which ascended and descended the foothills of the walls of the valley must have been comforting to the Continental Army. It had gone through literal hell while starving and shivering through a winter at Morristown that reportedly saw no less than 26 snow storms. Washington was not only fighting the British, but a severe moral problem within his own ranks. The infamous Pompton Mutiny was to take place a few months later just up the road, now known as Union Boulevard, in Bloomingdale. In a famous letter to Colonel John Lamb the Commander-in-Chief had lamented on June 29th:

then ended at Ratzer Road, were encampments of virtually every major battalion of the Continental Army. To the north and east the right wing of the Army spread out from Berdan Avenue to the site of present-day William Paterson University. Here was also the location of the Flying Hospital. To the south and west the left wing were extended from The Forks (Two Bridges), along Fairfield Road and Parish Drive. Each had their own flags and colors, thus the entire valley was ablaze with reds, blues, greens and yellows.

The lord of the manor was Colonel Theunis Dey, who headed the Bergen County militia. In 1780 Wayne was in fact in that county.

This empty lot, just on the Lincoln Park side of Two Bridges, was the site of Colonial Army's quartermaster, post office and ammunition depot.

"We have at Pompton and Mount Hope furnaces between five and six thousand 18-pound balls, and three thousand shells for the French 9-inch mortars, but I have not been able to have them transported to West Point..."

Between July 1st and 29th the future, if there was to be a future, of the world's newest nation was largely placed on the shoulders of those who chose Wayne as the place to headquarter the main body of the Continental Army. It was a good choice for many reasons. Although northern New Jersey was never the site of any major battles during the war, there was always a fear that the British were but a day or so away from a full assault on the interior of the state. They occupied Manhattan and Staten Islands and were gaining confidence as more and more troops were sent over from England. It is almost inconceivable to believe, given the presence of so many Tories in the state, that London was not fully aware of the struggles Washington and his troops were going through. Defending the interior of New Jersey was vital to defending the entire war effort. It's strategic position between the New England and Southern colonies, between New York City and Philadelphia and between the North (Hudson) and South (Delaware) Rivers was unquestioned.

For two long winters, the army barely survived in Morristown. Efforts by the British to attack through Springfield were surprising repelled by local militia and a motley crew of sloppily-dressed soldiers. An approach from the north was their next step. The Hudson River was relatively narrow near the fort at West Point, thus crossing was fairly easy. There were decent enough roads from there in the direction of Morristown. If the fort was lost, the passes in the Ramapo and Watchung Mountains near Wayne were probably the last bastion of hope. They had to be protected.

The Americans constructed large embankments to partially blockade the approach through the Ramapo Valley to the north of Wayne valleys. General Parr's elite rifle corps guarded the Great Notch, with additional troops sent a few miles to the south to guard Crane's Gap, the small passageway in First Watchung Mountain where Bloomfield Avenue passes from Montclair (then Cranetown) to Verona (then Vernon Valley).

Wayne was almost equidistant between West Point and Morristown, situated along the so-called Revolutionary Highway. Now U.S. 202, the road extended from near Valley Forge, northwest of Philadelphia, passing not far from Trenton and Princeton, through Morristown, through Wayne, and on to the Hudson River Valley just below West Point. The Ringwood, Long Pond, Mount Hope, and of course Pompton Iron Works were close by Wayne. There was an ample supply of fire and building wood, and food supplies in the heavily wooden foothills and mountains. The area was also not far from another important point in the war effort. At New Bridge in Riverdale, the Zabriske (later Von Steuben) home was used to guard the old wooden bridge over the Hackensack River. Taking a look at the steel replacement bridge that replaced the original structure 100 years ago, one would hardly believe that such a short span would have been so important, but it was. The Hackensack River is certainly not considered a major American, much less major New Jersey River. Many portions of it seemingly could be crossed without much effort. However this is now and that was then, and travel by wagon, horseback and on foot was far more arduous than any late 20th century man or woman can imagine.

For many months the British and American armies played a sort of war tag, each trying to take control of New Bridge. The route there was rather easy from Preakness---along what is now the Hamburg Turnpike through Paterson and Passaic (nee Acquackanonk), across another wooden (and later steel) bridge over the Passaic River (Acquackanonk Landing) and east to Hackensack River and then north along the western bank to High Bridge just above New Barbados (Hackensack). Once the bridge was crossed the route proceeded to Liberty Pole (Palisades Avenue, just north of Englewood), allowing easy access to Fort Lee, the strategic Bull's Ferry Blockhouse a few miles further south, and Pawles Hook (Jersey City).

From the Dey Mansion, one of Washington's most

enthusiastic and creative generals, a Pennsylvanian named Anthony Wayne seemed constantly anxious to make up for a series of clouds on his otherwise Stirling record. He was charged and then exonerated with bungling a major battle near his hometown in Eastern Pennsylvania at Paoli, and received added flack from another strategic botch at Germantown. While at the mansion, he again had some problems when his planned attack on the Bull's Ferry Blockhouse led to the unnecessary loss of several lives and a huge embarrassment for the Americans. A small group of defenders successfully held off the charge of several hundred troops, armed with cannons and other assault weapons.

Nevertheless, Wayne more than made up for his problems when he engineered a successful victory at the strategic Stony Point on the Hudson River below West Point. He was considered enough of a war hero to stand above all of the other famous dignitaries who visited Bloomburg (the Dey mansion) in 1780 and of course to have the entire region named after him 67 years later.

The course of the war clearly changed during Washington's relatively brief stay in Wayne. He and his troops came with little hope of success, and left with total victory on the immediate horizon. Today, the media would be bombarding the public with retrospectives on how things went at Preakness. Many of the participants would undoubtedly have been the subject of *Where Are They Now* segments on war heroes and villains. Certainly all Americans would remember where they were the day they heard peace and independence was finally achieved with the formal surrender of Mother England.

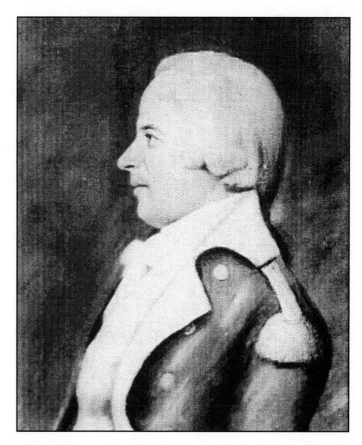

Two portraits of General Anthony Wayne. Top photo was probably painted later in his life, perhaps in the early 1790's, shortly before his death. While he may have been called "Mad" Anthony, he undoubtedly was sane enough to make a lot of British generals nuts themselves with his skillful tactics.

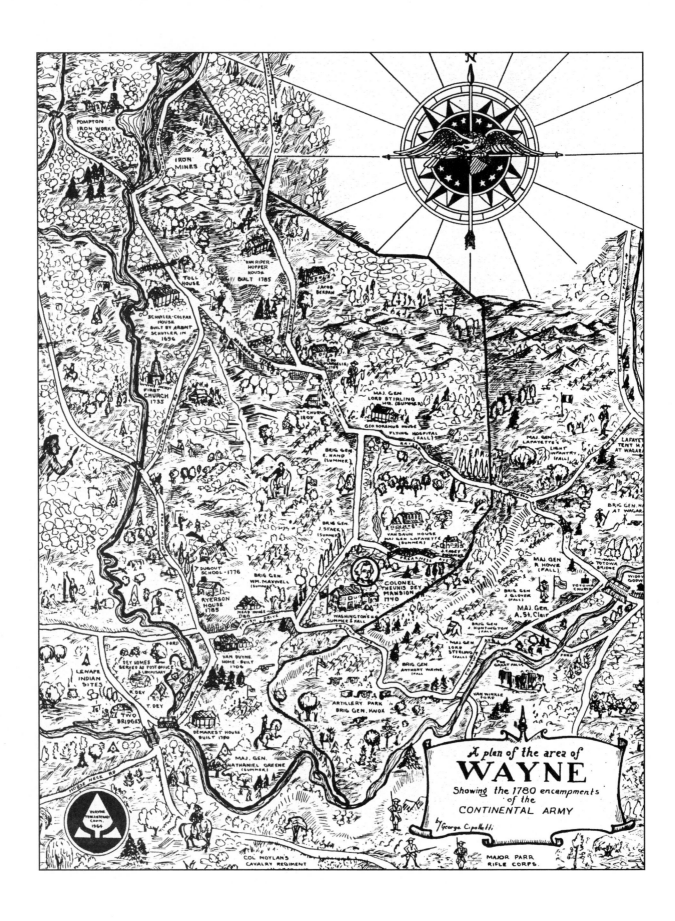

Historical Highlight
"Mad" Anthony Wayne

It is probably easier to understand why one of a number of other possibilities were not selected as the new Township's name in 1847 instead of naming it in honor of a man who was never a resident of the area and had been dead more than half a century. Absent a clear record of the debate which led up to the choice, one can only speculate. Preakness and Schuyler had to be considered. Although the former was obviously very popular, the name used to identify the eastern valley for possibly centuries before, those who resided in the western and first-settled valley probably balked at the idea. Likewise,

"Mad Anthony," namesake of the Township, was crazy "like a fox."

while choosing the latter would have been a fitting tribute to Captain Arent Schuyler, those in the Preakness Valley probably vetoed it for much the same reason....it only described about one-third of the area. Other communities had already taken the name of two of the three major rivers, the Passaic, Pompton and Pequannock, while the fourth, the Ramapo, had long been associated with a population of half-breeds who inhabited the northern mountain ranges. The Ramapo Mountain People who resided in ramshackle abodes were not exactly considered country ladies and gents.

Many communities favored being named after American presidents, but the most popular---Jefferson, Madison, Monroe, etc.---were also taken, or about to be taken by none-too-distant neighbors. And apparently the majority of the voters resisted the obvious inclination to name but another New Jersey town after the

Father of our Country. After all, there are more than twenty different Garden State communities named Washington. Almost as widely adopted was the name Franklin. No less than three communities within ten miles of the region went by that name. And at the time, naming towns after geographic or geologic features was yet to be commonplace.

Pennsylvania-born Anthony Wayne was obviously a very popular American general. But so were many others of equal or higher rank (Brigadier-General) who served the Commander-in-Chief during his 1780 stays at Preakness, and who probably had more notoriety. So why was the Township named after a man who was born (on New Years Day, 1745) and died (on December 15, 1796) in the Quaker State, and who had a turbulent career? The best guess is that many of the voters' grandparents and great-grandparents probably associated with the man who some say personified the American Spirit of '76. The colonists who fostered the Revolution were rambunctious rebels, traits also used to describe Anthony. Like him, they had minds of their own. And also like him, many probably had been persecuted by the authorities who controlled their lives until they battled for independence.

Another reason may have been that Wayne led the

American army to a victory at a battle at Stony Point on the Hudson that just may have been the turning point in the war.

Anthony Wayne tasted the agony of defeat along with the thrill of victory, time and time again. He was the owner of a tannery and an extensive property owner in his home area, a farm outside of Paoli, Pennsylvania, about twenty miles from Philadelphia. In 1776 the grandson of Irish immigrants was commissioned as a colonel in the 4th Pennsylvania Regiment of the Continental Army. He was soon rushed into battle in Canada to help rescue General Benedict Arnold's beleaguered forces. Wayne apparently impressed enough of his superiors to quickly rise in the ranks and was appointed commander at the important Fort Ticonderoga. There, against all odds, he held the fort against the attacks of the British led by General Burgoyne. This early success led to his promotion to Brigadier-General. Additional success followed, particularly at the Battle of Brandywine Creek. Perhaps too much success.

Many believe that General Wayne had become too overconfident, and this overconfidence almost ruined his career. Near his birthplace, his troops were the victims of a surprise attack by British General Grey, the infamous Paoli Massacre. Anthony was the scapegoat, and was found guilty of "carelessness and neglect" by a court of inquiry. Despite the fact that he was completely exonerated by general court marshal, his reputation was badly damaged the day he was in charge when 300 Continentals were killed by forces of the Crown who suffered only six casualties themselves. His chance to regain that reputation came in another important battle at Germantown. Whipping his Pennsylvanians into a frenzy with the cry "Avenge Paoli," this was simply not the time or the place and another bitter defeat followed.

Had not talent been thin, Anthony Wayne's career may have been over at this time. But he was to be given another chance very soon. Leading a courageous stand in an apple orchard outside Monmouth, New Jersey in June, 1778, the general was credited with saving the day for the Americans, and thus was able to right his career. A year later he gained what was probably his greatest victory. Just above what is

Haverstraw, New York, below West Point, Wayne's careful planning outwitted the Brits, and this time the calls to "Remember Paoli" had the desired effect.

From that point on, Anthony Wayne was a trusted, if still sometimes criticized, assistant to the Commander-in-Chief. He was assigned to Preakness and was instrumental in drawing plans for many mini-battles and to protect the interior of New Jersey from the major English assault that never came. Despite another embarrassing incident when troops under his command failed to take a blockhouse overlooking the Hudson across from Manhattan at Bulls Ferry defended by only a handful of British defenders, Wayne was on scene when ultimate victory was achieved.

After the war Wayne continued to serve the country with dignity. Perhaps his most noteworthy stint was after being appointed to serve as Commander-in-Chief of the down-sized American Army by President Washington in 1791. The army had suffered a string of defeats at the hands of the Indian Confederation, who up until then had successfully repelled all American attempts to move into the Midwest. Under Wayne the army effectively ended the Indian resistance at the Battle of Fallen Timbers despite being outnumbered 2 to 1. He then negotiated the Treaty of Greenville in 1795, which required the Indians to cede to the United States most of Ohio and large sections of Indiana, Illinois and Michigan. Wayne died while still on duty the next year.

Oh yes, about the "Mad" nickname. He certainly had a reputation of always being ready to rush into battle. He sometimes seemed preoccupied with other than things at hand. But he was obviously sane enough to have become one of the country's most respected generals by the time he died at the age of only 51. The story goes that he was given his nickname by a former neighbor who himself had a peculiar moniker--Jemmy The Rover. The young man was called that because of his pension for desertions from the army. After being arrested one time, he had hopes that Wayne would come to his rescue, but when Anthony failed to intercede Jemmy was quoted as remarking:

"Anthony is mad. Mad Anthony, that's
what he is. Mad Anthony Wayne."

Historical Highlight
The Dey Mansion

Most travel books list only one place of any historical significance in Wayne---The Dey Mansion, George Washington's Headquarters. Many ignore the Van Riper-Hopper and Schuyler-Colfax Houses, and certainly none make mention of most of the hundreds of other historical places memorialized in this book. While we have elected to use the oldest-surviving, and probably first-erected home on our cover, the second oldest-surviving one certainly deserves the recognition it so frequently receives.

The Passaic County Parks Commission, present owners of the former abode of George Washington's good friend, Colonel Theunis Dey can honestly make a claim that even the White House itself cannot---"Washington did sleep here."

Compared to virtually every mid-18th century home in Northern New Jersey, one can imagine how impressive the mansion must have been when it was built by Theunis and his father Derck more than a half-century before Washington's arrival. The walls were built of brick and mortar, fastened together by immense oak timbers with huge wooden pins. The outside of the two

The great house, before (top) and after (in 1936) being extensively renovated.

story structure dimensions are 50'X30'. A large hall, 12' wide runs through the center portion of the first floor. On both sides of the hall the Deys built two large rooms with fireplaces faced with brown sandstone. In an era when ceilings were not particularly high, this villa had a 9' high one on the first floor and 8' high one on the second floor. The distinctive double-pitched gambrel roof covers four good-sized attic rooms. It is believed that many of the building materials were imported not only from distant American but even foreign regions. The brownstone which adorns much of the house came from the local quarries in Little Falls along the Passaic River. Several dormers were later added, but removed in 1933-34 when a major restoration took place.

Located at 199 Totowa Road, when built the home did not have that address. It was situated in the same place it now stands, but in those days most homes were identified not by a street address but a name. While there are extensive records pertaining to this building, there are varying versions of exactly what the Deys called their home. Some indicated it was known as "Bloomsburg," while at least one other identifies it as "Bloomsbury."

In 1801 Wayne's most famous landmark was sold by the Dey family. Until it was acquired by its present owner in 1918, its title was passed around as if it was a hot potato. The chain of title shows no less than twenty owners, not even counting inter-family transfers. They are listed in this order:

1740-1801, the Dey family; 1801-1813 the Neafie family; 1813-1861, Marynes J. Hogancamp and family; 1861-1864, Isaac Yeomans; 1864-1865, Anthony Gillan; 1865-1866 Sarah M. Tainter; 1866-1875, Maria Millington; 1875-1883, John M. Howe; 1883-1889, Henry Heeseman; 1889-1891, George C. Islieb; 1891-1892, Heeseman again; 1892-1901, Ellen Petry; 1901-1902, Heeseman a third time; 1902-1906, William H. Belcher; 1906-1907 Albert French; 1907-1909 Franklin Murphy (Governor of New Jersey); 1909-1912, Edward S. Wright; 1912-1918, Edward A. Pfister; 1918-1923, Michael and Elizabeth Allsheimer; 1923-present, Passaic County Department of Parks.

This real estate version of musical chairs could possibly be attributed to several facts. First of all, several

owners probably purchased it solely because of its fame, and once they held it for a short while, that allure departed. Secondly, so large a dwelling required expensive maintenance and care, not to mention huge utility bills and the great costs of upkeeping the land, which at one time included more than 352 acres. The land was slowly lessened, as smaller parcels were sold off from time to time. It is reported that it now includes 56.31 acres.

During these many exchanges, until the parks department purchased it three quarters of a century ago through their agent, Arthur S. Sullivan for $73,000.00, the most anybody else ever paid for such a large piece of local history was the $19,700.00 the Tainters paid Mr. Gillan. As shown by Mr. Heeseman's three periods of ownership, there were a few foreclosures along the way.

The Dey family has long departed Wayne. There is some controversy whether or not Theunis is buried in the family cemetery on the original property due to the absence of a gravestone. In his magnificent and detailed study on early Preakness, Reverend Labaw states that the old Colonel's remains were indeed interred here.

The land surrounding the mansion had been cultivated from the days the Deys moved in until it was transformed into its present usage as a county park and public golf course. Dey's son Richard inherited the estate and rose even higher in the military ranks than his father. When he was tragically killed after falling from a horse in Fairfield in 1811, he attained the rank of General. Richard did not move far away after the sale, only a few miles south to the banks of the river near the Little Falls. The exact location of his new home is unclear, but it is likely it was on the Wayne or Totowa side. (A small portion of the Township was ceded to Totowa when the latter also broke away from Manchester in 1898). A very descriptive statement of the general area was given in an advertisement placed in The Centinel of Freedom, a Newark newspaper when Richard put this property as well up for sale the year before he was killed. On Tuesday, August 7,14,21 and 28, 1810, the ad read as follows:

"For sale-33 acres of land adjoining the Little Passaick Falls in Bergen County, and State of New Jersey. Upon the premises are erected a good stone, and two frame dwelling houses, a barn, saw mill and out houses. The situation is one of the best in the United States for the erection of water works of any description, and may be at a moderate expense so constructed as to command the whole water of the Passaick River.
There is also a good free stone quarry, and there are large tracts of timber and woodland in the neighborhood of it. It is distant ten miles from Newark by the Turnpike Road, six miles from Paterson Landing, from whense boats ply to the city of New York. 10,000 dols of the purchase money may remain on mortgage for any reasonable length of time, on payment of the interest annually.
    Apply to Anthony Dey, No. 19 Pine Street, N. York, or on the premises to Richard Dey."

Apparently there were no takers, and shortly after Richard's death was reported in the same paper, a second advertisement was placed a week later on October 22, 1811. It said:

"For Sale--the property at the Little Passaick Falls, lately occupied by General Dey, deceased, containing fifty-two acres, with the right of erecting a Toll-Bridge over the river. A large quantity of land adjoining can be procured if the purchaser requires it."

The exact date that a wooden covered bridge was erected over what is now Union Avenue connecting Little Falls and Wayne is unclear. It was probably erected by Robert Beattie, owner of the famed carpet mills, who cut the wide road through the area to con-

nect Little Falls and his properties with the original Boonton Line (which passed just north of where U.S. 46 now crosses). This was apparently the site of the suggested "Toll-Bridge" mentioned in the advertisement. The "Turnpike Road" was obviously the Newark and Pompton Turnpike, constructed five years earlier. The idea for a "water works" was apparently a good one as the New Jersey Water District plant was built here some years later.

The Dey Mansion was partially destroyed on at least one occasion by fire, was reportedly in a terrible state of disrepair during the Depression, and probably not too far from seeing the wrecking ball on numerous occasions. Fortunately, it has been saved, authentically restored, and is now open to public tours.

Colonel Theunis Dey was related by marriage to Arent Schuyler's descendants. There is some question where he is buried. One report states it is in an unmarked grave on his former estate.

Historical Highlight
Cannonball Road

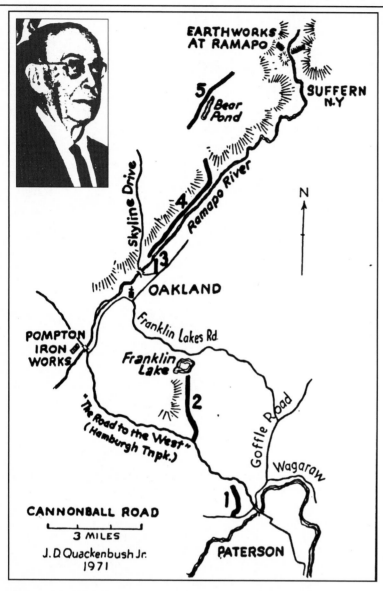

Longtime local resident J. D. Quackenbush in 1971 published an article for the Passaic County Historical Society contending the famed "Cannonball Road" ran through the heart of Wayne as this map he drew indicated. The exact route is to many still a mystery.

Perhaps only the invention of a working time machine in the future will solve the greatest historical mystery of the Wayne area. "Where exactly did the Cannonball Road run?" Most historians agree that during the Revolutionary War, the Colonial Army surreptitiously built and used a secret road from the Pompton and other nearby ironworks to the Hudson in the vicinity of West Point.

The road was used to carry cannonballs and other ammunition to the battlefronts, and anticipated battlefronts. U.S. 202 has been called the Revolutionary Highway. It richly deserved that moniker as along it more battles were fought and more sites were used as Washington's headquarters than any other road during the entire war. It was obviously well known to the British, particularly that portion of it between Pompton and Bear Mountain, locally called The High Road, The Road To Oakland, and now Terhune Drive. So well known that it would have been foolhardy not to have an alternate road between the ironworks and the Hudson.

In his classic work on the local iron industry, Vanishing Ironworks of the Ramapos, author James M. Ransom devotes a full chapter to discussing and trying to end this now 200 year old secret.

Many explorers, hikers, historians, archeologists, cartologists and others have discovered a series of half-obliterated and old wood roads across numerous ridges in the mountains between Wayne and Stony Point, where "Mad" Anthony Wayne had his greatest success. Most of them appear to be shored up, as if their builders anticipated them having to bear very heavy loads. Such as cannonballs?

There is additional evidence that these dirt trails seem to have been carefully leveled, filled in in spots, as if a considerable amount of money was spent by whomever took on the task. The Indians certainly didn't go to these extremes. Farmers certainly would not have taken their crops up to the ridge of the mountains when there were sufficient valley roads to bring their harvests to market.

Above the Pompton Lakes' New York and Susquehanna Railroad station is a road called Cannonball Road. It ends at the Dupont Plant a few miles to the north. A few years back an odd object was

found protruding out from the road bed. It turned out to be a cannonball. Was this the secret road? There is more evidence that it was than any other contender.

However, in 1971 John D. Quackenbush, Jr.. wrote an article published by the Passaic County Historical Society that theorizes Cannonball Road, or at least one of the Cannonball Roads, went through the heart of Wayne. A long-time resident of the region when he wrote the article, Quackenbush claimed to have found a number of unrelated segments of what he believed was the secret road, which if extended would form one continuous road. But his road does not run from the Pompton Ironworks, but surprisingly, Totowa. Beginning behind Second Reformed Church the Quackenbush route entered eastern Wayne and crossed Hamburg Turnpike and cut through the middle of what is now the North Jersey Country Club. He claimed that many oldtimers referred to this road before later development obliterated it, as "Cannonball Road." What makes his claim somewhat believable is that each of these segments had similar characteristics that such a military road would require: They were 4 or 5 feet wide, without any steep grades, the higher portions dug away and low spots filled with stones covered with dirt. Given the fact that this route would not have served any other purpose, then why did someone expend so much time and money for a dirt road apparent-

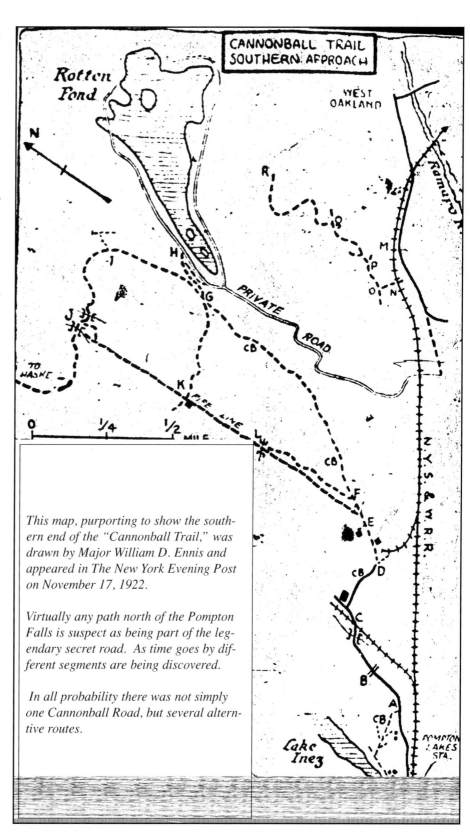

This map, purporting to show the southern end of the "Cannonball Trail," was drawn by Major William D. Ennis and appeared in The New York Evening Post on November 17, 1922.

Virtually any path north of the Pompton Falls is suspect as being part of the legendary secret road. As time goes by different segments are being discovered.

In all probability there was not simply one Cannonball Road, but several alternative routes.

ly heading nowhere but towards an uninhabited area of the county? Is it possible that there may be a few can-

nonballs buried along the fairways of the posh country club?

Chapter Seven
The Big Roads, Canal and Iron Horses

Looking northwest in Mountain View around 1910, Meads Basin, Hixon's Mountain View Hotel and the wooden bridge of the Newark and Pompton Turnpike over the Morris Canal are all in view. The D.L.&W. tracks ran just to the north (right) of here. Today (below) things have dramatically changed.

The term "Colonists" left the local jargon when America escaped from being anyone's colony. Just over the mountain from Wayne, Alexander Hamilton founded the nation's first industrial city, named after William Paterson, a New Jersey governor. Under the guidance of the Society For Establishment of Useful Manufactures (S.U.M.) the power of The Great Falls of the Passaic was harnessed and directed into three man-made falls and raceways, the moving water from which newly constructed manufacturing mills were powered. In 1793 the first cotton mill was built, and Paterson became known as Cotton City at first, then Locomotive City and finally Silk City. Over the next century and a few years it was the national

This path leading to Farmingdale Road at Eldorado is paved with stones, indicative of an ancient road. In that Slingerland Bridge, the first in the Township, crossed the Pompton River just west of here, this may have been the road leading up to that bridge.

center of those three industries. Other northeast cities were industrialized, all in a move to end the technological dependence on Mother England following the end of political dependence that was accomplished with the long and hard war.

By the beginning of the war, New Jersey had emerged as having more roads than any other single British colony. Highlighted by the Kings Highway linking New York and Philadelphia, a series of post roads, and industrial highways, the state was soon considered America's Main Street. The farming and iron industries heavily contributed to this situation. Each forge was a miniature industrial village, usually built in previously totally rural areas in order to provide the much needed timber required to fuel the furnaces. A

tavern, the actual legal term, was built every few miles or so to accommodate the massive number of travelers. Since more often than not taverns were converted houses, they were referenced simply as houses by Jerseyans. Over time, however, they developed into much more elaborate edifices, some having ballrooms, resident fiddlers for dancing and wealthy innkeepers. By 1784 there were 443 licensed taverns, roughly one for every hundred and seventy male inhabitants of New Jersey. Although supported to a great extent by travelers, who came by in their large Jersey Wagons and the growing number of stage coach lines, virtually each one was a place for the locals to argue their ethnic, religious and political differences.

The heavy use of the state's roads caused the hastily and crudely built byways to easily fall into a state of disrepair. Few were willing to spend the money or devote the manpower to maintain them in decent order. Not long after the settling of the state, the official machinery for creating a road system was in place. But local boards failed to act, and early settlers were reluctant to pay taxes for roads they seldom used themselves. Two years after the reunification of East and West New Jersey in 1702 an act was passed naming Commissioners of Highways, overseen and chosen by Justices of Peace. This helped the industrial cities develop roads in and through their communities. However, relatively rural areas like Wayne, which did not even have an organized government until 1847, did not benefit very much.

By the end of the war, Wayne still had relatively few improved roads. Most were the main drags first used by the Indians, later traders, trappers and farmers, and finally the Colonial Army. As discussed earlier, the first of these was an important branch of the Minisink Trail, which ran along the Passaic, Pompton and Ramapo Rivers before crossing near the Pompton Falls and continuing on to Sussex County and New York. This was sometimes referred to as the Pequannock Road. A second is what has been called the Old Pumpton Road (aka Preakness Road). This road appears to have entered the area in the northeastern portion of Preakness Valley near where Hamburg Turnpike now does after twice crossing the Passaic

River, first near Acquackanonk Landing (Main Avenue and Gregory in Passaic) and a second time south of the Great Falls in Totowa. The general path of the Paterson and Hamburg Turnpike appears to have closely followed this earlier route.

The Old Pumpton Road in Wayne is believed to have run above the line of present day Ratzer Road, itself cut through in 1771, where it continued across the valley to a point near the site of the Preakness Reformed Church. It continued along the general route of upper Jackson Avenue, where it probably split into two branches. One branch undoubtedly went to the Brockholst Mill/Pompton Furnace at Pompton Falls after intersecting with the aforementioned branch of the Minisink Trail, presumably along the route of Black Oak Ridge Road. The second branch presumably crossed the river at a ford close to where Pompton Plains Cross Road now does. The first church in Wayne was located on present day Shore Road between North and South Roads to the northwest of George Kuehm's Farmview farm. Records indicate it was erected along what is described as a "public road near a convenient ford in the river." At least at one point in time, another crossing was just across the Slingerland Bridge, the first bridge in the Township. That point was near the northern end of North Pequannock Avenue, slightly above where Black Oak Ridge Road and State Route 23 now cross. The public road described in the church records may have been either an earlier route of Black Oak Ridge Road, or what has been called Schuyler's Road.

While the precise time is almost impossible to confirm, it appears that a third early road may have run from Little Falls in the general direction of present day Riverview Drive to where Totowa Road has long intersected with that road. It then ran along the general path of Valley Road and Church Lane. There may have been a toll crossing at one point along this road over the Passaic River above the Little Falls.

One theory concludes that a road perhaps even older the Old Pumpton Road may have entered the Pompton Falls area near present day Terhune Drive (Route 202),

The Riverview Drive overpass across U.S. 46 (upper photo) and the Newark & Pompton Turnpike bridge over the Pompton River (lower photo) both contain sculptured markers identifying both highways by their former State Route names. The photo below is of the latter bridge taken in 1925.

The northeast corner of Black Oak Ridge Road and the Newark and Pompton Turnpike still contains evidence of the junction when it was heavily traveled before State Route 23 was realigned in the mid-1930's. Note the old turnpike obelisk.

The bridge over the Pompton River connecting Lincoln Park and Mountain View, in 1925 (above) and today (below).

branching off from an old trail which cut across southern Bergen County.

Early maps indicate that at the time of the Revolutionary War, there was obviously a road between Two Bridges and the Dey Mansion, which continued along present day Totowa Road to the Passaic River. This route was probably the forerunner of Fairfield Road and Parish Drive (nee lower Preakness Road). In addition to the two turnpikes discussed below and the successors of those discussed above, mid-19th century maps show only a handful of other roads in the 26 square mile Township. They included Berdan Road, Hinchman Lane (parallel and about a half mile east of Church Lane), Preakness Avenue and Two Bridges Road, forerunner to State Route 6, which followed present day U.S. 46 and Minisink Road to Totowa. Wayne may not have benefited much from the Road Commissioner system, but it certainly did from the Turnpike Era. This period was ushered in at the advent of the 19th century as an organized effort to upgrade the state's overused, but neglected highways. A Turnpike was a private road by which access was gained by paying a toll at various points, causing the tollkeeper to turn the pike which blocked the roadway. The first such road in this state was the Morris Turnpike, linking Elizabeth Town with Morristown and Newton in Sussex County. By 1829 the state legislature chartered fifty-one turnpike companies, resulting in more than 550 miles of improved roads being built and maintained. The latter stages of this era coincided with another, the Canal Era. The legendary Morris Canal, along with the far more successful Delaware and Raritan Canal, was built. The former connected the Delaware at Philipsburg with the Hudson, 104 miles away. The lat-

ter connected the lower Delaware near Trenton with the Raritan River near New Brunswick. Both eras came to a screeching halt with the successful debut of the railroad. The John Bull steam locomotive pulled the Camden and Amboy cars diagonally across the middle of the state, and was soon joined by tens of other lines running in every conceivable direction, extending to virtually every nook and cranny of the state. (The John Bull was saved and is on permanent display at the Smithsonian Institution's National Museum of American History in Washington, D.C.).

The view along the old Newark and Pompton Turnpike before it became State Route 23 hardly looks like today's superhighway.

Preakness Road (above) was renamed "Parish Drive" after LeGrand Parish. This early postcard shows a portion of road which Revolutionary War soldiers marched on between their supply center at Two Bridges and Washington's headquarters at the Dey Mansion in lower Preakness.

Before Wayne was served by portions of this legendary rail system, it benefited from two of the state's longest turnpikes which still pass through from the south and east, meeting at Colfax Corner in Pompton Lakes.

The one mode of transportation that missed Wayne was the trolley. It could not negotiate the hill and ended on Broadway in Paterson.

Weinmann's Roadside Market was typical of the numerous roadside businesses which served both turnpikes when the automobile became popular and Americans "took to the road." It survives today along Hamburg Turnpike.

In 1806, both the 19 mile Newark and Pompton and 44 mile Paterson and Hamburg Turnpikes were chartered and built. The Township was the perfect location for these largely industrial routes. Iron and timber from the Highlands could now be more easily shipped to Paterson, Newark and New York City along both Big Roads. So could the crops of Sussex, Morris and Passaic County farmers. A stage line began to run along the Paterson and Hamburg Turnpike connecting Sussex County with Newark and Jersey City. It alternated several times a week between this road and the Union and Morris Turnpikes which paralleled the P&H, through Union, Essex, Morris and Warren Counties. Another line later ran along the N&P. One of the most noted stage stops on the upper turnpike was at the Norton Inn, just east of the Pompton Furnace and Falls.

The Township was also arguably the most important stop along the Morris Canal. Meads Basin got its name from the small water basin on the land first settled by John Mead, one of the original Schuyler-Brockholst land purchasers. Located across from where Gabriel's Hotel and Restaurant has stood since 1909, originally known as Hixon's Mountain View Hotel, the basin was surrounded by a depot, general store, blacksmith shop and, later on, a post office. Here mule-drawn canal boat crews could unwind, rest, and find ample grub and grog, and even spend the night if they wished. Just to the west, the Pompton Feeder brought water from Greenwood Lake in upper Passaic County, picking up iron loads at the Pompton Furnace. Picturesque wooden bridges dotted the entire route of the main and feeder canals, wherever an important road passed over it, or where the canal itself passed over a river or major stream. At the point where it entered and where it left Wayne, elaborate aqueducts carried the industrial waterway over the Pompton and then Passaic Rivers.

In 1865 the first of two railroad lines finally reached Wayne. The Morris & Essex's (and later Delaware, Lackawanna & Western's) Boonton Line carried both passengers and freight through the Meads Basin/Mountain View station just southeast of the intersection of the Newark & Pompton Turnpike and Parish Drive, and just east of the canal. Less than a decade later, a second line, the Montclair Railway, erected two stations in the Township. One was at what is now Mountain View, a few hundred yards south of where the main and feeder canals met. The second was aside the Laflin & Rand Powder Works in Old Wayne (see below). Later known by a variety of other names, including the New York and Greenwood Lake Branch of the Erie Railroad, this single track line extended from its beginnings at Pavonia Station on the docks of the Hudson River in Jersey City to its last stop at Sterling Forest on the New Jersey/New York borderline at Greenwood Lake. It literally ran from ferry to ferry. At Pavonia, passengers could catch one to cross the Hudson River to Manhattan. At Sterling Forest, another could be caught to take vacationers to a variety of fancy hotels dotting the entire shoreline of the beautiful lake, often

Located at 6 Fairfield Road, just north of where IS 80 crosses high overhead, stands a well-worn old home with a straight line of trees standing between the front porch and the roadway. Little do most present-day passsersby realize that this rather lost old home was once a popular stagecoach stop and tavern, boasting "the longest bar around." It has stood nearly for most of the last two centuries. For many years it was known as "The Maples." The trees were in the middle of a circular driveway that the coaches used to drop off passengers. In earlier days there was no U.S. 46., so Fairfield and Two Bridges Roads were the major east-west thoroughfares across the south end of the Township.

1892 Colton Road Map of Passaic County shows the few major roads which ran through Wayne.

called Lake Geneva of America.

   With the railroads, turnpikes, canals and improved Indian and Colonial Roads, by the late 19th and into the early 20th centuries, Wayne was clearly a heavily traveled crossroads of the entire northern portion of New Jersey.   It was also by then well on its way to becoming a legally, if not actually, unified community as well.

Two views of Mountain View Erie station are shown 90 years ago, looking north with the A&P in the distance. Note the tracks ran west of the station, unlike today.

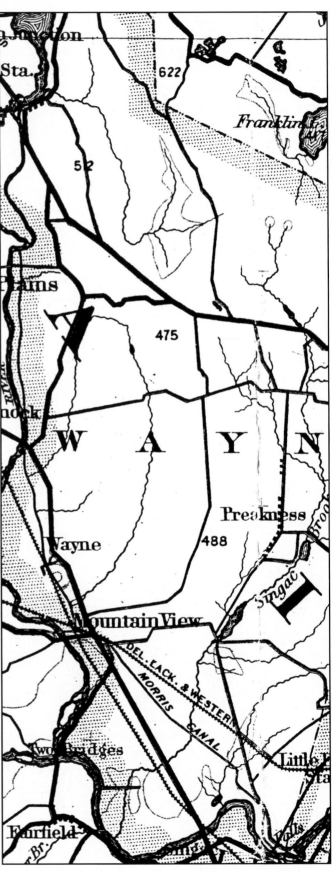

Wayne's First Railroad Station, The Old Morris & Essex/ Delaware, Lackawanna & Western at Mountain View....the original "Boonton Line."

Located south of Parish Drive and west of Boonton Avenue, the original station survived more than 100 years. Preakness Road, renamed for LeGrand Parish, crossed here.

Today the site is decayed and deteriorating.

The railroads passed over the main channel of the Morris Canal and Pompton Feeder via two iron drawbridges, just north of Route 202

The D.L.& W. crossed the main channel with a drawbridge that was lowered and elevated to allow canal boats to pass.

The feeder canal was crossed by the Erie over a bridge (below) which flipped up or down.

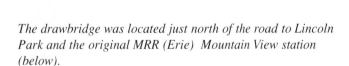

The drawbridge was located just north of the road to Lincoln Park and the original MRR (Erie) Mountain View station (below).

The old Erie tracks continue to the right but go nowhere today. The new ones go to the left and west following the D.L.&W.'s old "Boonton Line."

A grass path is what is left of the Pompton Feeder north of Mountain View. Here it crosses the abandoned D.L.&W. tracks. The large elevator drawbridge was on this site.

This is the spot where the flip bridge of the main channel of the Morris Canal was located, just above Boonton Avenue.

Buried in the concrete just northeast of the present intersection is what may be the last remnants of the flip bridge, this small piece of iron buried in concrete.

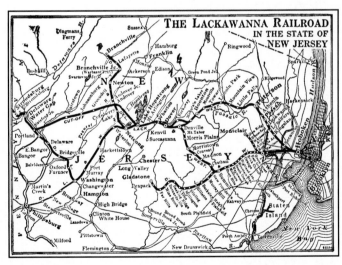

By 1944 railroad service in New Jersey had already been curtailed from its peak at the turn of the century. Nevertheless, as this map printed on the back of Delaware, Lackawanna and Western Railroad time table shows, it was still extensive, especially compared with how it is today. The D.L.&W. served Wayne, but this map shows the local stop only as "Mountain View." As was often the case, "Wayne" was rarely part of the common vernacular. "Pompton," "Preakness," "Totowa," and "Mountain View" often meant "Wayne."

Historical Highlight
Paterson and Hamburg Turnpike

It is a matter of conjecture and opinion whether the Newark and Pompton (N&P), or Paterson and Hamburg Turnpike played the more significant role in the transformation of Wayne from a colonial, rural outpost to a modern suburb (a term many residents would probably take issue with). One thing is certain, both were very important to the development of the Township.

Across the street from the 1696 Schuyler-Colfax House is one of the original toll keeper's homes, shown (top) in 1936 and today. It was probably constructed around the time the P&H was built (1806). In front was a tollgate or "pike."

The Paterson and Hamburg Turnpike (P&H) was incorporated one week after its southern and western counterpart. It originally was twice as long as Israel Crane's Big Road, stretching from Acquackanonk Landing (Passaic) at the Passaic River through Paterson, Wayne, Pompton Lakes, and onto Hamburg in Sussex County, a 44 mile course. It was arguably the most important road in this portion of New Jersey, and certainly the northernmost major turnpike. It was later extended further northwest to Deckertown (Sussex) and southeast all the way to Jersey City. One of its incorporators was the famed Ironmaster, Martin J. Ryerson.

The route followed the approximate path of the Old Pumpton Road in Wayne, except where that old trail dipped to the south to pass by the site and later location of the Preakness Reformed Church. For its day, the P&H was a mighty highway, linking the Sussex County farms and the Morris and Passaic County ironworks with industrial Paterson, Jersey City, and the ferries which crossed the Hudson to Manhattan. At Pompton Lakes it linked with the Ringwood Turnpike (now State Route 511) and thus the Long Pond and Ringwood iron mines and works, and Greenwood Lake (Long Pond).

The P&H, along with the N&P, played significant roles in early New Jersey public transportation. As early as 1803, three years before both turnpikes were chartered, a stage coach route followed the path of what was to be the N&P. It stands to reason that this helped inspire the investors in that Big Road to build it. The P&H did not have stage service until another twenty-nine years passed, but in 1832 what was known as the Western Line ran from northwest New Jersey to the New York Metropolitan area, alternating on different days between the P&H and the Newark & Morris and Morris Turnpikes.

While turnpikes were significant improvements over the old colonial roads that preceded them, which themselves were significant improvements over the original

In the front yard of the Schuyler-Colfax House is this pylon, rescued from alongside the turnpike which ran by. It is an original example of the early concrete, sculptured signs which indicated distances. This one notes the distance to "Hoboken," the end (or beginning) of the extended portion of what originally was a 44 mile route from Acquackanonk Landing (Passaic) to the rural hamlet of Hamburg.

Indian trails which preceded the colonial roads, they were far from the modern, paved roads we have today. Most were hard-packed dirt paths, shored up with rocks and timbers. Their quick deterioration and expensive upkeep led to the age of the plank road. These were literally wooden roads, sort of a long boardwalk. The planks were laid sideways across the road after the bed had been leveled off. At first they seemed to be the perfect solution to this and many other state's needs for better highways. However, this solution also proved short-lived as the timbers rotted, heavy wagons caused ruts to develop, and the cost of maintaining and repairing them was exorbitant.

The eastern portion of the P&H, extending fifteen miles from Paterson to Jersey City was made into a plank road, reportedly the longest of all such wooden roads in New Jersey. It was first called the New York and Paterson Plank Road, later shortened to the name which a portion of the original route maintains, the Paterson Plank Road. This was one of the few plank

roads built to be competitive with the railroads. It was backed by Paterson businessmen, who felt their business was hurt when the Erie Railroad leased the old Paterson and Hudson River Railroad (second oldest in the state to the Camden and Amboy). These businessmen believed the Erie neglected freight service, thus they reverted to relying on the reestablishment of a good land highway.

The disappointing performance of the plank roads was more than made up for when a British innovator by the name of Macadam, developed a method of paving roads covering the surface with a gradually smaller series of rock from the roadbed to the surface. Fairly large boulders were covered with smaller rocks, which were covered with even smaller rocks, and then

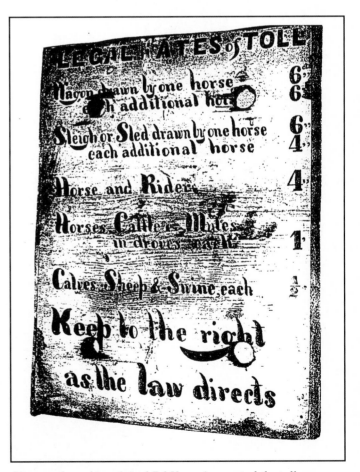

Signs such as this original P&H version posted the tolls users would have to pay before the "pike was turned," allowing access.

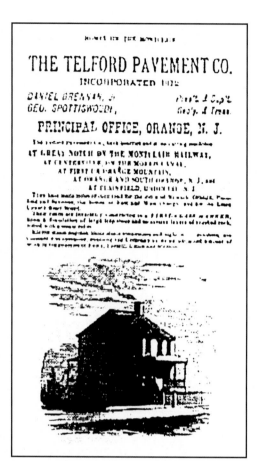

An Englishman by the name of "Macadam" invented a process whereby the roads could be improved by laying varying degrees of crushed rocks to "pave" the roads. At the Great Notch the "Telford" company quarried and crushed rock, which were transported on the old Montclair Railway to both pikes.

Before being replaced by a Grand Union supermarket during the middle of this century (now CVS pharmacy), the Norton Inn, shown here in an old newspaper photograph, stood for about 100 years at Terhune Drive and the P&H. This mid-century newspaper headline and photo headlined its fall to "progress."

gravel. A layer of dirt covered the entire concoction, which was then compressed to give a relatively smooth ride to the heavy wagons and early horseless carriages. The roads were pitched down from the center and small ditches were dug where shoulders now are, allowing rainwater to drain off, preventing major flooding. The macadamized road was the surface of choice until well into the 20th century when asphalt and concrete became widely used. At the nearby Great Notch, the Telford Paving Company operated two large steam-powered stone crushing machines. The gravel produced was then transported along the Erie Railroad to help macadamize the turnpikes which it crossed.

The P&H, now generally known as simply the Hamburg Turnpike, is still a major road in Wayne. Unlike the N&P, it has never been realigned, nor radically changed. With a close look, many of the old buildings which were built along it during the 19th and early 20th centuries can still be found today.

Norton Inn, Once a Stagecoach Stop, Soon To Make Way for Grand Union Super Market

At Terhune Drive (then "The Road to Oakland"), in 1900 the turnpike was a lovely country road.

A snowy night in 1935 along the desolate pike.

In 1946, roadside food stands began to appear. This photograph was taken on the Ramapo River bridge. near the corner of Terhune Drive and the turnpike.

This 1910 photo shows engineer Charles Lundmaster aboard Erie engine No.1014, class H-4, about to depart the Ringwood Station of the Greenwood Lake branch of the Erie. It had just loaded up with iron ore from the nearby Peters mine and was about to start its journey down the mountain and through Wayne. Passenger service to Ringwood ended in 1939, as only one a month made the trip that was once among the most popular jaunts in New Jersey. While freight service continued for a while, it too was canceled and the tracks laid dormant until 1961 when two locomotive were moved to Midvale, after which the tracks were removed.

Historical Highlight
Newark and Pompton Turnpike

As the 20th century winds down, the Newark and Pompton Turnpike (N&P) runs only a short distance in Wayne from State Route 23 in a slightly northwest

Israel "King" Crane.

direction to the Pequannock border at the Pompton River. And it has not technically been a turnpike, a private toll road, for more than 125 years. However, for more than 100 years that name included a route from the Passaic River bridge in Singac through Mountain View, up to its present location. In fact, originally the turnpike covered a total of 19 miles. It ran along Bloomfield Avenue from the point where that major Essex County road intersects with Broad Street in Newark to where it intersects with State Route 23 in Verona. From this point it divided into two branches. The southerly branch continued along Bloomfield Avenue to the Passaic River on the West Caldwell-Pine Brook border. The northerly branch ran along Route 23 (Pompton Avenue) to Singac, where it then followed the general path of the Wayne branch of the Minisink Trail through Pequannock, Pompton Plains and Riverdale, to Colfax corner, where it met the Paterson and Hamburg Turnpike.

"The Big Road," a popular term used for this and virtually all other turnpikes constructed during the era (1801-1829) when such private roads proliferated in New Jersey, was built, maintained and owned for much of its lifetime by Israel "King" Crane. Crane was a sixth generation descendant of Jasper Crane, who helped settle Newark in 1666, and great, great grandson of Azariah Crane, founder of Cranetown (since 1860, Montclair) in 1694. He was northeastern New Jersey's version of the great industrialists like Cornelius Vanderbilt and Jay Gould and Andrew Carnegie (although reportedly was simply too moral to ever be called a robber baron). His accomplishments are worthy of a book of his own. In addition to being the first merchant in Montclair, he operated a huge stone quarry in Newark, was a partner in Paterson's first cotton mill, and was the Essex County director, and part-owner of the Morris Canal. His 1796 Federal-style mansion survives today at 110 Orange Road in Montclair, and houses the Montclair Historical Society.

The N&P was incorporated on February 24, 1806. Four toll gates are known to have existed, one in Newark at its start (or end, depending on the direction taken), another atop Crane's Gap on the Montclair-Verona border along the crest of First Watchung Mountain, one at the end (or beginning) of the south branch at Pine Brook, and the fourth at Four Corners (Main Street and Pompton Avenue) in Singac. If there was ever any toll gate in Wayne, no record of it appears to have survived. The apparent absence of one could be explained by the report that soon after the turnpike was built, its official course was shortened by six miles to end (or begin) at Meads Basin (Mountain View).

In 1870 the toll gates were removed and the N&P became a toll-free, public road. In Wayne, however, the name remained along its entire course until it was designated as State Route 23 following the enactment in the late teens of New Jersey's state highway act. For a time the present route of the N&P in Wayne was designated State Route 8.

The course and nature of the road has gone through

Although barely recognizable, the last surviving of the original four turnpike gate houses, shown here in 1908, was located near the northwestern corner of present-day Main Street and what is still called the "Newark and Pompton Turnpike."

two major changes during this century. Originally it ran under the railroad just past the point where Route 23 intersects with Willowbrook Avenue (north of the present BP service station). It continued in a northerly direction until it intersected with Two Bridges Road (later State Route 6, and now U.S. 46), and then continued over what is presently called simply the Service Road into Meads Basin. In that hamlet it followed the course of what is now Boonton Road, where it passed by wooden bridge over the Morris Canal, and later the Delaware, Lackawanna & Western Railroad tracks.

The southern segment south of U.S. 46 remains as Old Turnpike Road running from the former site of the Carlton Inn, a popular tavern, (now Ballys health club) to Hobson Road (reached by passing through a weath-

ered, tiny concrete tunnel below the railroad tracks). A walk or ride along this half mile segment is like taking a trip back 100 years. Several of the original buildings that served the N&P remain, including a turn of the century gasoline station and auto repair garage (vacant and deteriorating), and several Victorian homes that are visible in an old photograph (presented here).

North of Meads Basin the road continued until it made a sudden turn to the northwest just past the site of what for many years was the Mountain View Brick Company. It continued past the DeMott-Ryerson General Store and Post Office and the Blind Man's House, making another sharp turn to the north.

In 1936 State Route 23 was reconfigured and dramatically improved. From the present location of Willowbrook Avenue it was realigned to run west of the railroad, before passing under the tracks at the now spaghetti-like S.R. 23, U.S. 46 and I.S. 80 interchange. It continued west of the old turnpike road, over a viaduct at Mountain View. This major alignment probably began the transformation of Mountain View from the commercial and social center of Wayne into simply the relatively quiet hamlet it is today. At the current N&P overpass, the new road continued in a more northerly direction until it crossed over the Pompton River and the abandoned Pompton Feeder Canal into Pompton Plains. The second major change occurred in the mid-1970's when the route became a high-speed superhighway. The route was significantly widened, resulting in the loss of many historic homes and commercial structures, particularly those in and south of Mountain View.

State Route 23 today bypasses old Mountain View/Meads Basin.

Old Turnpike Road (above) was heavily travelled in 1926. The same approximate location (below, l.), just east of the railroad tracks and south of present-day U.S. 46, is one of the last vestages of the original Newark and Pompton Turnpike. Abandoned service station on road, shown in 1996 (below, r.).

At this point, just north of the present BP service station, and opposite Willowbrook Avenue, the road used to go straight, under the tracks and along what is now Old Turnpike Road, and then along the Route 23 Service Road into Mountain View.

Route 23 being improved in the mid-1930's.

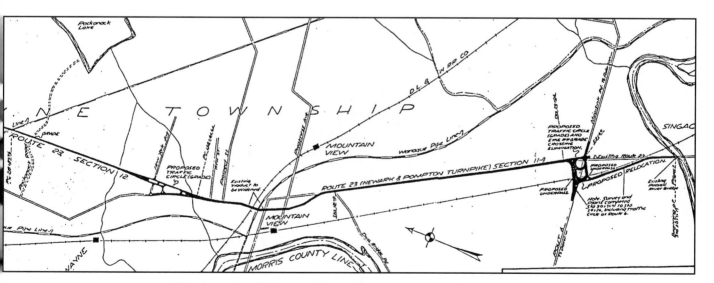

The planned realignment of Route 23 on a 1933 state highway map.

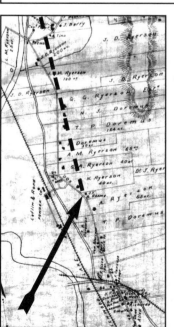

State Route 23 no doubt started life as an Indian trail and evolved into one of Wayne's first colonial roads. In 1806 it was improved and became the Newark and Pompton Turnpike. As shown on this 1877 map, the road passed right through Mountain View Center. It was a toll road until about 1870. Early in this century it was designated "State Route 23." In 1936 part of its route was reconfigured (dotted line) just above Mountain View (arrow). The old route retained the turnpike moniker, but was officially designated "State Route 8."

Historical Highlight
The Norton House

THE NORTON HOUSE, POMPTON, N.J.

Halfway between the vital Long Pond and Ringwood iron mines and forges and New York City for the better part of a century was Wayne's Norton House (aka Inn). Built at mid-century along the Paterson and Hamburg Turnpike, it was a familiar site for stage coaches and later automobiles well into the 20th century. Wayne had several such taverns along its two turnpikes, including the Carlton Inn where Bally's Health Club is located (at Old Turnpike Road and U.S. 46), along with The Jackson (Casey) House and Al Henn's Tavern, both further east on the northern turnpike. But the Norton House was by far the best known, especially among travelers. It sat in what is now the parking lot of a CVS pharmacy on the northeast corner of Hamburg Turnpike and Terhune Drive (U.S. 202), probably the most historic intersection in the long history of the Township.

The Inn was situated on 3.27 acres of land. It had approximately 18 rooms, a dining room and a legendary bar. Outside was a tie post for horses. In the early years of this century, it hosted perhaps its most famous guest, Elizabeth Nesbeth, the lady on the red velvet flying trapeze. The young beauty was hiding from the press while the most famous early trial of the 20th century raged on in nearby Manhattan. Her husband, Henry Thaw, was being tried for murdering her former lover on the roof garden dining room on the second of what was to be four Madison Square Gardens. The victim was none other than the most famous architect in America, Sanford White. As famous as the Norton Inn was, it was still located so far out in the country, no one was ever the wiser.

The Norton House was razed to make way for a Grand Union supermarket. Along with it went nearly a century of Wayne's history.

The Norton House, aka The Norton Inn, was located just across the Ramapo River from the historic Pompton Ironworks, now the parking lot for a CVS pharmacy. It was the social center of the area known as "Pompton Falls" and for a time "Schuylers Basin."

As stage coaches, and later buses and cars rounded the bend coming in from the northwest, it was a sight (below) for sore eyes (and other body parts).

Historical Highlight
The Morris Canal

In 1912 the canal was still a recognizable landmark in Mountain View, part of a "blue ribbon of water" that stretched across the state between the Delaware and Hudson Rivers.

The most spectacular engineering project of 19th century New Jersey was a blue ribbon of water, barely nine feet wide, stretching 104 miles between the Delaware and Hudson Rivers. Why would a five foot deep trench be so acclaimed? The project becomes amazing when it is considered that one could ship a load of iron ore or coal from the Delaware and send it in a relatively-straight line across northern New Jersey. This portion of the state contains virtually every topographical feature on earth hills and mountains, gorges, rivers, ponds, lakes, brooks, streams, with elevations rising nearly a thousand feet above both rivers. Yet the Morris Canal crossed everything in between the formerly-named South and North Rivers. How it did it is what was so impressive.

Minor to moderate changes in elevation were handled by constructing a number of typical canal locks. They were dug between two elevations along the planned water route and boxed in with steel, concrete and a gate at each end. A boat could enter the lock from the lower elevation and the gate behind it was closed. The gate to the high end would be opened to allow water to rush in and the water and boat on it would rise up to allow the boat to continue on its journey. To go from a higher to lower elevation, the opposite method was used by opening the lower elevation lock to allow the water in it to drop.

As we have said, this was a rather typical method of building canals in an area where the elevation changes slightly or moderately. The Morris Canal was one of the first to use the so-called Inclined Plane. To allow a boat to go up or down a large hill or small mountain, rails were laid on the hillside. The boats were detached from the mule teams that pulled them, removed from the water and placed in a wooden cradle on the rails. Boat and cradle would then be pulled up or down the hillside by iron chains (later wound wires).

A canal linking the coal fields of Pennsylvania with New York City was suggested many times before Morris County resident George P. McCullough came

up with an idea that he was sure would work. He came up with the idea on how it could be done while fishing

Looking east from Meads Basin toward the D.L.&W. railroad station south of Parish Drive, the canal ran north of the tracks .

one day in 1822 on Lake Hopatcong. "Why not use the water of this lake as a source for the canal?" he apparently thought to himself. He soon enlisted a top engineer and had enough political muscle to see others look upon his idea with great favor. One of the things he had going for him was timing. The coal-rich hills and mountains of Eastern Pennsylvania and the iron-rich hills and mountains of Western New Jersey contained millions of tons of both natural resources, but it was simply too expensive to ship it to New York and the other Northeastern industrial cities along the Atlantic coastline. The iron mines, furnaces and forges of Morris and Warren Counties were almost out of business, losing out to foreign competition. The only way to get the coal and iron to the Atlantic was to haul it by wagon, a far too slow and expensive way to ship it. But since a canal boat could hold ten times or more cargo than could even the largest wagon,

and mules or horses could easily pull the boats, even with such a large load if it was floated on water, all concerned were interested.

Within two years, the State of New Jersey commissioned the Morris Canal and Banking Company. 1100 men began to hand dig the trench and build the locks and inclined planes soon afterwards. By 1831 it reached Newark. It was later extended across Newark Bay to Jersey City.

The canal entered and left Wayne over two of the most impressive structures on its entire course. It entered the Township at Mountain View, coming in from the west just north of Boonton Turnpike (U.S. 202). A wooden aqueduct was built over the Pompton River, just north of the present Route 202 automobile bridge. It passed under a black steel drawbridge and tracks of the Erie Railroad and under a wooden bridge carrying the Newark and Pompton Turnpike, before bending around Gabriels and into Meads Basin. From there it headed

It paralleled Mountain View Avenue (Boonton Turnpike) and cut through the heart of Mountain View.

did a good deal of business.

The canal was never a great success. In fact it was really quite a failure. Only during a few years following the Civil War was it ever relied upon as McCullough and his fellow promoters thought and hoped it would. The reason for this is that no sooner was the canal completed (1831) than the first railroad was commissioned by the state

The main channel entered and left Wayne over two of the most spectacular structures along the entire 100+ mile course. The Pompton River (above) and Passaic River Aqueducts (r.) carried the boats across the two larger waterways.

to the southeast, crossing under another bridge carrying Parish Drive and over a small aqueduct at Singac Creek. At Two Bridges Road (U.S. 46) it crossed under still another bridge and then left Wayne at the Passaic River over an even more impressive structure than the one it entered the Township over. The Little Falls Aqueduct was actually two forty foot spans built upon a stone edifice composed of brownstone quarried just to the east along the Passaic.

Meads Basin was the site of an entire complex of stores, hotels and other buildings which were built on the south and west shores of the canal. Since entire families (and pets) lived on the boats, stops like these

(1832). As a canal boat could handle many times the load of a wagon, a freight car could handle even greater multiples of coal and iron than could a canal boat. And where it took a canal boat many days to cross the state, the railroad could cover the same route in a number of hours.

Instead of celebrating its centennial anniversary in

The Pompton River Aqueduct was a river built over a river. Most of the mule teams matched the same color animals. A mismatched duo was called a "Jersey Team."

The span was situated a stone's throw north of Route 202.

The southeastern end of the canal in Wayne passed under a steel truss bridge that carried Union Boulevard (l.), cut through in about 1875 by Robert Beattie. This view looks northwest. WayneTownship extends a thin finger, here between Little Falls and Totowa (sometimes referred to as the "Minisink Park" section).

The loss of the truss bridge, along with the original covered bridge (l. and below), deprived the area of two real pieces of local history.

1924, the Morris Canal instead saw what has been described as civic vandalism as it was not only abandoned, but destroyed. In the hands of the State of New Jersey, what could have been a magnificent greenway or recreational paradise was blasted into oblivion. Not one bridge, plane, lock or aqueduct was saved. Many portions were filled in. Why? There are many reasons, virtually all of them involve greed, shortsightedness, and pure stupidity. The

This is the spot where a plug of rock suddenly gave way 12,000-15,000 years ago quickly emptying Lake Passaic, formed by the Wisconsin iceberg.

State was afraid of having legal liability for deteriorated bridges and aqueducts. Cut-throat developers convinced the political leaders that the canal would be a breeding ground for mosquitoes and a dumping ground in every community along the route. While a number of citizen groups attempted to save the canal, they were simply too small in number and too outspent by the competition.

In Wayne the main canal bed is still very much distinguishable. It runs from behind the stores on the north side of Boonton Avenue, behind the convenience store across from Gabriels, under Parish Drive and along the western edge of North Cove Park. It continues until it becomes obliterated near U.S. 46, but again can be found running west of Riverview Drive as it approaches Union Boulevard. In the Pompton River, all that is left of the wooden aqueduct is a lot of debris. On the spot the old Little Falls Aqueduct once spanned, is the New Jersey Water District Pipeline bridge. In the community park in Little Falls east of Wilamore Road are several large remnants of the structure, thankfully saved from the wrecking ball and explosive charges.

The main channel passes just behind the strip shopping mall on Boonton Avenue. This view looks toward Route 23, where the path makes a sudden right turn, as did the canal itself.

When the canal was ordered abandoned, boats were left in the basins to rot (above, r.).

This location across from Gabriels was the site of Meads Basin.

Historical Highlight
The Pompton Feeder Canal

Mr. Smith's Lockhouse was located just north of present day Pompton Plains Cross Road and west of the Kuehm's farm, where the Ramapo and Pequannock Rivers form the Pompton. Today (below, r.) one would hardly believe the location was ever anything other than the small dirt path it is at present.

In back of the small strip shopping center on the north side of Boonton Avenue, just west of State Route 23 and just east of the New Jersey Transit tracks, is a grass path that leads north. One venturing on this out of the way path will see that below it runs the New Jersey Water District Main Pipeline. The pipeline was built to help meet the area's continued need for more and more water. 100 years ago this path was a trench filled with water, stretching from Pompton Falls to the main channel of the Morris Canal.

The so-called Pompton Feeder had multiple purposes. First and foremost it was supposed to be the main source of water for the eastern portion of the canal.

Just north of the Lincoln Park bridge in Mountain View was this wooden structure (above) at the spot where the feeder and main canal met. It was used to allow the mules to be walked over the feeder. In the distance is the drawbridge of the D.L. &W. railroad tracks.

Looking south above the Jackson Avenue Bridges (now the site of Pompton Plains Cross Road bridge).

Greenwood Lake was dammed and significantly expanded, with the plan being that it could do what Lake Hopatcong was doing in the western portions of the State. The second purpose was to allow canal boats to load up at the Pompton Ironworks and bring the iron manufactured at the famous forge to points south and east.

From Pompton Falls to a point just north of where Pompton Plains Cross Road connects State Route 23 in Pompton Plains with Black Old Ridge Road, the canal used the so-called driftway of the Ramapo River. At the point where the Pompton River is formed by the confluence of the Pequannock and Ramapo Rivers, a feeder dam was constructed, along with a lock. Their purpose was to allow navigation, but also to control the amount of water flowing south to the main channel of the canal. At this spot, just behind the George Kuehm farm (Farmview) was the lock-tender's home.

Perhaps the most notable event in the history of the Pompton Feeder took place in 1838. Brigades of mili-

tary mourners in full dress mounted the canal boats at Meads Basin and traveled all the way up to the backyard of the Schuyler-Colfax home on Hamburg Turnpike to attend the funeral of General William Colfax.

Like the main channel, the Pompton Feeder was also abandoned in the 1920's. The lock was filled in as was much of the trench south of the feeder dam. Today the location of the lock and locktender's house is virtually obliterated, with little evidence of its past visible.   However by entering the path behind the locked gates just north of Pompton Plains Cross Road and just west of Farmingdale Road, and taking about a 50 yard walk, one can find some evidence of the lock. It appears as a few foot long concrete strip where another path leads to the west toward the falls.

This strip is actually one of the buried walls of the old lock and is likely to continue ten feet or more into the soil. Further along the trail the original towpath is evident, along with a gaging station, a square concrete booth where canal observers could determine the height of the water passing by.

A dam was built, creating the "Feeder Falls," shown here at the turn of the century (above) and today (below). It is reached by a dirt path (the former route of the Pompton Feeder), off Pompton Plains Cross Road, opposite Farmingdale Road.

Above the Feeder Falls, the original towpath is still intact in spots.

Virtually hidden in the woods above present Pompton Plains Cross Road (formerly lower Jackson Avenue), the feeder canal started at the feeder dam. It is reachable only on foot along a narrow dirt path just west of the post office. At the turn of the century it served as another of Wayne's special recreational places. Note the old house on the island in the background of several of these early 20th century photos. It probably housed the man responsible for controlling the amount of water from the Ramapo river that entered the feeder canal.

The original feeder dam (l.) was made of wood as this photo taken around 1900 shows.

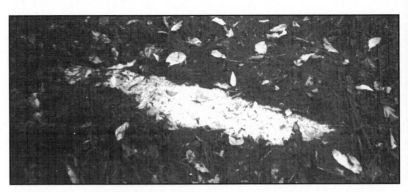

Along the dirt path north of Pompton Plains Cross Road is this piece of concrete buried in the dirt. It is part of the original lock, and may extend almost 20' into the earth.

This "Gaging Station" remains today along the old tow-path above where the Pompton River is formed. It was used to measure the level of the water in the feeder. The remnant of another one is just north of where the former Feeder Canal now runs under the Route 23 bridge over the Pompton River.

1906 USGA map shows path
of the Pompton Feeder.

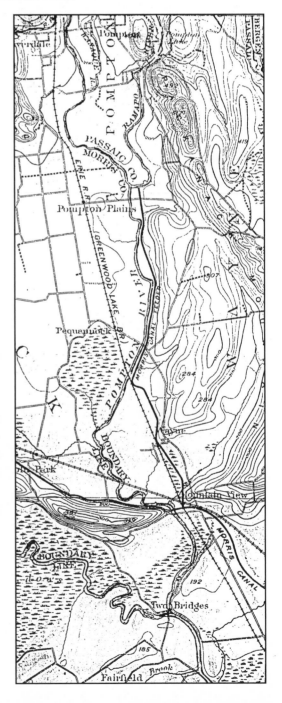

This long beautiful path covers the North Jersey Water District Pipeline between Route 23 and Pompton Plains Cross Road, just west of Farmingdale Road. Here the feeder mules had a chance to pick up some speed (but probably didn't).

Historical Highlight
The Montclair (Erie) Railway
aka The Greenwood Lake Branch

"RAILROAD SMASHUP" The story behind this simple but dramatic headline in the New York Times on February 6, 1866 was to play a major part in the development of Wayne, five miles or so to the north-west of the site of the subject train derailment in neighboring Montclair. Julius Howard Pratt was a Montclair resident, having moved to what was then known as West Bloomfield in 1857. Pratt was a Connecticut-born businessman who worked in Manhattan after his family's ivory comb business in the Nutmeg State went under. He was a fascinating mid-19th century entrepreneur whose resume included a stint seeking his own earned fortune in the gold fields of the Sierra Nevadas in far-away California. California was simply too hos-

Julius Pratt, the forgotten founder, shown here in 1901 at the age of 80.

The original Mountain View Station, shown here in 1910, was the smallest on the entire line.

tile an environment for the Yale-educated romanticist and dreamer. The food was bad, but the comfort level was simply horrendous, and he soon was on his way back to Connecticut where he remained until the discovery of hard rubber as a substitute for ivory doomed the family business.

He purchased a large parcel of land in West Bloomfield and built a typical Victorian home which he christened Applegate. The house survives to this day as a mortuary at 48 Elm Street in Montclair. In 1860 he led the fight to break away West Bloomfield from the Township of Bloomfield, and is credited with coming up with the name Montclair that same year. In 1868 the new Township of Montclair was formed using Pratt's suggested name, French for clear mountain.

Like many Montclairians who worked in New York City, Pratt commuted every day on the Newark and Bloomfield Railway, which came to town in 1856, before being taken over by the Morris & Essex (M.&E.). The M.&E. was far more interested in freight business than passenger business and Pratt and his fellow commuters were outraged by the shoddy treatment passengers received on that line. A passing freight train was always given preference over a passenger train, resulting in constant delays and poor service. On that fateful day the year after the Civil War ended, Pratt was aboard a railcar that derailed when the bridge over Bloomfield Avenue collapsed just as his

Before a community effort led to the present elaborate station, this old one stood after replacing the original "shack." By the 1920's, it was a popular stop, about the half-way point between the Hudson and Greenwood Lake.

Lackawanna & Western Railroad D.L.&W.), which was in the process of leasing the entire M.&E., including the recently built Boonton Line. In 1872 a station on the Boonton Line was erected at the newly named Mountain View.

Nevertheless Pratt and his syndicate prevailed. They were helped in large part by their success in raising over $4,500,000.00. 90% of it was the result of the sale of corporate bonds, and the rest by the personal contributions of Pratt and his new partners. By 1874 the line was completed, covering 40.9 miles. It serviced the ironworks at Long Pond and Ringwood, the latter by a short spur line. Initial plans called for the new railroad to link up with the New York & Oswego

train approached the structure. He came within an inch of being severely injured, if not killed. After surviving, he resolved to build his own railroad. The authorities in Bloomfield were resistant to supporting another line, forcing Julius to look to his neighbors in the former Cranetown and Speertown (Upper Montclair) to invest in his dream venture.

In 1867 Pratt joined with four others, Samuel Wilde, Joseph B. Beadle, Henry C. Spaulding and Albert Pearce and obtained a charter from the New Jersey legislature for the Montclair Railway Company (M.R.). When his partners got cold feet, he simply bought them out and organized a syndicate with business associates in New York. Following the lead of such enterprises like the Morris Canal and Banking Company and the Newark and Pompton Turnpike Company, the Montclair Railway Company issued bonds. He convinced the state legislature to allow the communities along the planned course of his line, from Jersey City to Greenwood Lake in upper Passaic County, to issue municipal bonds, which they did. The plan was met with strong opposition by supporters of the Delaware,

Midland Railway (N.Y.& O.M.), which was scheduled to extend south from Middletown New York in Orange County to the Village of Greenwood Lake.

Evidencing how much the "Wayne" name was overlooked, this 1910 photo is of the only railroad station in the Township that was referred to as the "Wayne Station."

Pratt's timing was atrocious. The Financial Panic of 1873 caused the ill-managed N.Y.& O.M., which had also operated the New Jersey Midland Railway, into bank-

ruptcy. Since the N.Y.& O.M. had guaranteed the bonds of the Montclair Railway, Pratt's dream crumbled at virtually the same time it seemed to be realized. It too went under. Abram S. Hewitt, one time mayor of New York and partner with his father-in-law, Peter Cooper in the Ringwood Ironworks, had been one of the biggest supporters of a railroad which would allow movement of his company's goods to the major industrial cities in the New York Metropolitan area. When the MR went bust, he became Pratt's biggest antagonist, and used his political and business contacts to worm his way into being appointed receiver for the defunct line.

After a brief period of time when the railroad was shut down, soon after it opened, it was sold in foreclosure and reorganized as the Montclair and Greenwood Lake Railway in 1876. That venture did not last much longer than the first, and it too bit the dust before reemerging under new ownership as the New York and Lake Erie & Western Railway. It would remain under control of the Erie, through trial and tribulation, until it was taken over by New Jersey Transit a century later.

For most of the time is was simply called The Greenwood Lake Branch of the Erie Railroad.

The Ringwood Lake spur was one of three branches the line was eventually to encompass. One was the former Watchung Railway, completed in 1872, which ran from the Forest Hills Station of the Erie in North Newark to West Orange. It was rechristened the Orange Branch. The other was the Caldwell Railway, built in 1892, and running from the Great Notch to Essex Fells, where it was soon to link with the even shorter Roseland Railway, and later the Morristown & Lake Erie Railway (M.&L.E.). By 1905, the 4.5 mile Caldwell Branch and its connection with the 12 mile M.&L.E., allowed service all the way to Morristown.

Two stations along the main line were built. One at Mountain View, and the second alongside the Laflin & Rand Power Company in Old Wayne. The line proved a boon to Wayne, and especially its recreational facilities along the Passaic and Pompton Rivers. At the halfway point between the Hudson River (with ferry service to and from Manhattan) and Greenwood Lake (with ferries to all major resorts around the lake) was the Singac-Mountain View area. This stretch of southwestern Wayne boomed, especially on weekends and holidays.

Until the Long Pond and then Ringwood iron mines and works finally ended two centuries of operations, the Greenwood Lake line was vital to their survival. In addition, it hauled large quantities of ice cut from a frozen Greenwood Lake in the winter down

The Wayne Station at Laflin and Rand Powderworks. This photograph which appeared on an early 20th century postcard was shot from about the Pompton Feeder, which ran just to the east of the tracks.

the mountain to Newark and New York.

In 1960 the Erie merged with the D.L.&W. to form the Erie Lackawanna Railroad, but any chance this merger would save either line was a case of too little, too late. Just as the railroad era had ended the canal and turnpike eras almost before they began, the automobile era greatly reduced the use of and reliance on trains. It took a much longer time, but piece-by-piece the Greenwood Lake Branch was dismantled. In about 1939 service to Greenwood Lake ended. In 1955 the last train to West Orange ran. In 1966 passenger service north of Mountain View concluded, as did that on the Caldwell Branch. For a while, Conrail used the northern portions of the line, but that too was short-lived.

When New Jersey Transit took over the Erie Lackawanna, it created a new Boonton Line. It incorporated the Greenwood Lake line between Hoboken (which has long since replaced the Hudson River station at Pavonia in Jersey City) and Mountain View, with the old western portion of the D.L.&W.'s Boonton line from Mountain View to Hackettstown. Julius Pratt was obviously distraught over his failed financial venture, but until his death at the ripe old age of 88 he took great pride in seeing his creation play so important a part in the development of northeastern New Jersey. Although few in Wayne ever heard of Julius Pratt, the entire Township owes him a debt of gratitude.

Montclair and Greenwood Lake
RAILWAY.

Leave	A. M.	M.	P.M.	P.M.	P.M.	P.M.	P.M.
New York...	8 30	12 00	3 30	4 30	5 30	6 30	8 00
Jersey City..	8 42	12 12	3 42	4 42	5 42	6 42	8 12
Pa. R. R. Jc	8 52	12 22	3 52	4 52	5 52	6 52	8 22
West End Jc.	8 55	12 26	3 55	4 55	5 55	6 55	8 25
Arlington....	9 07	12 37	4 06	5 06	6 06	7 06	8 36
Kearney......	9 09	12 39	4 08	5 08	6 08	7 08	8 38
New'k (W. av	9 12	12 41	4 11	5 10	6 10	7 11	8 41
Woodside Pk	9 14	12 43	4 13	5 15	6 16	7 14	...
Bloom'd ( ).R	9 17	12 46	4 16	5 18	6 19	7 17	----
Watsessing J	9 20	12 49	4 19	5 21	6 22	7 20	----
Glenwood Av	9 22	12 51	4 21	5 23	6 24	7 22	....
Washing'n St	9 24	12 53	4 23	5 25	6 26	7 24	....
Orange (P Av	9 26	12 55	4 25	5 27	6 28	7 26	...
Montgomery.	9 15	12 44	4 14	5 14	6 14	7 15	8 44
Bloomfield...	9 18	12 48	4 18	5 18	6 18	7 20	8 47
Chestnut Hill	-----	12 50	4 20	5 20	6 20	7 22	8 49
Montclair ...	9 23	12 52	4 24	5 24	6 25	7 25	8 51
Watchung...	9 25	12 54	4 26	5 26	6 28	7 27	8 53
Up. Montclair	9 27	12 57	4 28	5 28	6 30	7 29	8 55
Montclair Ht.	9 30	1 00	4 30	5 30	6 35	7 32	8 58
Great Notch.	9 35	-----	...	5 35	6 40	----	
Cedar Grove.	9 39	-----	----	5 39	6 44	----	
Little Falls..	9 42	-----	----	5 42	6 47	..	
Lindley .. .	9 44	-----	----	5 44	6 49	....	
Mountain Vw	9 52	-----	...	5 50	6 57	....	
Wayne	9 54	-----	----	5 53	6 59	----	
Pequannock.	9 59	-----	----	5 58	7 03	....	
Pompton Pl's	10 02	.. -	..	6 01	7 06	----	
Pompton	.....	....	---	6 06	7 11	....	
Pompton Jc.	10 10	----	----	6 13	7 20	...	
Midvale.. ..	10 18	-----	. ..	6 21	7 32	----	
Ringwood Jc.	10 24	-----	...	6 27	7 42	----	
Erskine.....	....	. ...	....	---	7 45	....	
Ringwood....	-----	-----	--	...	7 50	----	
Hewitt.... ..	10 35	-----	----	6 37	..	----	
Cooper... ...	10 40	. ..	----	6 42	----	----	
Strathmore ..	10 45	.. ..	...	6 47	----	----	
Lake Side....	10 50	-----	----	6 52	----	----	
Avington....	11 00	.....	....	7 05	----	----	

Saturday night train, 12 o'clock Midnight.

1876 Timetable (above).

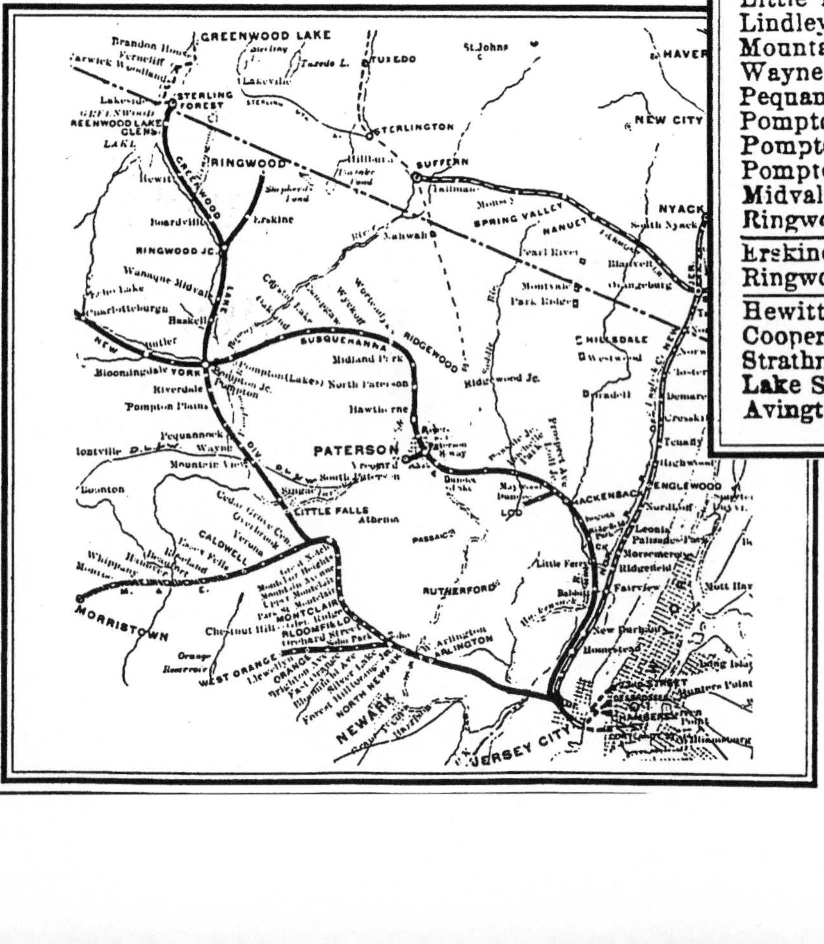

The route of the local railroads (l.).

Historical Highlight
The Red Building...
China Paradise

The Oriental motif of the building and sign of what for years was known as the "Red Building" on Hamburg Turnpike symbolized the transition of Wayne into a truly cosmopolitan community. Today, below, it remains a unique landmark..

Along *The Big Road,* the popular term for New Jersey's early toll roads, a distinctive red structure on the northbound side of Hamburg Turnpike marked one of the Township's most historic districts from 1968 to 1988. The stretch of land between the terminus of Church Lane and Berdan Avenue has a truly storied past. Two and a half centuries ago in 1759 Edo Merselis settled here and built his home where the Getty service station sits as the 21st. century approaches. It survived two full centuries until it was intentionally burned down by the fire department in 1959 at the corner of The Big Road and the former *Road to the Ponds* (Franklin Lakes/Oakland), now Berdan Avenue. To the southeast stood the *Grange Hall,* Wayne's social center where Preakness Valley farmers conducted business and held their social functions.

From 1919 to 1956 *Murchio's Flying Field* was located just across the turnpike as one of New Jersey's three earliest and busiest airports.

The Merselis homestead, the Grange Hall and Murchio's is long gone, but as their eras ended, the *Red Building* emerged as the new landmark on this portion of the highway.

In 1968 the new landmark was established, ironically by the Mark family. Jim and Boihar Ng Mark transformed what was already a historic Wayne restaurant into a little bit of China in what was formerly Dutch New Jersey.

Wayne has undergone numerous changes over the last 300 years. For the first 200 years the iron and explosive powder industries dominated the area. There was always farming but from about 1850 to 1950 it was primarily recognized as the farm belt of northern New Jersey. Valley Road farms were legendary. During this same era the south and western portions of the Township were known throughout the metropolitan New York area as a recreational paradise.

At the midpoint of the 20th century the farms began to be replaced with residential neighborhoods. Shopping centers swept the nation, and Wayne was no exception. If anything, it became a prototype suburban community with its tract homes, new schools and strip and regional malls. Behind the Red Building the Wayne Hills Shopping Mall joined a myriad of others. To the southwest the massive Willowbrook Mall was crowned as one of the largest indoor shopping centers in the state, if not the nation.

With this new development, Wayne became a far more cosmopolitan community. The Preakness Reformed Church no longer was the only house of worship in town. People of all kinds of religious, racial and ethnic backgrounds integrated Wayne as a very diverse and interesting place to live, work and visit.

The Mark family opened *China Paradise* in 1968 to introduce Wayne to a new taste and culture. It was a place where diners could enjoy distinctive Chinese and Polynesian cuisine, as well as sip exotic specialty

The Township joined the celebration of the grand reopening of China Paradise after the 1996 renovation. From left to right, Freeholder John O'Brien, Mayor David Waks, Tom, Jim and Boihar Ng Mark and secretary/treasurer Betty Mazziello stand in front of the historic restaurant located at 1082 Hamburg Turnpike (696-6464).

drinks rated the best in the entire state.

During the heyday of the airport across the road, the Airport Inn with its eye-catching airplane imbedded in the roof served the locals and tourists. It was replaced by the Old Heidelberg Inn. On the border with Pompton Lakes, the Norton Inn was a stage depot and place to rest and refresh one's palate for well over a century. The Mountain View Hotel (now Gabriels Restaurant) and Donahues Restaurant served Wayne's second turnpike to the southwest. Along the rivers *boat houses* built on platforms provided food, drinks and entertainment. Most of these are now gone, but Wayne still retains a reputation as a place where appetites can be satisfied, and diners entertained by a wide array of eateries with a multitude of atmospheres.

Italian, German, French, South American, African and even traditional American cuisine is offered along with the usual blend of fast food establishments one would expect in suburbia. For those desiring a true taste of the far east, China Paradise is the choice.

In 1988 the building was repainted and in 1996, improved and renovated. It is no longer the *Red Building*, but remains a landmark as the Marks, now joined by son Tom, celebrated their 30th anniversary.

Flying "The Coop"....
Henn's Tavern Leaves Its Mark

Shortly before it was purchased by one of Wayne's most significant developers, Spyros Lenas, Al "Henn's Tavern" occupied the corner of where Jackson Avenue met the Hamburg Turnpike (at Old Homestead Road). For well over a century it stood as a tavern, stagecoach stop and private residence.

Along with the legendary Norton House (aka Norton Inn) it was a landmark along the turnpike. About equidistant between the Pompton Lakes line to the northwest and Paterson to the southeast along the Big Road, it was also known as the "Halfway House" as well as the more lighthearted nickname of "The Coop," playing on Al's surname.

Just down Jackson Avenue sits the latest location of the Pompton Falls Fire Department. The land on which it sits was a testamentary gift of Mr. Henn.

In a 1966 newspaper article about the tavern, Frank's sister Mabel, who helped run the place remarked, "It was a real old-fashioned bar. Women were discouraged from coming in, and Frank didn't pour any gin and tonics, just whiskey and beer."

In 1906 Albert Henn, Sr. purchased a tavern that had stood for at least a half-century at the spot where historic upper Jackson Avenue met the equally-historic Paterson and Hamburg Turnpike. In latter years, Al's son Frank ran a tight ship, closing promptly at 9 p.m., even if it meant chasing out the clientele who were in the middle of their 25-cent whiskey or 1-cent beer. A visit here was like stepping back a century or more in time, to an era where virtually every New Jersey hamlet had a tavern---in many villages and outposts, the social and political center of the area.

The Henn tavern and homestead included a 32-acre farm when it was sold to mega-developer Spyros Lenas in 1966. Albert had purchased it from Joseph Terwilliger. For most of it existence, however, it was owned by the Smith family who obtained title in 1853 from one Samuel Westervelt.

Inside, the famous bar was a typical turn-of-the-century (and earlier) tavern.

The massive pot belly stove (above) heated the bar area without the aid of modern-heating mechanisms until its demise thirty years ago.

A few nostalgic views (above and below) that many a stage coach passenger saw as the vehicles they rode in pulled up for some grog and grub, and rest.

Chapter Eight
Birth of a Township

150 years ago this little white house, that now sits on a small rise on the south side of Hamburg Turnpike just west of Berdan Avenue, is surprisingly the birthplace of the Township of Wayne. Behind the front bungalow is a fairly-substantial extension. In 1847 it may have been much larger, as it once was home to a hotel.

Pompton, Pompton Plains, Pequannock, Totowa, Preakness and even Singac. At one time or another, places and things squarely within the borders of Wayne have been placed and misplaced linguistically in one of these places. On the other hand, the area that has been officially designated as Wayne for the last 150 years had in olden days been legally a part of Saddle River Township, then afterwards Manchester Township. At one time or another Wayne has been a part of three different counties, first Essex, then Bergen and eventually Passaic.

Prior to 1700 northern New Jersey was comprised of only three counties, Bergen, Burlington and Essex.

Burlington County not only included the land within its present borders, but all of Atlantic, Hunterdon, Mercer, Morris, Sussex and Warren Counties. Hunterdon split off from it in 1713; Morris split from Hunterdon in 1739; Sussex split from Morris in 1753; and Warren split from Sussex in 1824.

Bergen County, which was created in 1675, stretched from the Hudson to Hackensack Rivers, from about Kill Van Kull to the New York State line. It also included all of present-day Hudson County.

Essex County, incorporated in 1682, included everything west of the Hackensack River to the Burlington (now Morris) County line, and included present-day Union County.

Both Bergen and Essex were part of the Province of East New Jersey until the 1702 unification of the two portions of the state. In 1710 Essex County ceded its land west of the Hackensack River to Bergen County, including present day Wayne. For 127 years thereafter this area was part of the immense Saddle River Township, named because of its geographical configuration. That township had broken away from the even larger New Barbados (Hackensack) Township, which was founded by several immigrants originally from the Island of Barbados in the West Indies.

break away from Bergen County and form their own, to be called "Pompton County."

At the same time residents of Acquackanonk, including two of its former portions, Paterson and Passaic, and the just formed Manchester Township, which included Wayne, banded together and filed their own

The Township's Municipal Building started out in 1812 (above) as a school; became the Town Hall late in the 19th century (r.); has been the American Legion Hall (below) since the new Municipal Building was built on Valley Road (lower r.) some time after the middle of the present century.

petition. The northern two township residents resented having to travel to Newark, the county seat of Essex County. Manchester residents had no interest in

In 1837 residents of West Milford, only independent from Pompton Township for three years, being the fiercely independent mountain folk they were, protested having to travel all the way to the county seat in Hackensack for official business. They joined with the residents of Pompton to petition the state legislature to

being part of either the proposed Pompton County, or remaining as part of Bergen County. They wanted to form still another county, Passaic County.

In a typical New Jersey political move, a compromise was worked out in which the five northern townships were allowed to become Passaic County, while Atlantic County was carved out of Burlington County. This made sure neither the northern nor the southern portions of the state gained any voting advantage in the State Legislature over the other.

Manchester not only included present day Wayne, but Totowa, Hawthorne, Haledon, North Haledon and Prospect Park. By 1908, when residents adopted the name Haledon, Manchester joined Acquackanonk in completely disappearing from all maps. Piece-by-piece all of its hamlets had begun to break away, starting in 1847 when Wayne Township was formally incorporated.

On February 20, 1847 the State Legislature was advised that the governor had signed the bill they had unanimously passed, entitled:

> "An Act to Divide the Township of
> Manchester, in the County of Passaic,
> and to Establish a New Township to be
> Called The Township of Wayne."

The white Henry Casey Home, with its peeling white paint, today stands solemnly by itself on a slight elevation just west of Berdan Avenue on the south (somewhat west) side of Hamburg Turnpike. At first glimpse it appears as not much more than a bungalow. However, a closer look indicates that the building, although quite narrow, has some depth to it. From the main portion, it appears that at one time an addition was added on. By all accounts, in 1847, and for years afterwards, it was significantly larger than it is today. This would explain why it was chosen to be the place where the first town meeting of newly-formed Wayne Township took place on April 12, 1847. An 1861 map published by G.H. Corey, Publisher, which appears to be the oldest-known formalized one showing the new Township, describes the Casey House as the B.R. Sisco Hotel. Seventeen years later, on a map published by E. B. Hyden, it was described as the B.R. Sisco Union

Hotel. This map was republished by the Passaic County Historical Society in 1926, and again by the Works Projects Administration (WPA) in 1938. Both errantly date it as being first drawn in 1880, two years after the actual date.

An early 20th century hand-drawn post card depicts an elaborate complex on the same apparent site that includes a dance hall, cafe, and a number of out buildings, including a storage house and an automobile garage. It is referred to as The Jackson House Preakness as the sign outside of the building on the post card also indicates. A 1956 book on the history of neighboring Pequannock Township, refers to what is now called Jackson Avenue and Pompton Plains Cross Road, as The Road to Jacksons. Wayne Historian Marcia Sills attributes this as being a reference to the old Jackson House.

Until the present, modern municipal complex was built on the west side of Valley Road over the last half of the 20th century, between Nellis Drive and Preakness Avenue, the town center was located in the former Meads Basin, which has been known as Mountain View for a century and a quarter. In the original Meads Basin 1812 schoolhouse, now the American Legion Hall, the first town hall was located. It remained there for many decades.

While the first truly municipal government of Wayne was not organized until 1847, there had been more than a semblance of a municipality for over 100 years. As with many early New Jersey settlements, the church was usually the center of the community's civil and social life. Prior to 1736, no house of worship was formally established in Wayne. Those who lived in the northern portion of the region worshipped at The Pond Church, originally a log cabin that later served as a cattle shed. Those in the south went to Fairfield's Dutch Reformed Church when it was organized in 1720. In Pompton Plains, there had been preaching since about 1711, although it was done in school house and private residences rather than a formal church building. Any other organized worshipping had to be done in Acquackanonk, or all the way to the east at the Church of Hackensack, established in 1686.

In 1735 construction began on the first formal church building within the boundaries of present day Wayne

Township. It was located between the east bank of the Pompton River and a public road leading to the Falls. As previously mentioned, this site has now been identified as being on the west side of Shore Road, between North and South Roads. While present day Black Oak Ridge Road, formally dedicated in the late 18th century as being that road which began by a large black oak tree, is considered to be a portion of the original branch of the Minisink Trail, most older roads were not so straight. Is it reasonable to assume, based on all available evidence, that the original trail, and public road referenced as the site of the first church, followed the present course of Shore Road, at least in part? Probably not.

The best visual evidence of this church is an old drawing which indicates it was an octagon. Apparently it was constructed as this area began to grow and the Pond Church began to deteriorate. Nevertheless, this original house of worship did not have a long life, as the congregation built a second and more permanent building across the river along what became Newark and Pompton Turnpike in the Pompton Plains section of Pequannock Township.

It was not until 1798 when Wayne truly had its own church. The Preakness Reformed Church was built that year on a small hill along a dirt path which was given what probably was its first name, Church Lane. Undoubtedly, this was a crossroads where the Old Pumpton Road intersected with the aforementioned old road that branched off to Totowa and Little Falls a few miles to the south. The property was a gift of Edo Merselis. Without the records of this church compiled over the years by its elders, Wayne probably would have forever lost recollection of most of its roots. The old church stood until it was tragically destroyed by fire in 1931, after which the present structure was built. At the only formal cemetery within Wayne, south of the church building, lies the remains of many of the

When the town center was situated in Mountain View, Wayne actually had a semblance of a downtown. Included was the old police station down the road from Gabriels and not far from the D.L.&W. railroad station.

town's earliest settlers.

While Wayne boasts its own university, a branch of another college, several trade schools, four high schools, along with an array of public and private elementary and middle schools, formal educational opportunities began in Wayne in a most inauspicious manner. Although no evidence has been found that any cavemen (or women) lived here, for a while the community had cave children. Or at least children who were sent to school in a cave of sorts. The year

the United States was born was the year the first school opened, or shall we say was dug in Wayne. On the south-facing hillside along present day Brandon Avenue in Mountain View, just north of where LeGrand Terrace begins to run to the south. Three

By all descriptions of the location of the "Dug-out School", the first educational institution in Wayne, this site at the north end of LeGrand Terrace, where it meets Brandon Avenue, seems to be the approximate site of that location.

Wayne's earliest schools included the present American Legion Hall in Mountain View, the Village School above CVS Pharmacy in Pompton Falls (above) and Preakness School No. 2 (below, r.) on Hamburg Turnpike and Church Lane. Among those lost were the first Preakness School (r.) and the old Lower Preakness School (below).

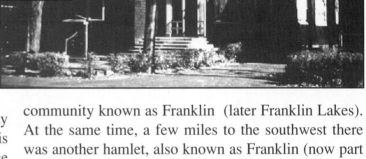

This 1881 pix of the Mountain View Methodist Church, along with a later version (below) represent the religious diversity that began in the Township well after the Preakness Reformed Church made its debut in 1798. Today the Township boasts a wide variety of houses of worship.

years later this dugout school was improved by the construction of a heavy stone structure that was reputed "to look more like a fort than a school." While the parishioners in The Ponds may have had to share their church with cows, Wayne children may have had to share their school room with a horse. It is believed that General Anthony Wayne stabled his horse in this building in 1780.

By 1812 population in the community had risen sufficiently to consider expanding the learning opportunities for its youngsters. The Franklin School Association was formed. Why that name was chosen is anyone's guess. However, it appears Benjamin Franklin, and his son William, governor of New Jersey the year when the Declaration of Independence was signed, made Franklin a very popular moniker. A map drawn of the general region around this time supports this proposition. What is now Wayne is surrounded on the north by the

community known as Franklin (later Franklin Lakes). At the same time, a few miles to the southwest there was another hamlet, also known as Franklin (now part of West Caldwell). And to add just a little more confusion, present day Nutley was also called, you

The Volunteer Fire Company, No.1 began extinguishing blazes in Wayne more than 100 years ago.

guessed it---Franklin.

The new school association was followed by five separate smaller districts, or schools: (1) Franklin School #13; (2) Jefferson School #14; Preakness School #15; Washington School #16; and Lafayette School #17. Where and even if schools number 1-12 were ever built is a fact that has apparently been lost in time. What is known is that Franklin School #13 became School # 1, and was established in Mountain View.

It should become apparent by now that the former Meads Basin had evolved into the center of activity in Wayne Township.

Police Captain Magee tries out his spanking new Model -T Ford patrol car on the streets of the hamlet of Mountain View as it began to emerge as a vacationer's paradise.

The Casey House 60 years ago (above) and today (upper r.)

An early-20th century post-card (below) depicts what is believed to be the Casey House at a time when it was expanded and served as the "Jackson House." After Casey it became Sisco's Union Hotel.

Preakness Reformed Church Fire and Stone

From 1851 until 1930 this handsome structure stood on Church Lane. It replaced a 50 year old rough-hewn edifice which served as the first permanent house of worship in Wayne. A mysterious fire destroyed the building. Definitely arson, the former paster of the congregation was the number one suspect, but no one was ever charged.

Religion played a far more important role in Colonial America than it does today. A settlement was considered complete only after its first house of worship was completed. The church building was much more than a place to pray. In most instances it also served as the town's social, government and business center, sometimes in competition with the local tavern. (A tavern was not simply a bar; many included large meeting rooms, dancing and dining halls and rooms for rent). In early New Jersey there were three major religions and thus the first churches in most of the settlements were either those of the Friends, the Presbyterians or the Dutch Reformed. In the south, many towns were built around their Friends Meeting

Hall, which did not take on the appearance of what we usually think of as a traditional church building. Most of these buildings had no steeples or spires. In the north the predominant churches were either the English Presbyterian or Dutch Reformed. The former were represented by the construction of First Presbyterian Churches which initiated formal services into the settlements. The latter by the Dutch Reformed Churches. The Presbyterian edifices, at least after the church societies were wealthy enough, were often elaborate, Gothic-styled buildings, completed with the aforementioned steeples and pointy spires. The Dutch Reformed were usually sturdy structures built of locally-quarried stone or molded clay bricks, topped off by

Many early residents are now resting for eternity in the only cemetery in Wayne, adjacent to the present church building. Included are Edo Merselis, whose generous gift gave the congregation the land upon which they built the original structure.

Above the front entrance was a brownstone tower, just slightly higher than the roof. The land was situated on a rise along the old road coming from Totowa. Curiously the church was built a year before the deed was executed; thus it appears Merselis either promised to donate the land and finally got around to it the next year, or simply rented the parcel to his fellow colonists.

a simple, somewhat-rounded steeple.

Since agrarian northern Essex and Bergen Counties were primarily founded by Hollanders, the first church in a community was more likely to be a Dutch Reformed one. Wayne was no exception. However, it took a few years more than a full century before the first permanent church society was formed in the area. Church goers previously had to travel to Ackquackanonk (1690), Fairfield (1720), The Ponds (no exact record, but before 1700) or as far away as Hackensack (1686). In 1736 what would become the Dutch Reformed Church of Pompton Plains was initially built on Shore Road in Wayne, but it later was relocated in that community, west of the river on what became the Newark and Pompton Turnpike.

In 1798 the Preakness Reformed Church society was formed by the Demarests, Van Sauns, Van Ripers, Berdans, Spears, Van Winkles, and the other Dutch farmers who helped pioneer Wayne. On June 7, 1799 a parcel of land was donated by Edo Merselis to the church founders. The deed to that land was recorded in the Bergen County records at Hackensack. The first edifice consisted of rough-unhewn stone, laid up in mortar, made of hard clay, with straw intermingled.

Adjacent to the building was what remains as the only cemetery in Wayne. The old tombstones include the names of many historic Wayne families, including that of the church's benefactor.

The original, crudely-constructed building began to crumble by the middle of the 19th century and a committee was formed to plan a replacement. In 1852 Preakness, in fact all of Wayne, had a handsome new church building. This one was much larger and made of brick. It included a beautiful mahogany pulpit. It only took about $100.00 to completely furnish it. As Wayne grew, so did the congregation, which not only served as the spiritual center of the new Township, but which kept intricate records of births, deaths and other vital statistics. When Reverend Labaw wrote and published his classic Preakness and the Preakness Reformed Church in 1902, he didn't have far to go to do much of his indepth research.

Labaw was not only a man of the cloth, but, as his book evidences, was a talented historian, scholar and writer. From 1899 to 1927 he served with dignity and grace, and appears to have personified holiness. His immediate successor did not serve and leave the con-

gregation with exactly the same impression that the Reverend George Warne Labaw did.

Alexander T. Paxson obviously had some big shoes to fill. He apparently tried too hard to fill them, immediately instituting major changes in the life and style of the church. He not only ordered physical changes to the property, but augmented changes in the liturgy. He also actively solicited new members, held bake sales and obviously shook up the older members of the 129 year old congregation. Within six months of his arrival the church entered a phase of distrust and turmoil. So much so that many members of the Consistory resigned. In less than three years, Reverend Paxson

was asked to leave. Within two days after the date of the decision to tell him that his services were no longer desired, and probably about the time he received the news, someone decided to burn down the 78 year old building. During the night of May 1 and early morning of May 2, 1930 the second church was completely destroyed. In his follow-up volume to Reverend Labaw's book, the late Reverend Albert A. Smith strongly implies who the arsonist was. He reports that in an interview he held on January 30, 1973 with several older church members it was noted that Paxson was "the only fellow at the fire who was dressed up; everybody else was in their pajamas--and that's all we care to say about it. But they found things (incendiary devices)."

On May 30, 1931 the cornerstone was laid on the third and present church building. It was completed the following October.

The Preakness Reformed Church is far from the only church in the vast Township. By 1948 there were seven churches in town, and during the second half of the 20th century many more appeared as the population became more and more diverse. In addition to Roman Catholic, Baptist, Methodist, Episcopal, Lutheran and other houses of worship where European and South American descended residents now pray, by the 1990's the Middle Eastern and Asian influence began to show. A Korean Methodist Church was organized on Alps Road and a Moslem mosque on Oldham Road. Today virtually every major religion, and minor ones, are represented by churches in Wayne. Needless to say, however, the Preakness Reformed Church on Church Lane continues with a tradition that celebrated its Bicentennial year in 1998.

The rebuilt church structure is now is entering its eighth decade. The congregation is celebrating its bicentennial.

Historical Highlight
William Paterson University

Hobart Hall on the campus of William Paterson University became the home of Garret A. Hobart's family after McKinley's Vice President from Paterson predeceased the to-be-assassinated president by two years. The photo above was taken in 1880 when the original owner and builder John W. MacCullough still lived there. Today (below r.) it has been greatly remodeled, and sits in the center of a massive college campus, but remains elegant and stately.

Throughout the Wayne area there are moraines, remnants of the glacial movements across New Jersey 12,000-20,000 years ago. Large single or a small clumps of boulders in the middle of fields and meadows. Gravel pits and bits of petrified wood. The northwest foothills of Preakness and High Mountain were particularly covered with scattered rocks and pebbles, along with deep scars cut into the land by the advancing ice. It is no wonder that a Scotsman by the name of John W. MacCullough felt that the area William Paterson University now occupies would be his new Alisa. It reminded him of Alisa Crags, his boyhood home, green uplands looking out to the ocean swells.

The first President and Vice President of the United States to both die in office were William McKinley (l.) and Garret A. Hobart.

Alisa Farms was obviously not at ocean's edge, but a short hike to the top of high mountain, the highest point in the three coastal Watchung Mountains, certainly brought an ocean vista. And vice-versa. Its peak was often the first sight of land weary sailors saw protruding above the clouds and fog after a long ocean voyage.

In 1877 MacCullough, a wool merchant, built a huge stone castle adjacent to Pompton Road on the Haledon-Wayne border. In 1902, the family of Garret A. Hobart purchased the estate from MacCullough who returned to Scotland to live out the latter years of his life. Hobart was the 27th Vice President of the United States and would have become President in 1901 when William McKinley was assassinated, but he too died in office two years earlier....of natural causes. Their next door neighbor was Robert Gaedis, a Paterson silk tycoon, who also built an elaborate mansion, across Pompton Road.

At the turn of the century, Paterson City Normal

School was close to celebrating its golden anniversary. In 1855 it was founded to give professional training to teachers of the city's public schools. In 1923 the State Board of Education designated the institution as the New Jersey State Normal School at Paterson. 14 years later it's name was changed a third time and the school became the New Jersey State Teachers College at Paterson.

By mid-century, while the city of Paterson was losing industry while gaining population, neighboring Wayne was going in the opposite direction. Its transformation from a farming to a suburban community was well under way. The college needed more room to expand, and the Hobart and Gaedis properties were available. In 1948 both were acquired and in 1951 the campus was moved to overlap the Wayne-Haledon border. The centerpiece of the new environment was the elegant Hobart manor house, already dedicated as a national historic landmark. Six years later the word "Teachers" was removed from all six state college names as the local institution underwent its fourth name change to Paterson State College. Two more were in store.

William Paterson was born in Atrium Ireland on Christmas Eve, 1745, and came with his family to British America two years later. His father purchased a general store in Princeton, New Jersey, just across from Nassau Hall, which became the site of the College of New Jersey (now Princeton University). Young Bill entered the Ivy League school when only 14 years of age and was graduated four years later. He began the study of law in the offices of prominent local

attorney Richard Stockton, and was admitted to the bar in 1768. He entered politics and had a meteoric rise in government. Soon after independence was declared, William Paterson was elected the state's first Attorney General under legendary governor William Livingston. His star continued to rise as he was chosen to be part of the state's five-party delegation that went to the 1787 Constitutional Convention. In September of that year he signed the new United States Constitution.

Paterson was later elected to the United States Senate, from which he resigned in 1791 to succeed Governor Livingston in New Jersey's highest post. His support of Alexander Hamilton's plan to incorporate the Society for Establishing Useful Manufactures (SUM) and form the nation's first industrial city at the foot of the Great Falls earned him immortality. After signing both the SUM corporate and the municipality's charters, he was honored when the name of the community was unveiled, The Town of Paterson. After serving only about two years as governor, President George Washington appointed the Irish immigrant to sit as an associate justice on the United States Supreme Court in 1793. He remained in service to this country for the last 13 years of his illustrious life.

In 1971 the name of the college was lengthened to The William Paterson College of New Jersey in honor of the state's first United States Senator and second elected governor. Twenty six years later the New Jersey Commission on Higher Education granted the school university status.

The William Paterson University of New Jersey enrolls more than 9,000 undergraduate and graduate students. The campus has grown to 300 acres, featuring 26 major facilities, including a 300,000 book library, and the vastly remodeled, but newly renovated and still beautiful Hobart Hall. It would not be out of character for this fine university to produce another great American like the two gentlemen whose names are emblazoned on signs throughout the campus, Garret Hobart and William Paterson.

This sign outside the campus gate (below) shows the great pride the school has in its biggest athletic accomplishments.

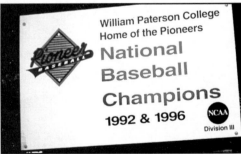

Paterson silk merchant Robert Gaedis built this Queen Anne mansion (l.) across Pompton Road from Hobart Hall. Photo taken circa 1900 shows Gaedis' Pond in foreground.

Site of the campus to be taken in the 1930's (above).

Aerial view of the campus in 1967.

Paterson Normal School in about 1910.

From the summit of High Mountain looking to the southwest, the view is breathtaking. Not only can the entire island of Manhattan be seen, along with the Verranzano, George Washington and Gothels Bridges, but Newark and virtually all points from the 360 degree panorama. From the ocean it has often been reported to be the first sighting of land for those coming into New York. It thus appears that the first view of the United States seen by millions and millions of newly arrived immigrants during the mid to late 19th and early 20th centuries was of Wayne.

Aerial view of the campus in 1952.

Chapter Nine
Meads Basin and Mountain View, The Great Junction

This spectacular photograph taken in 1910 is in marked contrast to the location today (below). Hixon's Mountain View Hotel served the Morris Canal (Meads Basin in foreground), the turnpike (between the basin and the hotel) and the two railroads with their stations within walking distance of the town center.

It is not very difficult to drive along U.S. 46 or Interstate 80, both bordering the region, or State Route 23, which crosses right through (or at least over) the center of Mountain View, and miss it altogether. Nowhere, except at the minimally-used New Jersey Transit railroad station, sharing a portion of a small one with the name Wayne, is there even so much as a sign welcoming anyone to Mountain View. Perhaps only those few passengers who use the Boonton Line, the last remnant of a railroad in the Township, even hear the word mentioned. (There is no rail service at all on weekends and most holidays).

Today the station is surrounded by a few older, some-what modified buildings. To the west of the tracks is a rather desolate street, Fayette Avenue. As one drives along the quiet road, somewhat dilapidated buildings jut out on the right side of the street at an unusual forty five degree angle. One has to look real hard to find the Pompton River, also hidden behind the mostly bungalow-style structures. Here and there are a scattering of small dirt paths leading between the homes to the river. Few use them, as there is really never much going on along the Pompton River---these days. An occasional overturned rowboat can be seen on both the Wayne and Lincoln Park sides of the water-way. The rotting remnants of numerous old docks line

Mead Homestead, Erected 1762, Mountain View, N. J.

Almost 100 years before Mountain View emerged as the municipal center of Wayne after the Township's formation, the Mead Homestead stood on the northeast corner of Preakness Road (now Parish Drive) and the old Indian path that became the Newark and Pompton Turnpike, State Route 23, and presently Boonton Road. It was operated as a popular hotel before burning down early in the 20th century.

Essex (M&E) Delaware, Lackawanna & Western (D.L.&W.) Rail-road. Just south of this viaduct, on the east side of the tracks is an empty lot partially covered with concrete and asphalt, some rotting timbers and wood splinters, and what is left of the crumbling foundation of the once-bustling Mountain View D.L.&W. station.

For about two miles south of Gabriels, beginning at the junction of Routes 23, 46 and 80, is a stretch of superhighway with but a few businesses located on the east and west service roads. For the most part, this is wide open, empty land.

With this present scenario in mind, it is hard to believe that the tiny Mountain View, nee Meads Basin, hamlet was once the crossroads of railroads, canals, state and federal highways, not to mention the junction of two of the state's most important and frequently-used rivers. It is also difficult to fathom that it was also one of the most-visited vacation spots in the northeast.

Gabriels Bar and Restaurant is perhaps the last living vestige of a far more active era in what for years was the seat of the Township government, as well as its social and commercial center. When John Mead first settled here and built his home on a hill overlooking what later became the hub of the community, he was followed by many other settlers who immediately saw the potential for farming, something the Indians apparently discovered long ago. Farms like the Van Duyne, which once encompassed 160 acres, spread out over the southern portion of the western valley, from Two

the shoreline, along with a few sandy, empty lots.

To the east of the superhighway, State Route 23, which passes above Mountain View over a viaduct, just past a 55 mph speed limit sign, is a small city street. Boonton Avenue is lined with a few older-looking buildings. Other than customers of Gabriels, with its Second Empire mansard roof, walking around the building to the adjacent parking lot, a few patrons of the rather innocuous convenience store directly across the street from the restaurant and bar, and an occasional customer of the candy-supply store just down the block, there is little foot traffic. During the rush hours, cars stream around the bend in the road just north of Gabriels, their drivers obviously anxious to get on Route 23, north or south. Few, if any, ever stop.

A few hundred yards south of the bend there is a bank. Its parking lot behind the building can be entered on Parish Drive. This was once the community's local school. Just up Parish Drive from the bank is another viaduct which goes over the dried up path of the Morris Canal and the abandoned tracks of the old Morris &

Built in 1828 the Wilson Store housed the post office. It was later acquired by the Shackleford family before being leased to Harry Hammond. It obviously was built in preparation for the Morris Canal, which reached Meads Basin a couple of years later.

one ever built.

Henry M. Mead, who died in Jersey City in 1849, is reported by the Passaic County Historical Society to have been the person who introduced Indian corn as a substitute for potatoes in Ireland. From 1844 to 1867 Andrew H. Mead ran a successful hotel on the northeast corner of present day Parish Drive and Boonton Avenue, on the site where the aforementioned bank is now situated. The hotel drew visitors who arrived via the canal and the railroad, both very short walks to the hotel's back door, as well as the Newark and Pompton Turnpike, which ran in front of the property. The hotel burned

Bridges to the Totowa line.

The Mead clan steadily grew and by the advent of the 20th century, they abounded in the area. Jacob lived in the small south wing of the house at 231 Parish Drive which LeGrand Parish, a multimillionaire inventor and business tycoon, expanded into one of Wayne's grandest showplaces. That small wing is probably the oldest house still standing in Mountain View, and possibly the first

Harry Hammond expanded his business and moved his general store and the post office across the street to this building on Greenwood Avenue and the pike. The building today (below) has several neighbors.

Hammond provided home delivery, and even published postcards for the tourist trade.

This small office building (above) once housed the A&P (above r.) which opened right across from the Erie station (r.).

to the ground when the local fire department was simply ill-equipped to extinguish an apparently fierce blaze.

On June 12, 1871, despite the continued presence of so many Meads still occupying, and probably dominating the hamlet, the name was changed to Mountain View. A month later it was formally adopted by the local post office, which was located in the general store just south of the earlier-mentioned convenience store. That general store

Preakness Road (Parish Drive) and the turnpike (Boonton Road) early in the century (l.) and today.

Parish Drive (nee Preakness Road) crossed over the Morris Canal.

In the heyday of the canal, the basin itself, the area in which the convenience store now is located, was surrounded by a bevy of businesses which profited from the industrial waterway's traffic. There was a blacksmith shop to the north, along with several merchant shops and a depot surrounding the small pond-like body of water. Cornelius R. Jacobus built the 2 1/2 story brick blacksmith shop north of Gabriels on the southern bank of the canal. After being modified numerous

was built in 1828 by Jacob and Nathaniel Wilson about the same time the canal was being dug. The next year Nathaniel was appointed postmaster as the Meads Basin post office was officially established in the general store. The store and post office was operated for years by the Shackletons, and then leased out by Harry Hammond. He later moved his operation to larger quarters on the corner across the street in the building now occupied by the candy supply concern.

Given the fact that the Meads were apparently wise merchants, they may have supported, or at least did not vigorously protest the name change for purely economical reasons. Mountain View quite accurately denoted the area as being one with a magnificent vista. In the same vein, Prospect Avenue which began to climb the south and east faces of Packanack Mountain just north of Meads Basin was also renamed. It became the more descriptive and romantic-sounding Alps Road. Mountain View and Alps Road are certainly more appealing names for a tourist destination than Meads Basin and Prospect Avenue.

times, it was a victim of the latest improvement of State Route 23.

Both railroad stations drew travelers, vacationers and visitors in large numbers, particularly during the first few decades of this century. As discussed in more detail later on, the Pompton and Passaic Rivers were teeming with swimmers, canoeists, rowboaters and even diners and dancers, who were entertained in floating dance halls and restaurants, such as the Imperial Boat House. That rather desolate stretch of State Route

Harry Hammond published this postcard of the Mountain View Church and Parsonage.

5318   MOUNTAIN VIEW CHURCH & PARSONAGE, MOUNTAIN VIEW N.J.   PUBL. BY H. L. HAMMOND.

23 between routes 46 and 80 and the viaduct above Gabriels, once was dotted with picturesque and unusual roadside stands and eateries. Klein's Grove sat alongside the turnpike, along with its handsome pond and footbridge. The quiet Fayette Avenue was anything but until at least midcentury. Those odd-angled buildings were built that way to allow maximum density and access to the bustling riverfront. Most were either vacation cottages, hotels, restaurants or boat houses.

The loss of Meads Hotel was more than made up for in 1909 when Hixon's Mountain View Hotel opened at the corner of the Newark and Pompton and Boonton Turnpikes. If location, location, location are the three most important factors of a good, solid real estate or business investment, then this popular early-century hostel had it all. Within walking distance were the two railroad stations and the Pompton River, and literally within a stone's throw was the junction of the two heavily-traveled turnpikes, and of course the canal basin. Just up the road the Pompton Feeder Canal ended its journey from the

Along the State Road, WAYNE, N. J.

Route 23 (above) was originally a country lane, incorporating portions of the Newark and Pompton Turnpike. What is believed to be Prospect Avenue (Alps Road) ascended Packanack Mountain (below). "Alps Castle" offered room and board further up the hill during the 1930's.

Pompton Falls and the former Pompton Iron Works. By the turn of the century, a huge steel works complex replaced the old furnace.

A short lunch at Gabriels today, with its turn of the century dark wood decor, and nostalgic photographs lining the walls, is the best way to step back in time and appreciate Meads Basin/Mountain View, as it was many years ago. If one listens real carefully, with a little imagination he or she just might be able to hear the whistles of the old steam engines which once rumbled by, or the shrill sounds of the mule skinners, shouting out instructions to their somewhat stubborn teams of animals.

POMPTON TURNPIKE, BUSINESS CENTER AND SCHOOL.   MOUNTAIN VIEW, N. J.

Mountain View shortly after the turn of the century was the business, social and government center of Wayne.

The pike and Rt.23 passed right through the center of town.

Although traffic is still steady today, it is mostly confined to the locals.

Aerial View of Mt. View Center
Mt. View, N. J.

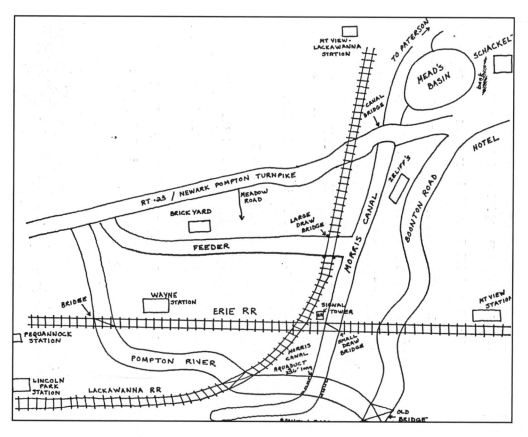

Aerial view of Mountain View (above) shows newly realigned State Route 23 which gradually caused travelers to bypass the hamlet. When the Township government moved to Valley Road several decades later, the hamlet no longer was "Wayne Center."

Map sketched out before Route 23 realignment emphasizes Mountain View's right to be called "The Great Junction."

MOUNTAIN VIEW BOAT HOUSE, MOUNTAIN VIEW, N. J.

Fayette Avenue was lined with facilities to accommodate the growing summer vacation trade during the first half of this century. The "Mountain View Boat House" was one of numerous recreation-orientated establishments lining both sides of the Pompton River.

The last reminder of the days when the present American Legion Hall served as the Township's Municipal Building are these bars on the basement window evident from the rear parking lot. Mountain View had its own dungeon, the town jail.

One of numerous gifts from philanthropist LeGrand Parish was the "Community Club," now the Fire Department, on Parish Drive just north of the former Town Center.

This is a later view of the Mead Hotel which was supplanted by the second Mountain View school. The latter building is presently occupied by the Ramapo Bank.

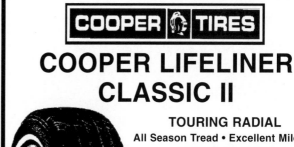

Historical Highlight
LeGrand Parish

Mountain View's benevolent millionaire.

LeGrand (French for "The Great") Parish may have been the wealthiest Wayne resident of his time, if not all time. His salary alone as compensation for his position as president of Lima Locomotive Works of Ohio was reputed to be $100,000 per year in the 1920's. This was at a time when a home in Wayne could be purchased for a few thousand dollars. In addition to this salary, Parish probably received even more in royalties thanks to his inventing and patenting an airbrake coupling device to connect railroad cars, along with several other important early-20th century railroad devices. The air brake helped revolutionize and solve many problems the huge iron horses had, particularly in trying to stop while descending a large hill or mountain with a full load.

By all accounts Parish was as generous as he was smart and rich. Perhaps the fact that he was born in Friendship, New York was an early omen to a man who is said to have given most of the produce raised on his large holdings in Mountain View to his less-fortunate, struggling and hungry neighbors. His former secretary once said, "I vividly recall the 'magic figure' of eight-hundred dollars. That was the amount of cash he liked to have in his pockets at all times to help out destitute neighbors. It seems that I was constantly running to the bank. As soon as his pockets were emptied out, off I'd go to the bank again." He also gave to the Township in general. Included in his municipal gifts was the land that became the Parish Oval. To Community Fire Company No. 1 he gave the land where the present fire station and Community House stands (east of the D. L. & W. tracks, on the north side of Parish Drive). However, his most generous gift was undoubtedly the 48 acres he gave to the Passaic County Park Commission for a park that now makes up that section of the Passaic County Golf Course, also adjoining Parish Drive. It is no wonder he was asked to serve as Park Commissioner.

Parish moved to Mountain View in 1914. He first lived across the street (then called Lower Preakness Avenue) from the Community House. Before long he was buying up every plot of adjoining land he could get his hands on. His holdings included most of the area bordered on the north by Alps Road, Parish Drive on the south, Maple Avenue and Parish Drive on the east and the D.L. & W. tracks and the Newark and Pompton Turnpike on the west.

He apparently did not give all of his money away, as he reserved the best 45 acres he owned for his main estate. Obviously with a historical perspective, he purchased the original Mead home at 231 Parish Drive, and added and added and added on to it. From a small, typical Dutch farmhouse, the residence overlooking the center of the hamlet grew into a magnificent mansion, complete with Italian marble, ornate frescos and surrounded by stately pine trees. Now owned and

occupied by the Methodist Church, the house remains as one of many memorials in Mountain View to probably its most distinguished citizen ever. Had he not died at the age of 67 in 1933, he may have even made a greater contribution. He was in the middle of a utopian plan to build a community of "deserving humanitarians." He began to allocate large lots for magnificently designed houses costing $20,000 in Great Depression dollars which he gifted to selfless individuals who had demonstrated a high order of service to their fellow man. Given his immense fortune, had not death taken the man, Mountain View just may have had to be known as St. Mountain View. Imagine a community consisting of hundreds of the type of individuals Parish felt deserved such an expensive gift?

Parish converted this 19th century original Mead home into what was undoubtedly referred to as "LeGrand Manor" (below). It overlooked his massive holdings and the Town Center. It now houses the Methodist Church.

Historical Highlight
Gabriels/Hixon's Mountain View Hotel

The operating licenses inside Gabriels say "1908," but most other official records say "1909." Whichever is correct, the venerable hotel, restaurant and bar has long been the centerpiece of Mountain View since it replaced an earlier hotel reputed to have occupied the same site. This photo may have been taken the day the establishment opened.

While only about a year away from its 90th birthday, the familiar Gabriels Restaurant with its traditional Second Empire mansard roof is one of the newest landmarks in Wayne featured here. By 1909 when it opened as Hixon's Mountain View Hotel, the Township already had numerous century-old edifices, and one that was more than 200 years old. Nevertheless there is a strong possibility that more people have passed by or caught sight of this building, which symbolizes Mountain View (and Meads Basin), than any other historic structure in the entire Township.

Since the mid-1970's State Route 23 has been a major superhighway. For the last few years it has been a major link between the two interstate highways (287 and 80) in northwestern New Jersey. Since Route 23 runs just west of Gabriels with its distinctive architecture, thousands of travelers have seen it everyday for the last two decades. But even before that it was alongside the major byways of Wayne, the Morris Canal (in its last days), the two railroads, and the old Route 23 and predecessor, the Newark and Pompton Turnpike (where it meets the old Boonton Turnpike).

When Joseph Hixon opened his Mountain View Hotel the hamlet was 38 years removed from being named after the founding family and the small basin that had been a major stopping point on the Morris Canal since the early 1830's. There was reportedly an earlier hotel on the property, but details of it are sketchy at best. However, the one down the block is well remembered. The Mead House had stood on the property on the northeast corner of Boonton Road and Parish Drive since 1752, almost 80 years before the canal reached Meads Basin. Despite the fact that the Town Hall stood diagonally across the street and the Township's first firehouse nearby, the volunteer fire department was simply too ill-equipped to handle a raging fire that totally destroyed that building.

It is believed that while the Township jail was situated in the basement of the Town Hall (originally the 1812 schoolhouse and now the American Legion Hall), a room upstairs in Gabriels was used for a courthouse. An employee of Gabriels claims that the outline of the judge's bench is still distinguishable in the room, now being leased to a tenant.

Gabriels has been somewhat modified since it replaced the Norton House on Hamburg Turnpike as the most famous hostel in town. The open porches have been filled in; however compared to many other Wayne landmark buildings, it still looks much like it did in old photographs.

NEWARK POMPTON PIKE 1910

No other photograph uncovered by the author depicts the"country inn" atmosphere of Hixon's in old Mountain View than does this one looking south along the Newark and Pompton Turnpike. The Morris Canal and Meads Basin (to the right) was just about out-of-business by then.   Today, a visit to Gabriels provides a real "taste of history."

In 1972 the establishment was still prominent along State Route 23, the last of the unique and colorful eateries along the old road. The latest improvements to the state highway took their toll on both the historic inn along with Mountain View's main business district.

Twelve years later (l.) it was still a survivor, this time from one of the worst of Wayne's many inundating floods.

Chapter Ten
Old Wayne

The first post office in Wayne was located along the Newark and Pompton Turnpike in the Ryerson-DeMott general store. The turnpike veered west and then north above Mountain View.

Just north of Mountain View, the Newark and Pompton Turnpike retains the name it has had for nearly 200 years, as it departs State Route 23 and goes off to the northwest toward Pequannock Township after crossing the Pompton River. The old road and the river form a peninsula many refer to as Old Wayne. Before Route 23 was realigned in the mid-1930's, the state route and then 130 year old turnpike were continuously one and the same. Just beyond the present junction, the road made a sudden turn to the northwest, resulting in such a hazardous condition, the location was known as Killer Bend, or Dead Man's Turn. It remained a real problem until the state route was improved in the 1970's, the same time the old Wayne Circle was eliminated. While this change drastically improved the flow of traffic along the western border of the township, it also eliminated the old Sears and Sisco houses on both sides of Route 23, as well as the old Blacksmith shop across from Gabriels. Unfortunately, these were the only three historic buildings listed as being in Wayne in the National Park Service's 1939

Historic American Building Survey (HAB). The others, including the Schuyler-Colfax House, are still listed as being in Pompton.

The term Old Wayne probably received that name because the first post office in the Township was not located in what became the town center at Meads Basin, but in the Ryerson-DeMott Store built over a century and a quarter ago. That post office amounted to little more than a small secretary desk, now on display at the Wayne Museum in the Van Riper-Hopper House on Berdan Avenue. The old store was located just north of Killer Bend. With the realignment and improvement of State Route 23, the road which kept the turnpike's original name (aka State Route 8 for a time), was also slightly realigned. As a result the former post office and general store building is now on Old Newark and Pompton Turnpike, a short street which runs off the main road. It dead ends at a grove of trees, just before the present Route 23. Across the street from it, now known as the Turnpike Tole House, is not only another old home, but one which was the

Today the general store is called "The Tole House," specializing in the well-known toy dolls. The turnpike became Route 23 and was realigned in 1936 to eliminate this stretch of road. The store is now along a short, dead-end street aptly named "Old Newark and Pompton Turnpike." This desk (below) was the actual post office inside.

subject of its own book during the 1920's, and national attention. Listed in *Ripley's Believe It Or Not* is the so-called *Blind Man's House*.

Frances A. Burnett in 1925 was a 65 year old sightless gentlemen who more than made up for his disability with his imagination, tenacity and sheer will. With virtually no assistance by anyone, he literally built the house with the gambrel roof by hand, despite being totally blind.

The DeMott family were among the earliest settlers of this region. Their homestead was located on Greenwood Avenue in what is now Pequannock Township. One of the region's earliest roads was located on the highland overlooking the Pompton River between the DeMott home and the north end of present day North Pequannock Avenue, at the point where Wayne's first bridge once stood.

The Ryerson family was more than simply early pioneers. One of their descendants, Martin Ryerson, rose to become one of the most prosperous and important men in the state, if not the nation. Born in 1751, on April 18, 1797 Ryerson purchased the Pompton Ironworks, and expanded his holdings soon afterwards by also buying land in Bloomingdale and the surrounding area. Before long he found himself lord master of the legendary Ringwood and Long Pond ironworks, as well as half owner of the Charlotteburg iron works and several other smaller concerns. His home was the elegant Ringwood Manor.

Prior to the 1930's everything and everyone of consequence who passed through Wayne or into Wayne from the south or north passed through Old Wayne.

Black Oak Ridge Road, believed to be along the path of the major branch of the Minisink Trail in Wayne, started its journey up to the Hamburg Turnpike and the Pompton Furnace just south of the point where the Newark and Pompton Turnpike cross-

"Beginning at a Black Oak Tree marked standing near the southwest corner of Aaron Schuyler's field Fence by Pompton Road, that leads toward the falls Pisake River, and from thence running by a line of trees to Poquanick River and from hence by a line of trees running along the east side of the land of George Ryerson tell (sic) it meets with the Old Road at the brook called Beaver Dam."

One would hardly recognize the original version (above) of the vastly-modified Ryerson House (below), still standing north of Old Newark and Pompton Turnpike road.

Packanack Lake Road also began in Old Wayne, originally marked with an elaborate wooden gate which the fancy Pierce Arrows, Duesenbergs, Cadillacs and Lincolns of the well-to-do passed through on their way to the newly built Lake in the Mountains when it was created and first developed in the 1920's.

Beginning in the 1930's the 665 foot tower of the WABC

es the old Pompton Feeder Canal and the Pompton River. The road may have been officially dedicated as early as April, 1707. The following description appears in official records:

radio station could be seen from miles away after being built in the marsh off what is now Vincent Street. Its construction was met with vigorous opposition by a citizens group led by the influential LeGrand Parish and the mayors and other government leaders from vir-

Built in 1784 the George Ryerson House (above) stood across the pike from the Abraham Ryerson House. In 1936 it was moved to Hathaway Lane in Essex Fells, where it was converted and expanded into the villa it is today (below). To the right of the former house is a rare photo of the Voice of America tower.

tions, at that time the major source of entertainment for most Americans. A compromise was eventually worked out where local homeowners were provided with a special anti-interference device that solved the problem. What started out as such a major problem for the locals, during World War II became a source of great pride and expression of patriotism. From here the Voice of America transmitted its propaganda and spirit-lifting broadcasts to our servicemen fighting for the survival of a free world in Europe.

Today the spire is long gone, and all that remains is a crumbling foundation of the old brick station building, surrounded by a chain-link fence with signs warning that it is "Property Of The United States" of which there should be absolutely "No Trespassing."

tually every surrounding community. (Wayne is so large that it borders 13 other municipalities). Their concern was that it was not only unneeded, but it would interfere with local resident's reception of other radio sta-

Another reason why the area became known as Old Wayne is that, of the three railroad stations situated within the Township borders, only the one just south of Ryerson Avenue was designated the *Wayne Station*. It was located at this spot for one major reason: this was the site of the Laflin & Rand Powderworks, the major business in Wayne for the good part of a century.

"Horseshoe Hollow," reportedly built with petrified wood, is also reported to be the only place in Wayne still zoned for hay rides. It is located further north on the former pike.

Historical Highlight
The Blind Man's House

Located across the street from the DeMott-Ryerson House, this home was built "In the Dark."

Wayne is blessed with numerous intriguing oddities. Many unique and unusual events have occurred here. Yet only one apparently qualified to be listed in *Ripley's Believe It Or Not*, the so-called Blind Man's House, or as others have called it The House Built in the Dark.

On what is now the corner of the Newark and Pompton Turnpike and the Old Newark and Pompton Turnpike in Old Wayne, diagonally across the original route of the byway from the former DeMott-Ryerson General Store and Wayne's first post office, is a handsome home with a large gambrel roof. This house was literally built in the 1920's by a 65 year old man by the name of Francis A. Burdett, who was totally blind--- believe it or not!

Burdett had sight for the first 50 years of his life, but lost it in a tragic industrial accident around 1910. As he was a jeweler (from Rhode Island), one can imagine how terribly ironic it was for someone who was able to make his living because of what had to be exceptional eyesight to suddenly find himself lost in the dark. But Burdett apparently could create his own light---at least in his mind. He may have lost his sight, but certainly not his vision---or his memory.

In 1925 he decided to build his dream house, all by himself. He started out by drawing up plans and constructing a cardboard model. For many blind people, this alone would qualify as a tremendous accomplishment. But not Francis, who had every intention of constructing a 25 foot wide home. And not just a rambling

one story ranch, but one that rose 29 feet in the air.

Virtually every tool, ladder and building aid used, the blind man built himself. He commenced by constructing three ladders between 10 and 23 feet high, along with a temporary house and workshed behind the main construction site. The shed was connected to the main house as it began to rise by a somewhat shaky platform.   Unlike conventional building techniques, Francis started his project by completely building the first floor, including the interior, before beginning the second.

Word soon spread from beyond just fascinated neighbors as onlookers came from as far away as Virginia. Members of the press swarmed around, obviously smelling a great human interest story. Some went so far as to light a match inches from Burdett's eyes, hoping to cause him to flinch and prove this was a con job par excellence. He never did.

The builder encountered many problems, as could be expected. The windows were one. He came up with a solution by sawing holes in the completed walls, attaching frames, and carefully adding the glass. This was a minor challenge compared to his intention to add a Dutch Colonial roof. Attaching a ridge board seemed virtually impossible. After much research Burdett was able to fashion a rope and pulley system where he could lift the completed ridge board above the second floor and then drop it into a pocket-like brace he had built using several 2 X 4's.

Amazingly, not only was the house completed, but it was clearly one of the nicest in the entire neighborhood. But it lacked one thing that every other house of the time had, something that Burdett simply didn't need.....electric lighting. Eventually this too was added, and Francis A. Burdett accomplished the seemingly impossible. A few years later his son-in-law, William Vahrenkamp authored a book in tribute, *The House the Blind-Man Built*. It included scores of diagrams and drawings showing exactly how his father-in-law completed his amazing project. It also illustrated how Burdett was able to carry on the everyday tasks even non-builders who are sightless rarely can accomplish---cooking, dressing, cleaning his home, etc. Under such titles as "Here is how the blind man cooks his dinner," Vahrenkamp included step-by-step drawings.

Today, the Blind-Man's House remains stable and secure. In 1986 it was even subdivided into multiple occupancy dwellings.

FRANCIS A. BURDETT
The Blind Builder
DECORATED WITH A FEW OF HIS PETS.

This amazing story was the subject of an animated book written by Burdett's proud son-in-law.

Historical Highlight
Voice of America

WABC was actually owned by the Columbia Broadcasting System. Shown here in 1946, it was the "Voice of America" during World War II overseas' broadcasts.

While Murchio's Flying Field filled the air with many student pilots who went on to defend America on the battlefields of Europe, another Wayne institution filled the air with patriotic support overseas. Not with bombs and bullets, but with words. During World War II the Voice of America (W.O.O.W.) broadcasts to Europe originated from a quiet spot in a marsh on the west end of Vincent Avenue in Old Wayne. Few communities had a high enough tower and powerful enough transmitter to cross the Ocean. But Wayne did!

Ironically, when WABC of the Columbia Broadcasting System announced its plans to build a 565' tower with a 50,000 watt radio transmitter the community leaders were outraged. They claimed it infringed on the freedom of every resident for miles around. Little did they realize that the objectionable facility would wind up doing just the opposite-help protect our freedom.

The site planned for the facility was a mile or so to the northwest of the old Laflin & Rand (and later Dupont) Powderworks. Another ironic twist is despite the fact the powder works was closer to the population center of the Township, and was the site of numerous, ear-popping, heart-stopping explosions, no organized protests appear to have taken place. Nor did too many community leaders stand up and do anything about Dupont and the old Pompton Ironworks polluting the air and water for miles around. Yet the radio station found the now-typical "Not in my backyard" cries of protest.

The forces against the broadcast facility were headed by the man who was probably the wealthiest and most famous local resident---LeGrand Parish.

The famed inventor/business tycoon, who was also Passaic County Park Commissioner appears to have corralled the mayors of Paterson, Caldwell, West

Today only crumbling ruins remain.

Caldwell, Verona and Totowa, along with other government leaders from Little Falls, Hawthorne, and even Wayne itself. He wrote and published a leaflet signed by all entitled *Affecting Radio Reception in Your Area, Committee of Municipalities Opposing the Erection of a 50,000 Watt Radio Broadcasting Transmitter in Wayne, N.J.* Parish urged residents to sign a copy of it and return it to him, assuming they agreed with his position. The publication contended that the station was really being built to serve "New York City, not New Jersey"; that it would "have a blanketing effect upon 85% of the radio sets located within a minimum distance of 6 to 8 miles within which lies a population of over 400,000 people." It was claimed "Real estate values and business will be depreciated because people will not desire to move into, or remain in, an area where radio reception is limited to one station only." Apparently new Wayne residents didn't have a problem moving into an area with two explosive powder works, one where iron sledge and waste had been dumped into its rivers for over 200 years, and one where there had never been apparently concern over other environmental issues. But Parish believed that asking them to accept but one radio station in town was simply too much to expect.

Parish, being the ingenious scientist and inventor that he was should have known that a simple device provided to each resident would solve the problem. It did, and the station was built. It served not only Wayne and the New York Metropolitan area for years, but the entire nation as well during the war.

While the base of the station was situated in an obscure location in the Township, everyone knew where it was. It not only rose from sea level to a point 80% as high as the peak of High Mountain, but had a very unusual design, narrow on the top and on the bottom, with the middle bowed out. It must have been a real topic of conversation for anyone who drove by on State Route 23, wondering what in the devil the odd steel tower was.

Today the station is long gone. However, surrounded by wire fence with warning signs for all to stay away, is a crumbling brick building that at one time had a certain air about it.

A rather fuzzy photo of the 665' tower appeared many years ago in Audio Magazine.

Chapter Eleven
Construction and Destruction: Wayne's Contradictory Industries

Laflin & Rand, and then DuPont, operated a huge complex of manufacturing plants, offices, recreational facilities and even housing along Ryerson Avenue in Old Wayne. By the time this photograph was taken in 1946 their powderworks companies had long been gone, taken over by Mack Molding.

Ironically, the two major industries situated in Wayne proper from the middle of the 19th to well into the 20th century were ones which had seeming contradictory purposes. Laflin & Rand, as well as the other powderworks in town, the J.R. Rand & Company, aka Rendrock Powder Company, product was explosives, the type used to demolish buildings and other unwanted structures (as well as to blast out tunnels and hillsides). The other major industry which existed here during about the same period produced not a product

that knocked things down, but which was used to build them-bricks.

The Laflin & Rand Powder Company was organized on August 24, 1869 under the laws of the State of New York. In 1873 a tract of 130 acres was secured just to the west of the Newark and Pompton Turnpike in Old Wayne, along present-day Ryerson Avenue. There the company (and its predecessor) built a huge complex which included not only a substantial manufacturing plant, but a recreation hall, bowling alley and tennis

Today, the massive complex is mostly boarded up. Is it ripe for a new and even more influential industry?

courts for the workers, along with housing on the surrounding acreage. (Several of the original workers' houses still exist along Ford Street, north of the complex). When the Montclair Railway was built in 1873 and ran just to the east of the facility, the Wayne Station was erected just south of Ryerson Avenue. An interesting innovation was attempted at Laflin & Rand, that

the company hoped would bring it even greater success than it had been having. It developed a process to purify common salt resulting from the conversion of nitrate and potassium chloride. A vacuum kettle was bought and a salt turned out that was practically chemically pure. The success led to the marketing of the product under Dickey Bird label. Unfortunately, the discovery of salt wells in Michigan, where fuel was obtained as a by-product of sawmills, made it uneconomical and the effort was abandoned here in Old Wayne.

In what some have called Preakness Hollow, the small depression in the middle of the unusual upside down, "U"-shaped crests on the north end of Packanack Mountain, the other powderworks plant in Wayne was situated. This is close to Tom's Lake (Captain Michael Kilroy Memorial Park) on Kiwanis Drive, north of Ratzer Road and west of Alps Road. Earlier it was also the site of one of the first sawmills in early Wayne operated by, who else, a Ryerson.

The J.R. Rand Powderworks Company, aka the Rendrock Powder Company, was organized in 1873. Rendrock was not someone's name, nor a geographic

The Rendrock Powder Company left few records in local logs, however this 1878 map, published by E.B. Hyde & Co. of New York shows its location in "Preakness Hollow," present site of Kilroy Park (pictured today, l.) on Kiwanis Drive.

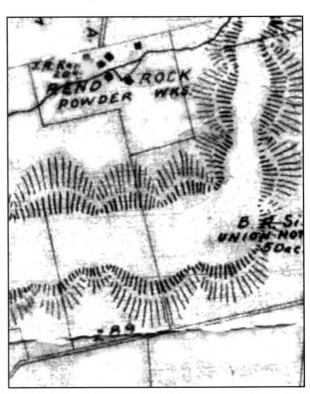

description, but a type of powder consisting of 40% nitroglycerine, 40% saltpeter, 13% treated wood pulp and 7% paraffin, the invention of one Treat S. Beach. Beach convinced Jasper R. Rand and Addison C. Rand, sons of Albert T. Rand, president of Laflin & Rand, to invest in his new powder and they built their mountain plant in 1874. Their dynamite was sold to iron mines in Port Henry, New York, rock contractors in the Empire State, other iron mines in Wisconsin and copper mines in Michigan. A supply of it was sold to help blast out the Bergen Tunnel in Jersey City, which allowed trains of the Montclair and other railways approaching from the west to navigate the obstructive Bergen Hill. Not long after the town's second explosive works was built, the company was forced to give up production of its name product when a patent infringement suit was filed against both Rand-owned companies, who they claimed were in cahoots. While

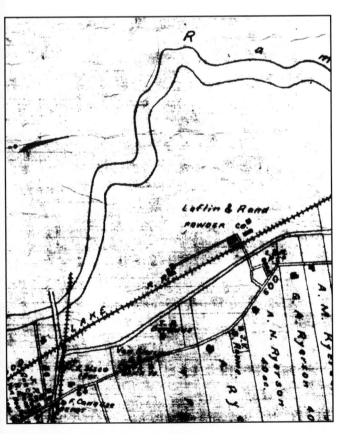

On the 1878 map, Laflin & Rand is shown in an area that was almost about as developed as it would ever become.

agreeing to cease production of rendrock powder, the J.R. Rand Powderworks almost immediately began production of another type of explosives called Rack-a-rock. In 1885 it was used for the huge Hells Gate blast, and assisted in the construction of portions of several West Shore, Lehigh Valley (Vosburg tunnel) and other railroad tunnels. Despite these sales, it never became very popular in this country, although the United States Army continued to use it as a demolition explosive until it was replaced by compressed TNT during World War I.

Wayne was chosen as the site for these two operations for several obvious reasons: It was close to major transportation, rivers, railways and turnpikes, yet it was also far enough out in the country not to frighten too many people when the periodic unintended explosions would rock both plants. In 1905, it was reported that 100 of Old Wayne's 205 inhabitants worked in the powderworks.

Laflin & Rand was eventually acquired by the Dupont Company which was primarily responsible for expanding the local facilities into a community within a community. The powderworks closed in 1925, replaced by Mack Molding Company. Today the facility is mostly vacant, the train station is long gone, as is the radio tower. Cars still stream by along the former turnpike, but most are simply on their way to other places.

The J.R. Rand Powderworks Company is rumored to have closed its local plant after one gigantic blast occurred, reportedly heard as far away as Manhattan. However, as late as 1927 *The History of Explosives in America*, published by Columbia University Press, reported that the company, which once was located in Pequannock, still maintained offices in New York City.

Wayne's second major industry had an even longer life. The lower portion of the Township, in and around Mountain View, along with in and around Singac, was not chosen because of its remoteness like the explosive industry. The reason was simply that here could be found a seemingly endless supply of glacial Pleistocene clays ideal for building decorative and strong buildings, walkways, walls, bridges and towers.

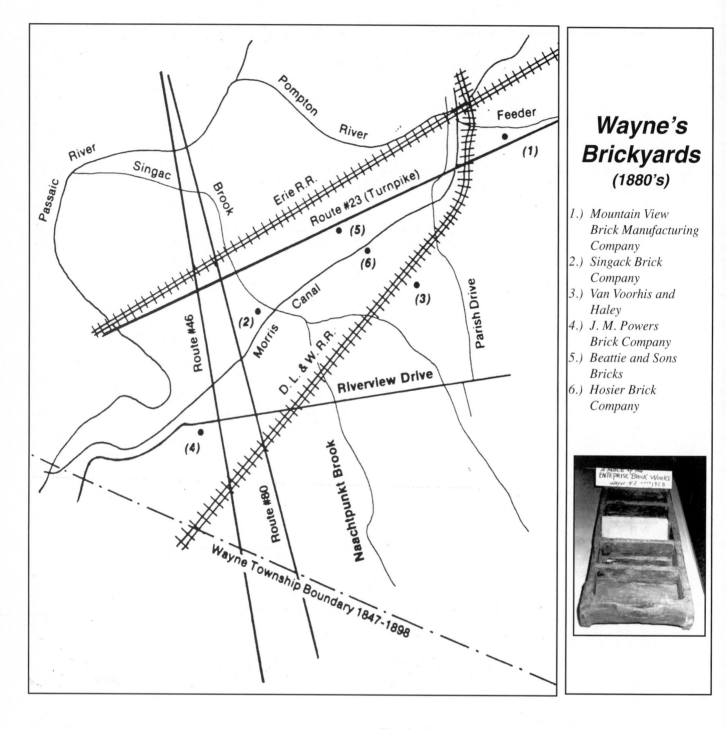

Wayne's Brickyards (1880's)

1.) *Mountain View Brick Manufacturing Company*
2.) *Singack Brick Company*
3.) *Van Voorhis and Haley*
4.) *J. M. Powers Brick Company*
5.) *Beattie and Sons Bricks*
6.) *Hosier Brick Company*

It was found 10 to 15 feet below the surface, covered mostly with sand, in beds twenty to thirty feet thick. The presence of iron oxide, probably the same compound whose presence explained the abundance of the ore which gave rise to the state's major industry for centuries, resulted in the brick made from the clay taking on a desirable red color when burnt.

Why was there so much clay in this area? The hint lies in the above mentioned reference that it was technically glacial clay. During the last Ice or Pleistocene Age, the massive glaciers which crept south from Canada brought with them considerable amounts of crushed rock and other debris. The debris was mostly sand and gravel of various shapes and sizes. Some of it was ground so fine, it was almost flour-like. This flour was the basis of the clay found in Wayne,

Van Varick heating is located on Route 23 on the former site of the Mountain View Brick Manufacturing Company. The brickyard and clay pits were situated across the highway in the parking lot of the former Mothers discotheque.

Brick Manufacturing Company which was formed in 1879. It included 120 acres of clay and sand. Many of northern New Jersey's most famous buildings were constructed using Wayne brick, including those in the historic mill district of Paterson, the Beattie Carpet Mills in Little Falls, the powderworks in Old Wayne, along with thousands of residential, commercial, church, school and government buildings throughout the New York Metropolitan area. Apparently Arent Schuyler discovered the clay as well, as his 1696 home on Hamburg Turnpike is not the type of traditional Dutch Stone Farm House once so prevalent in the area, but consists of mainly red bricks, probably of local vintage. The bricks were also used for railroad stations and streets.

A companion building material found close by was

which was created when the ice masses melted, leaving the ancient Lake Passaic.   Since the northern shore of this lake was in and around Singac and Mountain View, it was here that the most abundant and finest quantities of the clay was found. Similar clay was found in and about the Hackensack Meadowlands where another glacial lake once existed. A similar industry thus existed there as well.

The clay was hand dug in pits, shoveled into carts and pulled to a tempering ring by oxen. By the end of the 19th century huge steam-powered shovels did the digging and the loading. Each pit generally was 20 to 25 feet in diameter, and produced enough clay to mold 25,000 to 30,000 bricks. The main skill of the brickmaster was applying just the right temperature for just the right period of time to produce the highest quality brick. Slowly the fires would rise in temperature. By the fifth day, they would peak at or near 1800 degrees Fahrenheit. There were six major brickyards in Singac and Mountain View (see accompanying map). The first in Wayne appears to have been the Mountain View

Perhaps the last recognizable building left from the Wayne area's six brick manufacturing companies is this sole structure on Riverview Drive, south of U.S. 46, now technically in Totowa. Across the street ran the Morris Canal and was part of the Connors/Powers brick yards.

the beautiful brown stone quarried at the Great Notch and on both sides of the Passaic River just below the former Morris Canal Aqueduct. In an ironic twist, that magnificent structure was built with local rock andprobably taken down with local explosive powder. mills. Portions of it were saved and are on permanent display in the city park in Little Falls just to the east of town along the path of the canal.

Over the last three hundred years Wayne has had numerous industries. Thousands of years ago the Indians dried animal skins and picked local grasses to build their huts and long houses. Early on during colonization there were sawmills, gristmills and cider John Hinchman operated a gravel pit on his property adjacent to Hamburg Turnpike and Hinchman Avenue. Another quarry was located near the Pompton River south of Pompton Plains Cross Road. Of course the ironworks at Pompton continued for nearly two centuries. But if Wayne was known for any one industry, it would have to be farming.

William A. Hosier, Horseshoer was in operation as blacksmith just north of Gabriels on a small strip of land between Mountain View Avenue and the Morris Canal. The building (r.) stood for over 150 years, and was even listed in the United States Park Services "Historic American Building Survey," conducted in 1939. It underwent numerous cosmetic changes over the years (below), but was a victim of the most recent improvement of Route 23. Today the lot is empty.

Another blacksmith shop was located south of Gabriels on the turnpike. Here the old ramshackle building is being put to use in its last days (r.).

Chapter Twelve
Valley Road: Wayne's Main Street and Miles and Miles of Farms

"Wayne's Main Street," Valley Road, seen here in this old and rare 1900 photograph, was far different than it is today. It was lined with farms from foothill to foothill. In all probability, absent some of the buildings in the distance, this is how George Washington saw this portion of the Preakness Valley the many times he rode his famous white horse along this route. In 1780 the landscape was covered with the regiments of the American army.

If time travel was possible, one visiting Valley Road, the so-called Main Street of Wayne, one hundred years ago would probably not recognize it at all. At the time it ran only as far north as Ratzer Road. In order to reach the Paterson and Hamburg Turnpike from the Lower Preakness Valley, a traveler would have to turn left or right at Ratzer and venture a short way to either Church Lane to the west or Hinchman Avenue to the east. On a map, the three appeared like a giant "Y". The road was little more than a sleepy country back road, with sixteen large farms running to the foothills of the mountains to the east and west. Among these

families were familiar pioneer names like Doremus, Demarest, Berdan, Stagg, Berry and Terhune. The little two-room Preakness schoolhouse served the entire valley quite well.

A typical farm of the early 20th century was that of the MacDonald Family, on the east side of Valley Road above present day MacDonald Drive, obviously named for the family. The property encompassed 80 acres, including 50 which were cultivated and the other 30 which were either woodlands or meadows. A small brook on the land was well filled with trout. A larger spring down further in the valley often was used to

The MacDonald Farm was one of the smaller, but certainly very significant farms along Valley Road. Seen here is the barn (l.) and the family farmhouse (below).

Today, the MacDonald farmhouse is still there (below), but blended into the many other suburban homes that cover the old farmland. It is across the street from what is presently a Treasure Island store.

refrigerate milk and other dairy products the family used. As with many other so-called truck farms in the valley, the MacDonald Farm rotated their ground crops, which included corn, potatoes, tomatoes, cabbage, beets, carrots, and egg plant. There were chestnut, mulberry and apple trees on or near the farm. Cows and chickens were raised to be butchered for home use. Horses and oxen were the standard beasts of burden.

At the northeast corner of Valley Road and Preakness Avenue stood the Sanford Place, more formally called Preakness

Life on the MacDonald Farm in 1915 (above and r.) was in some ways more formal, in some ways more simple, but other ways much more complicated. The formal part was the dress. When one took a photo, they put on their Sunday best.

Lost Jewels. In 1997 Wayne lost two of what were undoubtedly its two most visible landmarks on Valley Road. The Nellis Farmhouse (l.) was razed after standing on Nellis Drive since 1840. It was one of the premier dairy farms in the valley, shown below in 1900. Also removed was the "Red Barn Farm" (below) with its classic gambrel roof. The latter is of more recent vintage, being constructed early in this century. It was particularly unique in the Township as it is reported it was an original Sears and Roebuck barn, sold through that company's famous catalog. At the time, one could purchase barns, homes, and even automobiles by mail order from Sears.

The last of the dairy farms, the Van Peenen (above and l.), which began in 1929, remains north and across the street from where the Red Barn was located.

The last major farm in the Township remains on Black Oak Ridge Road. George Kuehm's grandfather purchased the property in 1894. The family farmhouse, filled with what amounts to a small museum worth of antiques, also over 100 years old, still stands along with one of its earliest barns. Kuehm has an immense collection of Indian artifacts he has collected in the area for decades. Archeologists have discovered that one of the largest Indian temporary villages was situated just west of the farm.

George Kuehm's "Farmview" is not only historic, but the view of the mountains and western sky is awe-inspiring, particularly at sunset.

The Benson House on Valley Road is an unusual example of early American construction. The iron lettered street address on the south side of the building is actually four steel or iron rods which run through the building, securing the back and front walls.

The Grange Hall was located to the west of Preakness School No. 2 on Hamburg Turnpike at Church Lane. It not only was used for meetings of the "Grangers" (farmers), but hosted numerous fairs, shows and social gatherings.

Farms, the home of the horse ranch of Milton Holbrook Sanford, owner of the legendary Preakness racehorse. This prized animal was the 1870 winner of Baltimore's Pimlico Race Track's first Dinner Plate Stakes.   In the three year old colt's honor, the stakes race thereafter became known as The Preakness Stakes, becoming the first in time of what is now recognized as the middle jewel in thoroughbred racing's famed Triple Crown Series.   On the site of the shopping center where the A&P is now located, once stood the Preakness Race Track, also owned by Mr. Sanford. Years later during the early 1930's another Preakness Race Track operated diagonally across Valley from the Nellis Farm and directly across from the Main Branch of Wayne's Public Library.

Farming was obviously nothing new to Wayne, remembering Arent Schuyler panned the land as being ideal for agriculture. Centuries, perhaps millenniums before his arrival, the Indians raised corn and other ground crops in this area.   And also remember that Schuyler and Brockholst gathered together mostly wealthy farmers as their core of prime investors who settled here and set up farms. According to information filed with the State of New Jersey in 1860, 8,411 acres in Wayne was reported to be improved land, and 5,110 unimproved. Obviously the definition of what is improved and what is not improved was different than it is today, meaning the so-called improved land prob-

ably meant it was tilled, planted and harvested. An animal census revealed 364 sheep, 274 horses, 8 donkeys and mules, 615 milch cows, 211 working oxen, 602 head of cattle and 530 swine. Yields for the year ending June 1, 1860 indicated that 2,009 bushels of wheat, 8,205 bushels of rye, 22,987 bushels of Indian corn, 12,933 bushels of oats, 486 pounds of wool, 23,012 bushels of Irish potatoes, 4,412 bushels of buckwheat and 3,136 tons of hay were produced.   Add to this 75,004 pounds of butter and 1,690 pounds of honey and one can get a good idea how fertile the Lower Preakness Valley was. Since the average farmhand worked for only $12.00 a month, including room and board, the farmers did quite well for themselves.

In 1904 just to the north of School #2, the latter which is still standing opposite Church Lane on Hamburg Turnpike, farmers constructed The Grange Hall. For over half a century it held flower shows, square dances, 4-H fairs and meetings for other organizations. The Grangers throughout northern New Jersey met once a year for their Farmers Picnics, formal affairs in which they dressed to the hilt and traveled in their best formal carriages and early horseless carriages to such favorite meeting places like nearby Crystal Lake at Eagle Rock Reservation on the West Orange-Verona border line, or Verona Lake Park. While crowds of 5,000 or more were commonplace during the early years of the 20th century, they dwindled to but a few hundred by 1924 when the annual get-togethers were canceled.

Many of the farms in Wayne primarily grew and harvested crops, however there were also a number of dairy farms as well, such as the Van Peenen and Nellis Farms on both sides of Valley Road in Preakness, and the large Sheffield Farms over the hill along Black Oak Ridge Road, south of what is now Pompton Plains

Cross Road, bordering the Pompton River. This was a literal showplace. The public was invited to visit the milking parlor and view the state-of-the-art machinery. Among the sights included were two overhead pipes which carried pumped milk high above and across Black Oak Ridge Road over two specially built bridges to the bottling plant on the east side of the roadway. The Sheffield operation included numerous barns and outbuildings, and even their own fire department on the premises.

Just to the north were the Graham and Kuehm Farms, mentioned earlier, near the site of ancient Indian transitional villages. Of the hundreds of farms that once dominated the landscape in Wayne, the Kuehm's Farmview is the only one of any consequential size left. When George Kuehm's grandfather pur

chased the land from the previous owner in 1894, it would have had to be considered a relatively minor transaction. Today's acreage owned by the family, which seems far reaching when standing on the elevated roadway east of the farmland, would have been considered postage stamp-sized in comparison with virtually every other large farm in the entire Township 100 years ago.

The character of Wayne has changed more in the last century than virtually any other of the thirteen bordering communities. Certainly these changes have been far more drastic than any experienced by the older, more urban neighboring towns like Paterson, Montclair, Caldwell and Little Falls. One thing that has changed little is its astounding beauty.

Valley Road, 1939

Over the last three decades of the 20th century Valley Road has changed somewhat as this 1965 aerial photograph shows. Mainly, the open spaces have been largely filled in. However, the changes were far less dramatic as they had been over the prior three decades which saw the transformation of the valley from an agrarian into a suburban landscape.

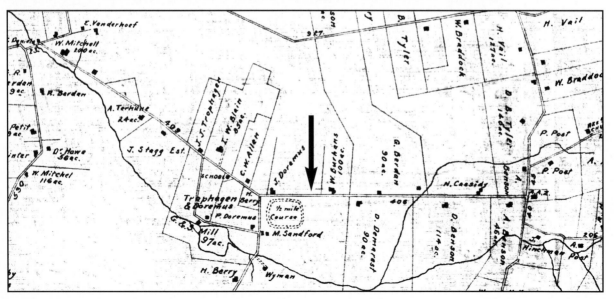

Valley Road (arrow) in 1877 was lined with farms, not stores, residences and municipal buildings as it is today. It ran from Riverview Drive to Ratzer Road.

Holy Resurrection Orthodox Church

On August 23, 1964, the first Orthodox Christian Divine Liturgy was celebrated in Wayne. This service took place in a temporary chapel in the Wayne Community Fire House. Services were subsequently moved to the Valley Road P.A.L. building. The Reverend Alvian Smirensky was assigned to lead the newly formed parish. He remained in that position until early 1968 when Father Paul Kucynda, the present pastor, was appointed. On September 13, 1969, after many years of planning, a new church building was finished and dedicated at 285 French Hill Road.

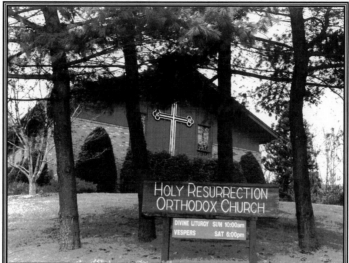

Our life as a Christian community centers on the celebration of the Divine Liturgy. We heard the Word of God, partake in the Sacrament of Holy Communion and rejoice together in the risen Lord at this weekly service.

We are a very active Christian community. Our parish participates in many worthwhile projects and sponsors many programs for personal growth and enrichment. We provide educational programs for adults and children An *Inquirer's Program* is also offered for those seeking to know more about our Orthodox Christian faith.

We have two ongoing group ministry programs. The *Small Group Enrichment* focuses on bible study and offers solutions based in scripture to many of life's challenges. "Dealing with Stress", "Troubles", and "Parenting" have been recent topics. The *Peer Ministry Group* coordinates our weekly coffee hour and other special events and receptions.

Vocal music is an integral part of our Christian life. We have several music programs. Many adult parish members participate in the *Adult Choir.* Our *Youth Choir* consists of children age nine to seventeen. Our unique *Early Childhood Program* is for infants, toddlers and children up to nine years old.

Now that you know a little more about us, please consider making Holy Resurrection Church your spiritual home!

Boathouses like H. Brownlee's proliferated along Wayne's rivers. This one was located in the Minisink Park section, just east of State Route 23, on the Wayne side of the Passaic River.

Historical Highlight
Sheffield Dairy Farms

Sheffield Dairy Farms was a large complex of buildings on both sides of Black Oak Ridge Road (at the corner of present Pompton Plains Cross Road). This 1922 aerial photograph taken from a biplane shows the main complex, the so-called "Sheffield homes," (top) where family members and key employees resided, along with the Graham Farm house (foreground). The building to the left, connected by the "pumping ramps," is today the controversial site of the United States Department of Energy.

Driving along Black Oak Ridge Road approaching Pompton Plains Cross Road is an obvious relic of the past. A large red barn-like structure closely parallels the east side of the roadway. Today it is an antique furniture store. For most of the first half of the 20th century, it was the main plant and headquarters of the Sheffield Dairy Farms, a major business and certainly a major Wayne landmark.

From the time Arent Schuyler began to cultivate his land in the Pompton Falls area, until well into the 20th century, agriculture was the predominant industry in Wayne. There was the brick industry, the explosive powder industry, and the iron and steel industry.

However, farming was number one. Most of the farms were so-called truck farms. They grew vegetables, corn, potatoes, squash, cabbage and the like. But there were also a number of dairy ranches, such as the Nellis Farm, the Van Peenen Farm and a few others. By and large the Sheffield Dairy Farms was the queen of this genre of land use. The WPA Guide to New Jersey was originally published in 1939 and often reproduced. It is still in print and serves as a wonderful look at the Garden State as it did during the height of The Great Depression. Included are over 40 Tours, mile by mile descriptions of landmarks along what are offered as the most scenic and interesting routes in the state. Tour 4 brings the reader south from Oakland along historic

U.S. 202 and 200+ year old Black Oak Ridge Road. The following description is included:

> "Three broad acres along both sides of the macadam road at 13.2 m are SHEFFIELD FARMS (milking parlor open). Sweet timothy and alfalfa smells make up its bucolic atmosphere for the modern buildings where milk is drawn from cows by machine and pumped across the road for\bottling. The luminous white milk houses are a cross between old Dutch mill buildings and the spare, trim, twentieth century industrial architecture."

Just south of the complex was a row of fairly large homes that the company also built, presumably for family members and high-ranking other employees. At the corner of Pompton Plains Cross Road, the middle link in the old Road to Jackson's linking the Newark and Pompton Turnpike with the Paterson and Hamburg Turnpike (which actually intersected in Pompton Lakes),   stood the Pompton Falls Fire Station, operated by Sheffields and on its grounds. The building remains, but is presently

The farm had its own fire house and equipment at the corner of Jackson Avenue (Pompton Plains Cross Road) (top). Today the building survives as a copy store.

The main building exists today as the "Red Barn" antique furniture store. Several of the old barns stand weathered on the old property. The United States Department of Energy's "Information Center" occupies the old packing building across the street.

radically   modified   and serves as a copy store.

Sheffield Farms would place large full page advertisements during the mid-1930's and early 1940's in Wayne Today,   the only major newspaper published in the Township.   Its distinctive trucks could be seen delivering dairy goods throughout the region for decades.

Today, the shell of the once-grand complex remains. In addition to the furniture store and the copy store, the building across Black Oak Ridge Road has been owned by the United States Government. Labeled the *Environmental Information Center* of the Department of Energy, the facility has long been the center of a controversy, as the once bucolic setting of Sheffield Farms has become an environmental hazard. Several of the old barns, hidden to the rear of the former complex, are still standing, but barely. Times have certainly changed.

The Sheffield milkman (above). The company delivered its dairy products throughout the area and heavily advertised in local papers.

Labeled "A modern dairy plant in Pompton Plains," indicative of the geographical confusion which has long existed about Wayne and its neighbors, this photo (below) appeared in the 1939 WPA Guide To New Jersey.

There was an elevated "milk ramp" from which milk was pumped across Black Oak Ridge Road to be packaged (above). The Sheffields came to Wayne in the 1890's and stayed into the 1950's.

In the early 1900's a few souls relax in front of the Graham Farm, just across old lower Jackson Avenue to the north. Most photographs of the day, even on the farms, showed residents wearing rather formal wear. Gettin' one's picture taken was worth getting dressed up for.

Welcome to
WAYNE LIONS CLUB

"THE TALKING NEWSPAPER"

Where There Is No Sight - Let There Be Sound!

Gibraltar Towers, suite 7D
Jefferson Street
Hackensack, NJ - 07601

Home   History

The visually impaired get all the national & international news via the radio & audio TV,but don't know what happens on main street four blocks from their home. Many volunteers read the news for the visually impaired, but the Free Talking Newspaper is recorded on cassette and can be played back when they want to get the Local News.
The Talking Newspaper, endorsed and sponsored by the Wayne, N.J. Lions, gives the recipient the Local News that they missed.

Start A Unit In Your Area!!
Need Info?
Phone: (201) 498 - 0396
Fax: (201) 498 - 0395
E-mail: talknews@aol.com

Let's Make This An International Project!

Also visit:

Designed by MarcSoft,LLC   *Top-of-Page*   *New Jersey*

www.officialsite.com/waynelions

Chapter Thirteen
Beauty and the Beast

The stark contrast between the activity level in the Pompton River, south of the Lincoln Park (U.S. 202) bridge is shockingly evident in these two photographs taken almost ninety years apart. Today (below), the river is eerily placid.

Wayne is still a Wondrously Beautiful Valley. In fact it is several wondrously beautiful valleys along with numerous wondrously beautiful mountains. The view at sunset over the Kuehm Farm with the western hills in the far distance framing Pompton, Pequannock, Wanaque and Ramapo Rivers in the near distance is awe-inspiring. As is the beauty of watching the sun go down over the Point View Reservoir from the tailored grounds of the Van Riper-Hopper House. Sunrise at Pines Lake or Packanack Lake is sheer heaven. Hidden from all except those venturesome enough to set out on foot along the deeply-wooded river banks

In 1997 (l.) the lower portion of the Pompton River is rarely, if ever, used. On the other hand, canoeing, row boating and swimming were commonplace for much of the first half of the century.

There are several "flood gauges" (lower l.) placed riverside along the once popular waterway to measure the rising levels of what can be a very difficult environment after a heavy rain or snow melt.

Bathing at Sandy Beach
Mountain View, N. J.

4728

or along one of the many dirt paths south of the Pompton Plains Cross Road, are incredibly beautiful swamplands and meadows, ponds, inlets, springs and creeks lining this stretch of the Pompton River. Similar, if slightly less spectacular beauty is available downstream. From the heights of High Mountain, all of the wondrously beautiful valleys and other stunning topographical features of Wayne can be glimpsed from almost a birds-eye view. If nearby Greenwood Lake has been called the "Lake Geneva of America" and northern New Jersey the "Venice of America," Wayne may qualify as the "Garden of Eden of America," or at least one of them. Consider how even more beautiful the landscape had to have been before the deletion of caribou and wild turkeys, and all kinds of exotic birds, fish and animals. One can only imagine how peace-loving the Lenni-Lenape must have been not to have continuously been

Virtually no one swims anymore in the Pompton, nor in the Ramapo below the Hamburg Turnpike bridge, which also became popular after the steel works closed down.

on the warpath to stop the invasion of the land-gobbling colonists.

A major contributor to the beauty of Wayne is obviously the three rivers which border the Township (a fourth, the Pequannock, barely touches it).   Of those three, the Passaic, Ramapo and the Pompton, the latter has probably had the single greatest effect, good and bad. This river is both the beauty and the beast, a sort of aquatic Dr. Jekyll and Mr. Hyde. When it has been good it has been very, very good. But when it has been bad, it has been awful.

Aquatic activities proliferated below the Morris Canal Pompton River Aqueduct (above), on the main channel of the canal itself (r.) and even in the Pompton Feeder (below). During the 19th century, commerce limited this.

Canoeing on the Morris Canal, Mountain View, N. J.

The bad times periodically persist to this day. They occur whenever a major storm or spring thaw follows a particularly snow-filled winter. There have been major, and we mean major, floods along the Pompton for as long as records have been kept, and obviously well beyond that time. The relatively shallow waters of the river and not particularly defined banks, simply cannot contain even a few feet of abnormal elevation, and the entire countryside can fall victim to terrible flooding. A flood upriver in the Ramapo in 1903 was

so severe that it literally overwhelmed the Pompton Falls, and took with it numerous bridges, including the main one in which Hamburg Turnpike connects Wayne with Pompton Plains. Route 23 has from time to time looked like Lake 23. At times every house along Fayette Avenue could qualify as a boat house. Meads Basin, for most of the time the size of a small pond, spread out almost beyond view during several particularly bad floods early this century.

But regardless of how difficult the rivers (and the creeks as well) proved to the locals from time to time over the last half century (and before), the benefits in good times more than made up for the ugly side of Wayne's fickle waterways. During much of this century, and a good portion of the last, Wayne has been a recreational paradise. Few places anywhere could match the natural resources the Township had to offer sun worshippers, health enthusiasts, fun-loving athletes, and vacationers.

The rivers have always been here, at least for the last 12,000 or so years. So have the streams and some of the brooks and ponds. However,

The dress-up set also had numerous venues to dine and dance. Big time bands often had gigs at Mountain View and Singac along the Passaic.

the four large lakes (the 4 P's) have not. They were created as the social and business equivalent of the basic economic principle of supply and demand. Pompton Lake, which Wayne borders, if not man-

made, certainly has been man-altered. By damming the Ramapo River in the early 18th century, the lake was significantly enlarged. Packanack and Pines Lake, and Point View Reservoir were each formed by a sim-

ilar, although much more complex process. Basically, giant holes in the ground were dug and filled by diverting and damming the streams which flowed past the spots where these bodies of water now exist.

Pines Lake were built strictly to provide a recreational paradise for those sufficiently well-heeled to afford to live there. So was the much smaller Lionshead Lake, created in the early 1950's.

These recreational facilities were supplied based on the demand that began to build in the early 1870's with the coming of the railroads, particularly the Montclair. Prior to the iron horses, only the super-wealthy segment of the population took vacations. Few, if any, chose Wayne. Generally, the only non-residents who passed through here were those who were going somewhere else---businessmen shipping their products to market, prospectors, traders, trappers, former and potential mine and farm workers, and businessmen who rode the stages to and from the larger coastal cities. The railroads

FAYETTE ROAD, BUNGALOW COLONY. MOUNTAIN VIEW, N. J.

Fayette Avenue was the site of vacation cottages, inns and small hotels. The "Fayette Inn" (r.) today is a boarding house. Fifty years ago it was occupied more by vacationers than locals.

The first two were created in the 1920's, the latter in the early 1960's. Pompton Lake was damned and thus expanded to increase the amount of hydroelectric power that could be generated at the falls for the ironworks. The reservoir was built as a back-up source of water during a drought. However, Packanack and

changed all that.

The promoters of the Montclair Railway, later the New York and Greenwood Lake Railroad, linking Manhattan with the beautiful mountain lakes, sponsored excursions on a continuous basis. More and more city-folk began to experience the natural wonders the interior of New Jersey offered. But as much of an

Hoffman Grove is reached from Route 23 west along peaceful Meadow Road, while passing under the concrete underpasses below the old Erie and D.L. & W. tracks. It was once a place to best experience the out of doors.

Stations to spend the night. As more and more became familiar with what Wayne had to offer, it evolved one step further, not just a stop-over, but a vacation destination in itself. While Greenwood Lake remained popular enough for many years to support a wide assortment of vacation hotels which ringed the lake, the lower Wayne area was ideal for shorter stays, ranging from a few hours to a full weekend.

The Singac area on both sides of the Passaic was relatively quiet for most of the year, but when the warmer weather came, all that changed. Given that the Little Falls side of the river was served by the trolley, it was more built up. Running along the south bank of the river all the way from Paterson to Coney Road a half mile or so west of the Newark and Pompton Turnpike, this was considered among the most scenic of all trolley routes in the New York metropolitan area.

There was an assortment of Coney Island-style pleasure parks along the way. Laughlin's Pavilion and the Continental provided elegant dining, as well as dancing. On the Wayne side of the river, fronting what is now

improvement the steam locomotive was over wagon or horseback travel, it was not initially all comfort. Riding in open rail cars behind the noisy and soot-spitting locomotives was no piece of cake. Many preferred to break up the forty four mile trek between the Hudson and Greenwood Lake into two segments, with stopovers roughly halfway in between.

That halfway spot being roughly the southern end of Wayne, they could choose to depart the train at either the Singac, Carlton Park (U.S. 46) or Mountain View

River Lawn Drive (almost hidden in the shadow of Wayne Towne and Willowbrook shopping malls), one could rent a canoe or rowboat at one of the numerous boat houses, or rent a comfortable bungalow at a reasonable rate.

At Mountain View, there was even a greater choice of places to stay and things to do. Joseph Hixon's Mountain View Hotel (Gabriels) was the more formal place to stay. However, on both the Lincoln Park and Wayne sides of the Pompton River, there was an abun-

The Indians called what is now the hill which encompasses North Caldwell, "Meelonagkas" in the deed which the Schuyler-Brockholst syndicate was given. At the spot that township touches Wayne, just across the Passaic River, was the location of "Grandview Park," seen here in 1916. Trolleys ran along the south and east side of the river from Paterson to Coney Road in Singac (Little Falls), virtually to the front gate of this and a similar nearby amusement facility, "Singac Park." Wayne residents had many thrills crossing the river and enjoying the wild rides. The "grand view" was Wayne.

side of the river or at Maximan's on Fayette Avenue along the east bank.

While Meads Basin and the Morris Canal itself provided summer rowing, swimming and canoeing, along with winter ice-skating,

The constant threat of floods, too-often realized, contributed to the demise of the recreational use of the rivers. These two scenes represent how bad things could get. Above, on the Pompton Plains side of the Pompton in the 1960's, and to the right, the same road south of Mountain View in 1936 appear as if Route 23 was in fact a river.

dance of bungalows, cottages and small hotels offering adequate lodging. Many chose to buy or rent these small dwellings for extended stays, and would often store their canoes at the Haviser Boathouse on the west

Klein's Grove along Route 23, south of Mountain View, was a private paradise that took full advantage of one of the many small ponds that the Wayne landscape has been dotted with since the last Ice Age.

was the main choice on that stretch of river between the Lincoln Park Bridge and Two Bridges. On weekends and holidays in particular, what is now an area where few seem to ever visit, during the first half of this century there were days when it looked like the Coney Island or Jersey Shore beaches during a summer heat wave. During the day, there were swimmers and boats everywhere. At night, for those who chose to dress up and spend a few dollars, elegant dining and dancing was provided by an assortment of floating and beach-front entertainment palaces.

For those who chose to travel by motor car, Wayne could provide a variety of interesting places to stay, eat or be entertained. The 1939 WPA Guide to New Jersey includes a descriptive picture of the way that stretch of the Newark and Pompton Turnpike must have looked north of U.S. 46:

> "a flat district of roadhouses and hot-dog stands, some designed with considerable ingenuity--rusticized shack-palaces, rambling Colonial Virginia manses, red and white doll houses--architectural apexes of a hamburger civilization."

The Colonial Virginia manse reference probably was to Donohues (Grill or Restaurant, depending on the name Jimmy Donohue put on a variety of signs which identified the road stop). This was not only a forerun-ner to the sports bar craze of today, but one could buy a hot dog Jimmy himself grilled in one portion of the building, or dress up in formalwear and attend an elegant wedding with a multi-course dinner in another. Of particular note is the fact that Donohues was often a hangout for the great Babe Ruth and other sports celebrities of the day. The Three Vets was another place for a good meal, although in a far less fancy setting. The Alps Castle up the hill on Alps Road pro-

vided still another alternative.   Except for the time in 1926 when a police officer was murdered there, the French Hill Inn on French Hill Road was popular as well.

Along Black Oak Ridge Road was The Cottage and even something for the kids. For patrons of the roadside stand of the Fox Farm, near Sheffield Farms, there was no charge to pet a variety of farm animals, or even have the thrill of holding a real live

from agoutis and kinkajous to peacocks and wildcats. And, as discussed earlier, a visit to the Sheffield Farms

Donohue's, Newark-Pompton Turnpike, Mountain View, N. J.

Donohue's (l.) and The Three Vets (above), which stood close to each other on the west side of State Route 23, were two of the most prominent roadstops referred to in the 1939 WPA Guide to New Jersey. The Cottage (below, l.) on Black Oak Ridge Road and the Preakness Grill (below) across the street from the Schuyler-Colfax House were other popular eateries in town. The latter building is still a restaurant today.

THE COTTAGE,
BLACK OAK RIDGE ROAD, WAYNE, NEW JERSEY

black bear cub.   Across the street was Captain Mack's Wild Animal Farm, which while not also free, was fairly reasonable in that they only charged a dime to experience exotic animals that ranged

The distinctive Airport Inn on Hamburg Turnpike adjacent to Murchio's Airport was another landmark, thanks to the small plane that was displayed on the roof. The first impression of many travelers was that a pilot seemed to have a few too many at the popular eating and drinking place.

Milking Parlor was always an interesting experience.

On Hamburg Turnpike, there was of course the aforementioned Jackson House early in the century. The Preakness Grill and Swiss Tavern, now the French Quarter Restaurant across from the Schuyler-Colfax

All the romantic spots in Wayne were not so public. River Avenue was known as "Lovers' Lane," as shown on this early 20th century postcard.

House. Later on there was Old Heidleburg Inn and the Airport Inn, with a small plane sticking out of the roof. The latter was named based on its proximity to Murchio's Flying Field, a local landmark from 1919 when flying was in its infancy to 1956, the dawn of the jet age. Thomas Murchio loved cars and planes, and offered the public the chance to enjoy both at his auto museum at Greenwood Lake, or at his airport on the present site of T-Bowl Shopping Center. At Pompton Lakes after the steelworks, which replaced the ironworks, closed down, and the canal was abandoned, northenders were offered many of the same aquatic pleasures those in the south had. Swimming, canoeing and boating became popular in the Ramapo River driftway below Pompton Falls although those with a little more sense probably did not choose to immerse their bodies in this waterway. After all, it was just down river from the spot where for the last two centuries iron and steel works dumped an assortment of by-product into the Ramapo.

The well-to-do were offered an assortment of ultra-private recreational choices. The North Jersey Country Club relocated from its second location along the Passaic River at Warren Point in Paterson to the former Greenbrook Farms, just west of the Garret Hobart acreage (now William Paterson University). Built on the foothills of Preakness Mountain, the members built an elegant Tudor clubhouse and transformed the rocky grounds into one of the finest golf courses in America. In the winter a ski jump was built for the more venturesome skiers who had been enjoying the club slopes when the ground was covered with snow.

The 10th hole fairway at the North Jersey Country Club was converted in winter to a ski run and jump, where several international teams practiced for the Olympics in Lake Placid in 1932.

or chateau at the beautiful Pines Lake. A more beach-like setting was offered at Packanack Lake, whose club-house offered even non-residents someplace to come to. It was advertised as the Mountain Lake Resort Closest to the City. A third alternative was offered at mid-century at Lionshead Lake.

While Packanack Lake, Pines Lake, Lionshead Lake and the two country clubs continue to be more popular than ever, recreational enjoyment of the rivers has all but ended. The Singac and Fayette Avenue bunga-lows, boat houses and other commercial facilities have been converted to perma-nent residences. Few visitors ever venture here, and certainly no vacationers. The floating and beach front restaurants are long gone, as are most of the jetties and docks.

The public Passaic County Golf Course was built surrounding the Dey Mansion in Preakness Hills Park; a second country club the private Preakness Hills Country Club was built near the corner of Alps Road and Ratzer Roads.

For those who wanted to live in an area where boating, swimming, dancing and dining was available day and night, every day of the year (weather-permitting), they could buy their way into a European Mountain-style setting by purchasing or building a mountain cabin

The Wayne side of the Passaic at Singac today still holds evidence of its earlier days of high water activities, as numerous boat houses are now used as permanent residences.

No one single factor for the decline of Wayne's prominence as a vacation-recreational paradise can be blamed. However, there are many which are responsible, including, if not limited to, the decline of the railroad era (itself brought about by improvement of other means of transportation and the corresponding development of distant tourist meccas), a series of devastating floods, as well as upriver pollution caused by Dupont and other industrial companies. By mid-century, the post-

war era in Wayne was well underway, and things were changing almost by the day.

Fox Farm on Black Oak Ridge Road near Sheffield Dairy Farms was an early, and much more exotic example of the many petting zoos which can be found today. As shown here, there was much less regulation of wild animals. It is rumored that a member of the Space family, who operate the immensely popular Space Farms in Sussex County, was involved in Wayne's microcosm of that huge present day complex.

© THE FOX FARM, WAYNE, N. J., BEARS GOING FOR A RIDE

SEE ME AND MY LITTLE BROTHERS AT THE FOX FARM ------ WAYNE, N.J.

Neither the 1939 scene which the WPA called "architectural apexes of a hamburger civilization," nor the one C.W. Dittig remembered on the map he drew for this publication, had not changed dramatically as late as 1964 as this aerial (above) and close up (r.) of the same photo shows. The stretch of State Route 23 between the 23/46 interchange and Mountain View Center Wayne was for much of this century a conglomeration of eclectic roadside businesses with much character. With the construction of Interstate 80 in the mid -1960's and the widening of State Route 23 in the mid-1970's, the route reverted back to a desolate scene similar to how it probably looked two centuries ago. Thus what was for many a cherished piece of the past was obliterated by so-called "modern improvements."

Another 1964 aerial view of the 23/46 interchange, this one looking east, demonstrates New Jersey's 20th century highway construction philosophy using jug handles, circles and other twists and turns to handle the busier intersections. Things only got worse with the use of elevated on and off ramps when a third major highway, Interstate 80, came through shortly after this photo was shot . When Willowbrook shopping center was built five years later, traffic congestion increased dramatically. Major revisons are again on the drawing plan as the saga continues.

point where only eagles dared to dwell. For $25.00 the Grand Tour could be theirs, a ride from the air over all of Passaic and Bergen Counties. Since 1914 the brothers Murchio owned and operated an automotive repair shop in adjacent Pompton Lakes. But that enterprise eventually gave way to their new venture, well-timed during the period when Americans were having a ball roaring through the 20's.

In 1922 business was so good that Tom and Joe bought the land and built a fieldstone hanger and soon operated what would become a landmark in Wayne for the next four decades. Murchio's Airport was one of only three airports in New Jersey, and for years vied with the other two, Teterboro and Atlantic City, as the state's busiest. Throughout the 20's crowds as large as 3,000 to 4,000 lined up on either side of the runway and looked above as stunt flyers and parachutists performed unbelievable aerobatic tricks.

The shrewd businessmen began to make even more money in 1924 when a Standard J-1 biplane hangered at their facility was hooked up with an electric sign and flown at night over the larger New York and New Jersey cities. The sign advertised the motion picture *Iron Horse*.

town a few miles north of Wayne along the route of the Greenwood Lake branch of the Erie Railroad, leased a 70 acre section of the Van Orden farm on Hamburg Turnpike. They began flying World War I Curtiss Jennies from a makeshift runway. For $10 an earthling could have a ride and see Wayne from a vantage

The year that other mentioned hall of famer hit 60 home runs and Charles Lindbergh took a jaunt across the Atlantic with a Ryan airplane equipped with a

MURCHIO AIRPORT   JULY 1939

Tom sits in front row (circled) along with many of the famous flyers who often flew in and above the field.

Gary. Gary was the designer and builder of the Garyplane, nicknamed Gary's Hoople. It looked like an old biplane which had flown and become stuck in one of the rings of a giant wooden barrel. The contraption even had skis and bicycle tires attached. Yet it was not this loony bird that led to a terrible accident that ended Gary's flying days, but a flight in a far more conventional craft. To get the "feel of the air" before taking off in another of his experimental crafts, one only slightly less innovative than the Garyplane, the pilot took off in an old JN-4 Jenny from Murchio's one day in 1922.

Wright-whirlwind engine built in nearby Paterson, the Murchio's expanded. They constructed two wooden hangers and designed and built four airplanes that would be used for short sightseeing flights. They also became dealers for Air King biplanes.

In 1937 a plane left Murchio's to accompany a huge German hydrogen-filled zeppelin which was due to land at Lakehurst in mid-New Jersey after a cross-Atlantic voyage. The tales of the demise of the Hindenburg that pilot must have told had to have fascinated his fellow flyers at Murchios for decades afterwards.

Murchio's offered blimp rides, parachute jumps and air tours for years. It certainly helped put Wayne on the map. In addition, famous pilots from around the world visited. It was the scene of numerous experimental flights and must have caused more than a few scares among the conservative parishioners of neighboring Preakness Reformed Church during Sunday church services. More than a few of the planes fell from the sky, including one piloted by one William

While flying above Wayne the plane was apparently caught in a down-draft and it plummeted to the earth crashing in Barbour Pond.

Tom Murchio died in 1950. Following the Second World War airplanes were no longer thought of as a novelty, and Murchio was able to profit by money would-be pilots were given under the G.I. bill to take flying lessons at Murchio Airport. The enterprise continued operation for the next six years after its founder passed away. In 1956 it was sold to a developer by the name of Gerrard Berman for the then high price of $2,000 an acre. Four years later Wayne's second and far-less known airport also discontinued operations, Totowa-Wayne Airport along Riverview Drive straddling the borderline of the two communities. Reportedly, a large iron plate had to be constructed and laid over Singac Brook to permit safe landings.

Alleys have long since replaced runways on the site of the former Murchio's Flying Field,which is now the location of the T-Bowl Shopping Center.

looked somewhat like a fish with its head cut off. The patent's name was adopted for the new community.

By 1928 construction was underway on a clubhouse and several homes. Later a sewer plant was built and water mains laid. The lake was stocked with fish and

the real estate company provided beaches, a picnic ground, tennis courts, a ballfield and riding trails. In just four days over $450,000.00 of land was sold by a horde of salesmen to prospective home buyers.

The Packanack Lake Country Club and Community

This photograph was taken from a plane flying out of Murchio's Airport in 1935. It shows the unusual shape of the lake.

WHERE YOU GET JOY OUT OF LIFE

When these brochures were published during the development of the lake and community in the late 1920's, the promoters obviously were quick to take advantage of Wayne's unusual topography. The lake was considered the largest mountain lake within 50 miles of Manhattan.

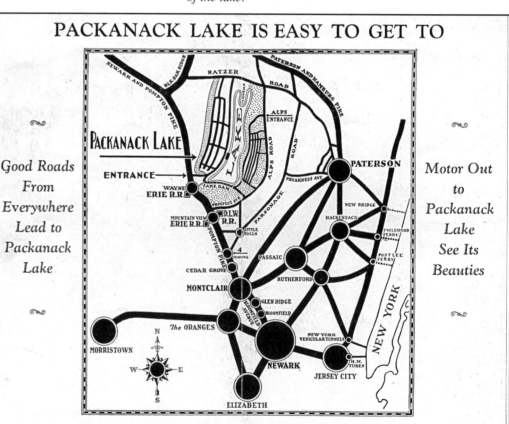

PACKANACK LAKE IS EASY TO GET TO

Good Roads From Everywhere Lead to Packanack Lake

Motor Out to Packanack Lake See Its Beauties

THE LAKE MIDST THE BIG CITIES

Our Main Gateway on Pompton Pike is very impressive and attracts a lot of attention from passersby. October, 1929.

When this wooden gate was built, Packanack Lake Road could only be reached via the Old Route 23, former route of the turnpike. Unfortunately, it is long gone.

Association, was formally dissolved, and full operation was assumed by the Club. Over the last forty years many improvements were added, including a golf course, all-weather tennis courts, a yacht club, children's park and numerous other embellishments.

Today, Packanack Lake is rimmed with modern streets filled with single family homes, and obviously not nearly as isolated as it was seven decades ago. However, it remains more popular than ever. Every morning and every evening during the warmer months, runners, joggers, walkers and bicycle riders exercise and enjoy themselves around the scenic perimeter of one of Wayne's real jewels.

Association was formed and a set of by-laws enacted. By the mid-30's a post office was added, bus service was provided and even a Civic Club and a dramatic club were formed. The community even published its own newspapers, the *Pack and Nac Monthly News,* which was renamed the *Packanack Life* in 1937. In 1942 the Civic Club published the popular Pack-A-News, which had a long run.

In 1944 40% of the homeowners formed their own corporation, Packanack Homes, Inc. and purchased stock at $100.00 a share. Before the 40's ended, Packanack Lake had its own Community Church, the Packanack School and paved roads.

The theme for Packanack Lake was that it was "Nestling in the Mountains, Yet Close to Big Cities." In 1956 Packanack Homes, Inc., which had turned over virtually all of the community's common land to the

The clubhouse and restaurant also featured an inn, which was advertised in local papers as one of the most beautiful places in the entire metropolitan area to stay. Barely 20 miles from Manhattan, it had many takers.

long advertised as "The largest and deepest lake within 20 miles of New York City." After the dam was completed construction began on the homes which were planned to line the shore. However, due to the depression and World War II, by 1944 only 150 residences had been built. Because of the shortage of construction materials during the war, many of them used logs obtained from a local saw mill.

Today more than 700 beautiful homes are eligible to join the private Pines Lake Association.

The first car crosses roadway built atop the dam in 1927. It empties into the "Glen" area to the south. Today this concrete bridge is still used, but large cars can have a real problem.

From the bridge the lake presents a gorgeous panorama today.

How many wish they had taken advantage of the bargain advertised in this 1944 promotional ad?

Historical Highlight
Donohues: The Hangout of The Sultan of Swat

Donohue's was arguably the most famous landmark in all of Wayne during the second quarter of this century. There was little interest in historical sites, and Americans were taking to the road. Situated on the southbound side of Route 23 about halfway between Routes 202 and 46 (then State Route 6), it was famous for miles around.

It may seem unusual to feature a long-gone business as one of the historical highlights of a town of almost too many to count. But Donohue's Restaurant (aka Grill) was by all accounts something really special. Arguably, during the 1930's and 1940's it may have been equally, if not more well-known than Wayne itself was. Often Wayne was identified as "the town where Donohue's is."

Located on the southbound (west) side of State Route 23, near the site of the present-day Oriental restaurant, the establishment was owned and operated by Jimmy Donohue. He was the commensurate host, not too full

of himself to cook up and personally serve hamburgers and hot dogs in the front section of the building which looked like a Colonial Virginia mansion. The huge inside rooms often were the scene of the best and fanciest dining in the region, as well as thousands of weddings, banquets and other important events. Whether it was indeed the "best restaurant in New Jersey" as its advertising claimed is subjective, but many certainly thought it was.

Donohue's may have been one of the first sports bars in the United States. Photos on the wall of Jimmy's office gave testimony to the fact that the establishment

was a favorite hangout of the most famous athlete in American history, none other than Babe Ruth. Ruth was a close friend of Donohue's and frequently visited the place, not only in his heyday when he was blasting homers out of every major league ballpark, but almost until his dying day in 1948.

Donohue's closed down soon after Jimmy passed on. According to Dr. Robert Brubaker, Chairman of the Wayne Historical Commission, his widow had the place set up as if it was about to host a gigantic banquet. Each table was set with the finest china and silverware--- and the doors were locked. It reputedly stood that way for several years, as what would happen to the Township's most famous eatery and catering hall was mired in the courts. It is not believed it ever opened again. When State Route 23 was widened in the mid-1970's all vestiges of the site were forever lost.

The magnificent Babe certainly knew about Wayne and Donohue's. Here (above) he stops for a snapshot outside Jimmy's eatery as the proprietor (center) and a friend also say "cheese."

Jimmy's office was a virtual museum dedicated to his hero, and other famous sports stars who frequented the "best restaurant in New Jersey."

Thousands of Wayne and other area residents celebrated weddings, anniversaries, graduations and a myriad of other celebratory events at the venerable manse-like Donohue's restaurant, seen here in the early 1950's. This section of State Route 23 was not the virtually uninhabited area it is today, as the old highway was lined with an eclectic array of roadside stops, farms stands, eateries, many of which were housed in unusual and interesting structures.

End of an era. *Arguably, the Wayne landmark best known to out of towners during most of the middle of this century finally succumbed when the building was ravished by fire in 1972 as this newspaper clip (above) and a photo taken from the paper show. But for all intents and purpose the end had already come when Mr. Donohue passed away and the famous restaurant closed its doors several years earlier.*

Donohue's postcards like the one above are valued collector's items.

This site (below) may have been the most famous along the entire 55+ mile State Route 23 for decades.

Historical Highlight
Fire Company #2:
Above and Beyond........

Heroic firefighter Glenn E. McCoog gave his life for the citizens of Wayne when he perished during rescue operations on the Pompton River during the 1983 flood. The present firehouse on the on/off ramp to Alps Road is dedicated to his memory. His helmet, recovered several days after he disappeared below the water in the Pompton River is kept in the company offices at all times, to remind everyone that Glenn is still there in spirit.

Five minutes before midnight on a cold February morning in 1924 a call went out to the volunteers of the barely two year old Fire Company #2 in Mountain View that a fire erupted in a bungalow near Wilkee's Race Track on the Passaic River. The present site of the Wayne Towne and Willowbrook malls was then primarily marshy swampland. Peter Van Ammers, 22, a dairyman, and Valentine Reder, 20, an employee of Tiffany & Company on 5th Avenue in Manhattan quickly responded in their Dey-Elder combination chemical and hose pumper. Making a sharp turn opposite Kayhart's Hotel on Fairfield and Two Bridges Road, their machine skidded and overturned, pinning the two young men under it. When help arrived, Reder was already dead; his partner died on the way to Paterson General Hospital.

The tragic event occurred less than two years after the formation of the *Property Owner's League Fire*

Company #2. The League was a social club comprised of residents of Mountain View and Lincoln Park, the latter then a part of Peq-uan-nock Township. Along with Fire Company #1, operated by another Mountain View social organization, the *Bungalow Club*, these two volunteer fire departments provided the only fire protection for Wayne residents for a number of years. Along with the pumper, a Model T Ford fire truck and some hand equipment, Fire Company #2 was responsible to not only fight fires but conduct rescue operations during the numerous floods that have long plagued the southwestern

---

WEDNESDAY, FEBRUARY 6, 1924

Two Firemen Killed on Way to Blaze at Mountain View

Combination Chemical and Hose Machine of Property Owners League Truck Company Overturns as They Round Curve Opposite Kayhart's Hotel.

portion of the Township. Their territory included Mountain View's renowned vacation paradise along the Passaic and Pompton Rivers, stretching from Singac to Black Oak Ridge Road. Ironically it included the building where Company #1 was headquartered, along what is now Parish Drive, just north of the old Mountain View D.L.& W. railroad station.

The equipment was originally housed in Marshall's Garage, a huge frame building located at the corner of Boonton Turnpike and Fayette Avenue. The entrance to the facility was two large double-swinging wooden doors, secured with a padlock. Each member of the company had his own key. In 1926 the social club was disbanded and deeded the equipment, including the old Model T and all funds remaining, to the treasury of the fire company.

Ten years later, the company built its own facility located at 122 Fayette Avenue, which remained its headquarters for the next twenty two years until 1958. Today a modern facility stands alongside the onramp to Alps Road, just east of SR 23. It is one of five such independent companies which serve Wayne. Senior Fire Inspector/Investigator Gregory J. Velardi, whose family have been Wayne residents since the 1920's, serves as the corporation's President.

The Department poses on Fayette Avenue near what would be their new headquarters 12 years later in this 1924 photo.

In the first 150 years of Wayne Township, three brave souls gave their life for their fellow-residents. On the brink of Company #2's 60th anniversary, a third hero joined Van Ammers and Reder in making the ultimate community sacrifice. Twenty five year old Glenn E. McCoog was knocked off his boat by a small bridge almost hidden by the murky fog as he and several other members of the company searched for those in distress along the Pompton River. His body was not recovered for 72 days.

As the next millennium approaches along with the 21st century, Wayne, with more than its share of corporate giants and huge shopping complexes, still remains a people town, protected by its five volunteer fire companies, like those of the heroic Company #2.

Today the fire company has a beautiful modern facility.

The 1984 flood inundated Mountain View, seen here from a photograph taken aboard a helicopter looking east towards Gabriel's Restaurant and the State Route 23 in Mountain View.

The former Wayne Center looked more like "Wayne Lake" (above).

No, this was not another water falls in Wayne, but actually State Route 23 spilling over.

If one could go back 15,000 or so years, and construct the buildings and roads that were in Mountain View in 1984, this is much like it would have looked, as ancient Lake Passaic covered this land.

This was not a pleasure row on the river, but what happened when the Fayette Avenue area once again became a river.

Three of Wayne's bravest have perished while trying to save Township's residents and property. Handsome, twenty two year old Peter Van Ammers, a graduate of the Mountain View School was one of the first two who gave theirs lives for their neighbors.

Anyone could obtain a free car wash by simply trying to drive along State Route 23 near the old Wayne Center in Mountain View.

Chapter Fourteen
Development of a Suburb

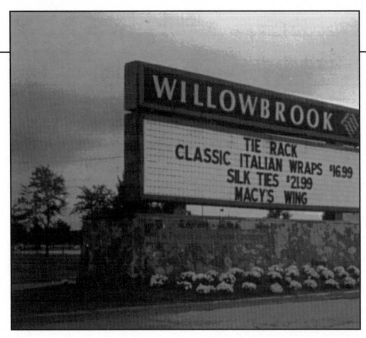 

The twin megamalls, Willowbrook and Wayne Towne Center, once again made Wayne the destination point it had not been since the decline of the summer and weekend vacation trade.

The transition of Wayne from a rural to a suburban setting occurred gradually during the course of the 20th century, although the most dramatic changes came shortly after the Second World War. In 1952, a decision by the New Jersey Supreme Court played a huge part in preventing Wayne from deteriorating into an overcrowded community of low-cost apartment buildings and shoddy residences. In a most controversial ruling the Court overturned a ruling first made by the New Jersey Superior Court throwing out a Township zoning ordinance fixing the minimum size of dwellings and placing certain properties in a residential district. Lionshead Lake, Inc. was the owner and developer of a large tract of land that it was developing around the expanded lake. It had argued that the ordinance enacted by the Township made it economically infeasible to build only fairly large houses in an area where it was expected many potential homeowners were looking only to purchase a second or vacation home.

The high Court disagreed and supported the ordinance, perhaps saving Wayne from ever having many of the same problems that affected other communities. The opinion rendered by Chief Justice Vanderbilt included an interesting description of the Township and comparison to Newark:

"The Township of Wayne is the most extensive municipality in Passaic County. It covers 25.34 square miles in comparison with 23.57 square miles of Newark. It has a population of 11,815 in comparison with Newark's 437,857. Only 12% of the total area of the township has been built up. Included within its borders are several sizable lakes (only one located within the plaintiff's development, e.g. having an area of about 145 acres) and as a result a considerable number of residences have been built for summer occupancy only. Although a political entity it is in fact a composite of about a dozen widely scattered residential communities, varying from developments like the plaintiff's where the average home costs less than $10,000, to more expensive sections where the homes cost from $35,000 to $75,000. It has little business or industry."

Since the population of Wayne forty five years later has almost quintupled, certainly much more than 12% of the land has been developed and most residents live here year-round, obviously there have been numerous changes in the interim.   What exactly caused that change is another example of a wide assortment of factors. Many are the same as those which caused the demise of the Township's position as a major recreational paradise and vacation spot. Others could have been the gradual sophistication of the population. Several famous residents played at least a marginal role in that sophistication. The first was Albert Payson Terhune.

A descendant of an old local Dutch family, Albert lived at a large house, Sunnybank, on the east bank of the Pompton River along Route 202, now Terhune Drive, a mile or so north of Hamburg Turnpike. He was a nationally-recognized author whose books about collie dogs made him famous and rich. Across the road from the Terhune place was that of the DeMille family. Movie mogul Cecil B. DeMille, who produced The Ten Commandments and other biblical classics, may just have been the most famous former permanent resident of Wayne ever.

The third prominent Wayne resident was LeGrand Parish. He was the inventor of a railroad air brake coupling device that contributed to him accumulating a large fortune. He purchased and greatly expanded the old Mead homestead at 231 Parish Drive (named after guess who?) into a grand white manor house which included 28 rooms, many embellished with imported marble.

The physical look of Wayne began to change with the emergence of first the railroad, and then the automobile. The reconfiguration of State Route 23 created a major north-south highway between the Newark and Pompton Turnpike and Alps Road. The significant widening and improvement of it during the 1970's into what is now almost a superhighway helped transform Mountain View into a secondary, often by-passed part of the community.

A second small airport was built on the Totowa-Wayne border, appropriately named Totowa-Wayne Airport, along Naatchpunkt (formerly Swamp) Road, now named the much easier to pronounce Riverview Drive.

The two things that define a suburb are residential developments and shopping malls. Wayne was the site of many of both during the last half of the 20th century.   A typical example of this growth was cited in a Paterson newspaper in 1954. It reported that plans were underway to build 86 homes on Valley Road, 231 in Sheffield Hills, 146 in Packanack Lake, 120 near the intersection of Alps Road and Osborne Terrace, 16 near Ratzer Road and Route 23, 36 at Sunnyridge in Pines Lake, 142 at the site of Murchio's Airport near Church Lane and Hamburg Turnpike, 35 at Lionshead Lake and 6 in the Perrin development just off Hamburg Turnpike.

Where there are homes, there must be shopping, and visa versa.   Thus it was only natural that numerous strip shopping centers and larger malls were constructed.   The Preakness Shopping Center and Berdan Shopping Center were built near the same time on Hamburg Turnpike. On State Route 23 Packanack Lake Shopping Center appeared, as did Valley Ridge Shopping Center on the former site of the Preakness Horseracing Track. For two centuries the Edo Merselis homestead dominated the corner of the Hamburg Turnpike and Berdan Avenue (and the paths which preceded both). After the local fire department allegedly burned it down for practice, the location became the site of the Wayne Hills Mall.

These shopping centers paled in comparison to the one which really put Wayne on the proverbial shop-til-you-drop destination. The Willowbrook Mall, including major stores such as Sterns, Bambergers (now Macys) and Sears, was proclaimed as "the largest indoor mall in the world," and today is reported to still be the second largest in the entire state. Adjacent to it is the Wayne Towne Center with giants like Fortunoffs among its anchor tenants.   The peninsula where these two neighboring malls are now located was once the site of the John Stagg farm, portions of it were later used as the Singac Driving Park. Here one could stop and rent a horse and buggy just for a leisurely drive

around the area. The Van Ammers' farm was located on Route 6, once called Two Bridges Road, and today

The Edo Merselis house stood on the corner of Berdan Avenue and Hamburg Turnpike for over two centuries after it was built in about 1759. Some contend it was burned down "for practice" by the local fire department.

known as U.S. 46. (The original route veered north at present-day Riverview Drive, and followed what is now Minnisink Road. Later the portion of U.S. 46 between this spot and Clifton was built).

Part of the significant growth in population had to do with what was done to the legendary farms along Valley Road. In 1997 the last truck farm disappeared, that of the Cialone Farm. Known for years as the "Red Barn Farm," the old barn which it was named for was reportedly purchased from a Sears catalog early in the century. Only Van Peenen Dairy Farm remains from the scores of large and small farms that once gave this stretch of Passaic County the look of America's heartland.

Wayne's school system grew at an even greater rate than its population, although it lost several of its most characteristic early school houses. The 1812 Mountainview School, later the municipal building, wound up as the American Legion Hall. The Preakness School has been transformed into a branch library, next door to the

old School #2, still standing on Hamburg Turnpike across from Church Lane. In 1953 the first class graduated from Wayne High School. Before the high school was built students had to travel to either Pompton Lakes, Montclair or Paterson Central High Schools. Between 1951 and 1967 fourteen other schools were built in the Township.

Plans have been underway for decades to build the West End Extension, connecting State Route 23 just north of where it follows a spaghetti-like maze of roads at U.S. 46 and IS 80, with Valley Road. If and when it is completed, the new Wayne municipal complex built after mid-century at Nellis Drive and Valley Road, would be only minutes away from what some called Downtown Wayne, the huge shopping malls on the banks of the Passaic.

There were of course numerous new church congregations that now give the community a far more diverse religious character than it had for so many years when the Preakness Reformed Church was virtually the only house of prayer in the entire Township. Likewise, branches of the police and fire department gave the community a far more civic appearance.

In 1955, another landmark event occurred that marked another major change in Wayne. That year a 99 acre site became the home of the United States Rubber Company's research center. Soon it was joined by scores of major industrial giants, the first being American Cyanamid, whose international headquarters were built north of the Hamburg Turnpike near Lionshead Lake. Today, with the second expansion of Valley Road, this time north of the turnpike, it can no longer be said that Wayne "has little business or industry" as Justice Vanderbilt stated in his 1952 opinion. In fact, the Wayne business community is a story in itself.

The Terhune Girls School (l.) was operated by the mother of Cecil B. DeMille as an acting school. The Gate House of the DeMille estate (above) remains across the road from the Sunnybank Park.

Top of the World

Led by adult manager Gene Cancellieri, only 21 himself, Wayne kids made national headlines in 1970 when they won the Little League Series Championship at Williamsport, Pennsylvania. Obviously the local rags were also quite impressed.

1966 aerial photo taken above intersection of U.S. 46 and Riverview Drive. Note the Totowa Drive-in, and the single runway Totowa-Wayne Airport, just south and west of where Valley Road begins.

Worldwide Headquarters in Wayne, New Jersey

A Manufacturing Leader Since 1956

World headquarters in Wayne, New Jersey.

Union Camp Corporation is a leading manufacturer of paper, packaging, chemicals and wood products. With over $4 billion in sales, it ranks among the nation's 200 largest industrial companies.

The company was formed in 1956 with the merger of Union Bag and Paper Corporation and the Camp Manufacturing Company. Union Bag and Paper Corporation grew out of the Union Paper Bag Machine Company, which was formed in 1861 by Francis Wolle. A teacher and minister, Wolle invented the first paper bag machine in 1852.

The Camp Manufacturing Company dates back to 1887 with the purchase of a lumber manufacturing operation that began production in Franklin, Virginia, in the 1850's. Camp entered paper manufacturing in 1938.

The two merged companies operated under the name of Union Bag-Camp Paper Corporation until 1966 when the company changed its name to Union Camp Corporation.

At that time, Union Camp was headquartered in the Woolworth Building in New York City. In 1969, the company moved its headquarters to the Valley Road extension in Wayne.

Union Camp has over 60 converting facilities worldwide, including six manufacturing plants in New Jersey — Clifton, Moonachie, Englewood/Teaneck, Norwood, Montvale, and West Deptford. The company also has more than 50 sales and office facilities worldwide, including three in New Jersey — Wayne, Montvale and Morristown. With over 19,000 employees, Union Camp has approximately 1,500 in the state and 450 in Wayne.

The company's four paper mills and 1.6 million acres of woodlands are located in the southeast.

Union Camp makes fine paper at this mill in Eastover, South Carolina.

Historical Highlight
Willowbrook and the Van Ammers, Centuries Apart

The Van Ammers farm (above) stood on the land that now encompasses the regional shopping malls on U.S. 46.

Not in his wildest dreams would Johannes (John) Van Ammers have imagined that the farm he built in 1918 in the marshy peninsula formed by the Passaic River in the southernmost portion of Wayne Township would someday play host to thousands of visitors--each day. Like many Township farmers, the Van Ammers were from Holland. Unlike many, they came not in the 17th, 18th or 19th centuries, but in the 20th. And, unfortunately, their brief stint as owners of what was to become a half century later perhaps the most valuable parcel of land in the entire Township was marred in tragedy and grief. Six years after they moved into their dream farm, blond, handsome Peter, one of their two sons, was killed when the fire truck he was riding

While generally thought of as a dairy farm, it actually was multi-dimensional. John loaded his crops on an old wagon and, by way of Minisink Road, drove to Paterson where he sold them. Neither U.S. 46, nor its predecessor, State Route 6 had been built.

on overturned on a bend at Two Bridges and Fairfield Roads. Four years later the family suffered another loss when the farm was foreclosed upon.

The peninsula formed by the river, and originally split by the Singac Creek, was for years owned by the Stagg family. Over the years, it was the site of at least two horse tracks, a drive-in theater and of course the Van Ammers and a few smaller farms. The Van Ammers had at least twelve cows, thus their homestead qualified as a dairy farm, however they also raised other farm animals for food and early photos show rows and rows of ground crops as well.

In 1969 the successors to the Van Ammers cashed in and sold the land to the developers of what was to be billed as "the world's largest indoor shopping mall," Willowbrook, the name taken from the old horse track.

The old farmhouse stood for decades along the road.

This 1860 portion of a map of Wayne Township, believed to be the first official one of its kind, shows the land that is now covered by Willowbrook, Wayne Towne and a few smaller shopping malls, was once owned by Thomas Stagg. The once significant Singac Creek was diverted and now empties into the Passaic north of U.S. 46. Note that Two Bridges Road, the predecessor to both State Route 6 and U.S. 46 connected with Minisink Road just east of the Township's border. This was the route local farmers took to sell their crops in bustling Paterson.

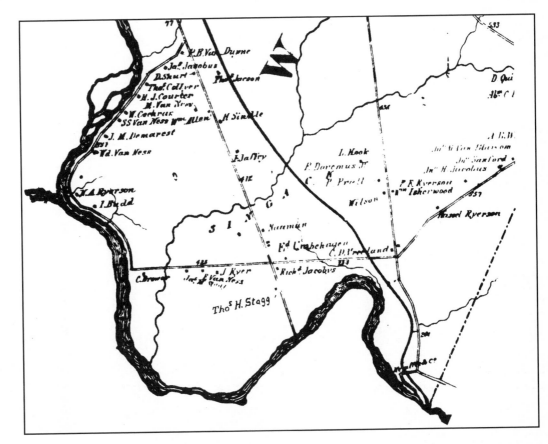

The Van Ammers, about 1918. From left, Johannes (John), Rema, Andrew, Johanna, Peter, Nelson and Marie. Rema later worked as a maid for LeGrand Parish. Peter was one of three firemen to give their lives serving the Township.

The family lived for a while at the present day site of Fenn's trailer park, the old Slanker farm. This photo is believed by the family to have been taken about 1912.

John shown here tilling the soil with two helpers, possibly Nelson and Peter.

In 1923 the family owned three Chandler milk trucks (l.). Peter, who was to die less than a year later, is seen on the running board of the first one in line.

Nelson (below) with two friends accompanying him holds fish caught in Passaic River. A half mile or so downstream, the waterway was long polluted by the Beattie Carpet mills.

Nelson was also married to a Marie. Here (above) he feigns writing her a ticket during one of the many jobs he held, a traffic officer. (Or was he just kidding? The old Dutch were believed to be real sticklers for the rules).

Years later in April, 1984, shown here a day after the river crested, the other side of the beautiful Passaic River reared its ugly head near where the farm once stood.

This photograph was taken from high above the intersection of Route 23 and U.S. 46 in 1966, before IS 80 or the Willowbrook-Wayne Towne Center malls were built.

&SONS

Approved Auto Repair

AUTO SERVICE, INC.

Greg & BonnieMaura Dwyer

11 Mountain View Blvd • Wayne, NJ 07470-6700

- *Brake Repair*
- *Maremont Exhaust Systems*
- *Steering & Suspensions*
- *Wheel Alignment*
- *A/C Service & Cooling*
- *Lube, Oil & Filter*
- *Monroe Shocks & Struts*
- *Sun Electronic Computer Analysis*
- *Tires & Computerized Wheel Balancing*

- *Clutches*
- *Engine Overhauls*
- *Tune-Ups*
- *Starters*
- *Interstate Batteries*
- *Alternators*
- *Radiators*
- *Heater Cores*
- *Towing*

Complete Domestic & Foreign Repair Center
Cars, Light Trucks & Vans
ASE Master Certified Technicians on Staff

**Telephone: 973-696-2548
Fax: 973-696-0134
Emergency Pager: 973-225-9309
24-Hour Towing: 973-694-1437**

Family Owned • Established 1978

International
PLANNING ALLIANCE, LLC
A Financial Services Organization

FINANCIAL, BUSINESS, AND ESTATE STRATEGIES FOR INSURANCE AND *INVESTMENT SERVICES

◆

"The Best Solution for Your Financial and Insurance Needs"

◆

Until recently, selecting the right insurance and financial portfolio meant doing a lot of legwork and getting a grab bag of results. But now, a unique new firm has been created to offer you a range of financial products and services that is truly global in scope – the International Planning Alliance, LLC (IPA).

From estate and business planning to personal financial services, IPA offers the finest service from some of the industry's most experienced professionals. Their staff of over 150 employees is dedicated to providing their clients with the most advanced and up-to-date planning techniques, while focusing on the highest level of personal service.

If you are in need of personal, estate, or business planning, IPA is the right place to start. If you've already set up your plans, it makes sense to get a second opinion from a firm that specializes in planning for your future. Give them a call!

David R. Alter, CLU	**Anthony J. Pascazio**
President and CEO	Vice Chairman
973-812-6924	732-469-0404
Gerald J. Clericuzio, CLU, ChFC	**Robert C. Kievit, CLU, LUTCF**
Chairman	Vice President – Agency Development
800-355-1919	973-812-6924
Howard Udoff, RHU	**Mitchell C. Beinhaker, JD, CLU**
Executive Vice President	Director of Advanced Markets
973-812-6353	973-812-6927

Historical Highlight
The Legend of Sunnybank

Albert Payson Terhune

of the Norton House. Mary was an established writer, who at only 16 years of age had written a novel *Alone*, that was widely acclaimed. She would be so prolific that during her life she penned a total of 25 books. It was obviously a talent that ran in the family. Despite her abilities, she would not wind up the best known writer in the family.

Albert Payson Terhune was only 21 when he traveled on horseback throughout the mountain and desert regions of Syria and Egypt, living among the nomadic Bedouins. When he returned he attended and eventually graduated from Columbia University and soon had himself a job as a staff writer for the New York Evening World. With a good education behind him, he took a real blue blood for a bride. Anice Stockton was a direct descendant of Richard Stockton, a New Jersey signer of the Declaration of Independence. (Stockton's huge home, Morven, for years was used as the official residence of the state's governor). She had more than just good lineage going for her. She was an accomplished linguist, pianist and composer. (Many of her over 100 songs were national hits).

Surrounded with all this talent, ability and the beautiful north Wayne setting, Albert reached the highest level of all. He began to write about one of his greatest passions---dogs--collie dogs. He was the James Herrot of his day. His *Lad, A Dog* and other books about his collies including Bruce and Sunnybank Bobby were best sellers. The former was made into a major motion picture.

There may have been something in the water there in that northern appendage of the Township. One of

While it was not always sunny from a climate point of view, the east bank of the Pompton River, formed in the 18th century when the Ramapo River was dammed for the ironworks, was a very bright light in Wayne for many years. For here lived Albert Payson Terhune, internationally-known author.

The year Abraham Lincoln was first elected President of the United States saw the Reverend Edward Payson Terhune bring his family to Wayne. In 1860 he and wife Mary Virginia Hawes Terhune built a summer house about a mile northeast

Terhune's childhood neighbors was Cecil B. DeMille, whose fame once he left Wayne for Hollywood exceeded even that of Albert. Among his megahit motion pictures was *The Ten Commandments*.

Unlike DeMille, Terhune never left Wayne. He passed on in 1942. Twenty two years later his Victorian Manor, Sunnybank, was simply too deteriorated to be saved and was razed. On the site, where many of Albert's collies are buried, is a beautiful Township park.

Terhune not only wrote about his cherished collies, he also raised them at Sunnybank. Here are a few of his favorites on the grounds.

In 1964 Sunnybank (l.) was so deteriorated it could not be saved. It was soon demolished.

This old photograph was saved from the home when it was demolished. It shows the property in 1925.

Historical Highlight
Witches, Ghosts and Goblins

The Demarest House of Fairfield Road has stood since 1760, making it the third oldest known still-standing house in Wayne. That is except when it was taken apart, board-by-board and reconstructed in 1850---to let the ghosts out. The 1936 photo (l.) shows the house in pretty much its original condition. The background photograph was taken in 1997. Is the white object to the right of the front door a Halloween decoration, or one of the purged ghosts trying to return?

The Legend of the Witch who Lived in Preakness

This is a story passed on from generation to generation as the families of the old settlers sat before their Dutch ovens, particularly on cold winter days when the fields where Indians and later Revolutionary soldiers once roamed were covered with snow. The witch reputedly lived in a gap between High Mountain and the Ramapos and would not allow any to drive cattle or sheep past her roadside shack unless she stood in the doorway to greet the drover. If her wishes were ignored, the legend goes on to say that the drover's herd would be spooked and his task would not be an easy one.

Many ills of the farmer were often blamed on the witch. For example, if a problem was encountered in attempting to churn butter, it meant that the witch had cast a spell over the churner. There was a solution, however. The spell could be broken and good butter made by heating a horseshoe until it was red hot and then quickly dipping it into the milk or cream. If a horseshoe was not conveniently available, an alternative was to grab a whip in one's left hand and swing it around the churn several times to scare away the trouble-making spirits.
****

The Legend of Sleepy (Pancake?) Hollow

Cockloft Hall on the Passaic River was located near the old Arent Schuyler home and copper mine, between Newark and Belleville. It was a popular gathering place for literary enthusiasts to enjoy each other's company, eat, drink and be merry. Here Washington Irving, William Irving and James Pauling are reported to have anonymously written the *Salmugundi Papers* of Washington Irving's travels to The Great Falls of the Passaic. His most famous character was Ichabod Crane who encountered the headless horseman in the author's *Legend of Sleepy Hollow*. Drawings of this supposedly fictional character look remarkably similar to the earliest known photograph of a member of Montclair's founding Crane family, namely the super-businessman, gaunt-appearing Israel "King" Crane. There is a long held rumor in Montclair that its first schoolmaster, Isaac Watts Crane, obviously a relative of Israel, was the inspiration of Ichabod. Washington Irving is said to have visited Cranetown in researching his book on his namesake, George Washington.

Ichabod Crane visited the countryside of Tappan Zee and borrowed a horse from a farmer, a choleric old Dutchman by the name of Hans Van Riper. He is said to have visited the kin of his benefactor residing on the farm near the old road from The Ponds to the Great Falls. Washington Irving Hopper was born on this farm in 1884. Awful coincidental isn't it?

****

The Legend of the Ghosts of the Demarest House

The Demarest House stands today along Fairfield Road as one of the true landmarks of Wayne. The Demarest family was among the earliest Hollanders to make their mark on northern New Jersey, and particularly Wayne. Only a few years ago the Township lost Gertrude Demarest Luks, who grew up in that historic abode. 150 years ago her ancestors dealt with alleged evil spirits in a much more complicated manner than did the butter churners of the Preakness Valley. They believed that the house was haunted, evidenced by colorful lights that could be seen in the windows of the top floor, but only from a distance. Maybe they tried to ward them off with a whip or heated horseshoe. Whatever methods they tried apparently did not satisfy them, so they went to really great lengths. The entire ninety year old house was carefully dismantled in 1850 in a most organized manner, literally board by board. It was then reassembled with few changes. The reason for this seemingly exercise in futility, was to rid the home of the ghosts.

Mrs. Luks theorized that the lights were probably reflections on the second floor glass windows of the sunlight which refracted off the Pompton River just across Fairfield Road. While at first this appears an intelligent, reasonable explanation, there does not seem to be any record of these bent rays reappearing when the house was rebuilt. Could it be that the orchestrated demolition and reconstruction worked? And if so, have the freed ghosts found a new home in another Wayne residence? Is it yours?

****

Historical Highlight
General William Colfax

Probably the greatest Revolutionary War hero ever to have lived in Wayne (although he never called it by that name).

One of Wayne's most distinguished citizens may have changed the entire course of American history. One can only wonder, in his position as George Washington's bodyguard, at the amount of times he saved the life of our most famous freedom fighter and first president.

It would be difficult to find another local hero who ever evoked as much respect from his neighbors and fellow soldiers as was evidenced by the mega-funeral held for him in 1838. It was nothing short of awesome. Picture full brigades of hundreds of soldiers, in full battle regalia slowly approaching the Schuyler-Colfax home in canal boats along the Pompton Feeder. Picture soldiers lined up along Hamburg Turnpike for as far as the eye could see mourning the fallen hero. The description of the scene as Colfax's widow looked on, given by William Berce in his 1964 study of early Wayne and its role in the Revolutionary War, *Under the Sign of the Eagle,* says it all.

"On top of his coffin were his favorite pistols (a gift from George Washington) and two swords which crossed each other and were tied with black crepe. His horse--boots and spurs suspended from the empty saddle--was led by a former orderly. The military detachments, weapons reversed, were commingled by officers wearing black bands around their left arms. Drums in the two bands were muffled with black crepe. Hundreds of persons lining the route gazed in silence as the procession passed.

"Through mingled emotions of shock, grief, and confusion, Hester's clouded mind attempted to grasp the significance of this bewildering spectacle. The procession moved with a deliberate, subdued cadence that was keyed to the doleful beat of unbraced drums and the strains of deep-toned instruments. Stretching more than three-quarters of a mile, the column was at once majestic, noble and martial--yet melancholy, pensive, and mournful--leaving the spectators with the feeling of having witnessed a scene of awesome grandeur....On the road ahead were the brightly uniformed-detachments of General Abraham Godwin's brigade, consisting of the General Guards, the Union Cadets, and two large military bands commanded by Captains Conger and Allen."

William Colfax was born in New London, Connecticut on July 3, 1756. He responded to his new country's call before his 19th birthday when he entered the military. Thanks to an enormous amount of gallantry in battle after battle, including the bloody ones at White Plains and Long Island, he quickly rose through the ranks. In 1778 he joined the elite corps of young soldiers assembled to guard and protect the life of George Washington, following several vicious attempts on the general's life. It was made up of between 180 to 250 men of "robust constitution, well-limbered, formed for activity, and men of established character for sobriety and fidelity." Adhering to its motto "Conquer or Die" proudly emblazoned on its gold-fringed battle flag of white silk, the group guar-

anteed that the Father of our Country would not face a premature demise which would have been the death knell for the Revolution.

Colfax continued his ascension and eventually commanded what some have described as the predecessor of the Secret Service. In doing so, he became not only one of Washington's most trusted aides, but best friends. The general became the godfather of one of his children and a frequent visitor to the Schuyler-Colfax homestead.

On one of his earlier visits to the home of another friend, Casparus Schuyler, Washington brought his young, handsome and dashing, six foot tall friend with him. There Colfax and Schuyler's beautiful daughter, Hester, reportedly fell in love at first sight. On August 27, 1783, their marriage forever fused the Schuyler and Colfax family names. (A grandson, appropriately named "Schuyler Colfax," served as Speaker of the House of Representatives and Vice President of the United States under Ulysses S. Grant).

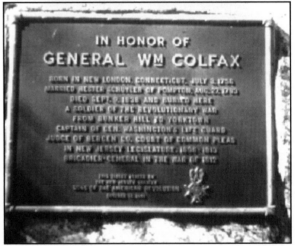

Wayne is not renowned for its statues and monuments, however its most famous war hero, General William Colfax, is remembered by a pylon gravestone (top, r.) and marker (r.) in the small grave yard, north of the Schuyler-Colfax House on the property.

The Washington Life Guard banner (l.) symbolized the special contingent of super soldiers who guarded the great general. Colfax was perhaps Washington's favorite member of the Guard.

Historical Highlight
Freedomtowne, U.S.A.

If Wayne ever elects to give itself a nickname, as so many other American towns and cities have done, perhaps there would be no more appropriate one than "Freedomtowne, U.S.A.". It would certainly be one that was well-earned. Four years into the life of this country, Wayne's strategic location and the loyalty, patriotism and spirit of its area residents played a vital role in our victory in the Revolutionary War. For more than two hundred years the Township has continued to step up in the name of freedom and independence.

The list is long of its contributions to the country's defense. While the Pompton Ironworks, which produced cannon balls during our first war was just across the Ramapo River in what is now Pompton Plains, portions of the complex were in what is today Wayne Township. Many, if not most, of its workers, not to mention its earliest owners, resided here. Both the Revolutionary Highway (U.S. 202) and Cannonball Road passed through here. Its two powderworks played a part in at least one war effort.

The summit of High Mountain is the highest natural point in, and was the place which afforded the greatest panorama of, the New York metropolitan area before the massive skyscrapers on Manhattan were built. It is no wonder that for these reasons it played a part, albeit still classified, in government surveillance operations during wartime.

During World War II, the Voice of America transmitted from its over 600' high tower in the marshlands of western Wayne.

In 1955 Wayne was once again called upon to play a role in our defense of freedom. Two sites in the Township were chosen to house components of a Nike missile system. The first site currently houses the Passaic County Probation Department, and is situated

Sketch from the cover of the Brubaker, Burns and Mahony Bicentennial booklet, "A Wondrously Beautiful Valley," symbolized Wayne's role in America's fight for freedom. That role has been repeated over in many ways.

just east of State Route 23 behind what is now Circle Lumber. Here a missile assembly and test plant was built, underground silos for Nike Ajax missiles and an assortment of barracks for the military personnel who resided on the base.

The second site was on a knoll above the northwest corner of Alps Road and Ratzer Road, virtually across the street from the Paris Inn restaurant. At this site were also a number of barracks, several other buildings, and a special radar tower. The tower provided a direct line of sight to the first site, and from here any missiles that were launched would be controlled and directed to their intended targets.

Contrary to common belief, the missiles were not launch-ready under the ground in a rounded silo. The underground area was primarily one of storage, more vertical than horizontal. If a launch had been ordered, the missiles would have had to have been brought to the surface, by elevator, set up on their own portable launchers and then launched.

These projectiles were far too dangerous to ship fully assembled and armed. As a result they had to be assembled at the lower site in a building that now is used to garage Passaic County equipment. The missiles were 35 feet long and weighed about 2,500 pounds each. They were designed by Bell Labs in nearby Whippany, primarily to shoot down enemy airplanes and incoming rockets. With a limited range of about 25 to 30 miles, at speeds of about 1,700 miles

In the trees across the road from the Paris Inn, and just above the roadway of Alps Road, one of the two old radar towers is visible for those who look up. Thousands pass by this location each day, few seeing the old remnant, much less appreciating its significance.

per hour, they could quickly reach altitudes of over thirteen miles (70,000 feet). Those who witnessed testing were astounded how fast they would disappear from view after launch.

The Ajax was eventually replaced by a more modern, more effective Nike Hercules, and the Wayne sites were closed in 1963. In their heyday, the two sites housed 130 people. Three other sites were also constructed in Riker Hills Art Park in Livingston and on River Road in East Hanover and Randolph, the latter two in Morris County.

The original towers atop Alps Road are still standing. For a time the site was used as a satellite campus for Fairleigh Dickenson University.

This old storage building (l.) was once used to assemble and test Nike Ajax missiles.

The entrance to the Passaic County Probation Department's Wayne location (l.), just behind Circle Lumber on Route 23, still includes the old gate and guard booth.

The missiles were not stored in traditional round silos, but in mine shaft-like underground caverns (r.).

The Township residents have long been ultra patriotic as is evident by the numerous war and military monuments throughout the area. The permanent Vietnam War Memorial (l.) is located in Mountain View just south of the American Legion Hall. In 1991 a temporary Persian Gulf War memorial (below) was erected near the Township offices.

Chapter Fifteen
Wayne Today, and Tomorrow

Just off Black Oak Ridge Road in what has become a typical Wayne neighborhood, waterfowl frolic on a fall afternoon in 1998, in and around an old pond once believed to have served a nursery. Even the Township's residential neighborhoods retain "The Beauty of Wayne."

As the area, known as Wayne for more than 150 years, braces to enter a fifth century of inhabitation, it is a very unique New Jersey community. It bears a resemblance to the fast-paced modern life of Southern California with its megamalls and superhighways. Yet, in many areas it could easily pass for portions of New England. The blend of the old with the new, the busy with the laid-back, and the urban with the suburban and rural give residents and visitors alike a great variety to choose from. Often chaotic State Route 23 runs not more than a football field in length away from one of the most serene and bucolic paradises one could

ever imagine just above the former site of the old Black Oak Ridge Road traffic circle. The land is so low along the Pompton River that flooding remains a problem, yet a few miles to the northeast High Mountain is the highest point in the New York metropolitan area.

For a township that is in so many ways 21st century, there is a remarkable number of 18th, and even a few 17th century remnants still to be found. The ground still holds many Indian arrowheads and tools that are thousands of years old that might not be discovered for many more centuries. In the densest populated state,

only a few miles from the densest populated community (Paterson) within that state, Wayne can boast miles and miles of backwoods' trails and park after park. And while a few of its historic treasures may have been lost to developers without too much of a forethought, there are still a remarkable number of historic structures and sites still relatively well preserved.

Wayne's commitment to its historical past is evident in the fact that unlike most of its neighbors which are lucky to have a small historic society made up of well-meaning, but underfunded volunteers, this Township supports its own Historical Commission.

While modern transportation has shrunk the distance between the various communities within a community that has almost always been a hallmark of Wayne, one still can return home to Pines Lake, Packanack Lake or even old Mountain View and feel quite isolated from the rest of the Township.

What the 21st century holds for Wayne can of course only be the subject of conjecture and speculation. However, no major changes seem in store in the foreseeable future. For decades there have been plans to build a West Belt expressly linking the Willowbrook-Wayne Towne shopping areas and State Roue 23, U.S. 46 and IS 80 interchange with Valley Road and the Preakness Valley. There have been other proposals to do some major engineering work to try to control the sometimes-still-rampaging rivers. Who knows as we leave the 20th century and second millennium A.D. if these plans will come to fruition.

Yet no matter what changes occur in the next century, and beyond, it is likely that Wayne will still remain a Scenic Crossroads.

Sadly, these two scenes of the Red Barn on Valley Road, outside (above) and inside (below) don't belong in this chapter. Had this book been penned only a few months earlier, we could point to the venerable 20th century landmark as a monument to the historic Valley Road farms which dotted the floor of the Preakness Valley. Yet the value of the land to add a few new residences and a few bucks to a developer was more important than the value to the community of having an important visual reminder of bygone days; the Red Barn was unceremoniously bull-dozed in 1997, leaving the Van Peenen farm as just about the last vestige of the agrarian pedigree of the Valley.

Unlike many northern New Jersey communities, Wayne has the look of a "turn of the century" (after 100 years, this term will soon have a new meaning) community. This scene is on Wittig Terrace in Black Oak Estates, one of numerous upscale neighborhoods in the Township.

This scene along David Scott Drive, not far from where congregations have worshiped for two centuries at the Preakness Reformed Church, was caused by what may have been the worst snowstorm to ever hit inhabited Wayne. It was the "Blizzard of 1996."

Virtually anyone who has driven along Fairfield Road in the southwest portion of the Township has encountered a scene similar to this one where the ever-present waterfowl believe they own the road. They certainly don't seem to have any fear of being run over. In all likelihood, a stagecoach driver or two as far back as 200 years ago also was forced to stop his vehicle as the cocky honkers and quackers crossed the road.

Place and Name Word Guide

An informative guide to pronunciations, derivations and alternate spellings of some of the most popular places and things in and around Wayne over the centuries.

Alps Road Once called Prospect Road

Berdan (family, avenue, etc.) Also spelled Baerdan

Berdan Avenue Once called "The Road to the Ponds" (Oakland, Franklin Lakes)

Bloomburg or Bloombury--The official name the Deys called their mansion

Brockholst (family) Also spelled Brockholles

Demarest (family, etc.) Demarist, des Marest

Dey (family and mansion Pronounced Die

Doremus (family, etc.) Also spelled Dooremus, Doormus, De Riemer, Du Remos

Mead Also spelled Meet

Meads Basin Earlier name for Mountain View

Merselis Also spelled Marselis, Merseiles, Mersieles, Mercelis

Minisink Also spelled Meenesink, Minissing means "the water is gone." This Indian term may indicate that they lived here even earlier than the earliest believed date in that the area was covered by Lake Passaic between 12,000-15,000 years ago

Minsi means People of the stone country

New Jersey Named after the English Isle of Jersey. Originally part of New Netherlands. Named Albania by the English. Also Nova Caesarea. Called Scheyichli by the Indians

Packanack Also spelled: Pacquanac, Pachganick, Pachgannick

Passaic Also spelled Pasawack (meaning valley), Passaick, Passawicke, Paassaya, Fishawack

Passaic River Also known as the Pequannoc Creek.

Pequannock Also spelled Pequannoc, Pacquanacs, Pacquannack. Named after an Indian tribe

Pompton Falls Called by Indians Awrigh

Pompton River Alternately called Pequannock River, Pompton Creek

Preakness (valley, horse, breeding stables, etc.) Pronounced Prake-ness. Alternate spellings include: Praquaness, Preaquaness, Perekenos Perikines, Perikeness, Prikenis, Parikenis, Parikenes, Parekenis, Parakenis, Pracaness,, Precaness, Priekenis, Prekniss, Preackness, Prakeness, Preckenis, Peckwas. The Indian spelling is believed to be Praqualess, meaning "quail woods," or Perukunces, meaning "a young buck." Some historians believe that it meant "of the deer."

Riverview Drive Once called Naachpunkt Road

Ryerson (family) Also spelled Reyerson, Reyersze

Singac (Creek, Brook, Region, etc.) Also spelled Sinkaak, Singack, Sinkaak

Terhune Drive (U.S. 202) Also known as The High Road, The Road to Oakland. Part of The Revolutionary Highway

Totowa Means "Heavy falling water" (i.e. The Great or Totowa Falls) or "Place where land (or water) splits"

Two Bridges Once called The Forks

Valley Road Once called Parsonage Road

Van Riper Also spelled Van Ryper, Van Reyper, Van Reypen

Van Saun Also spelled Van Saen

Watchung Means include hill, mountain, high place. Also spelledWachtschu, Wadchu

The Beauty of Wayne

The Township's southwestern gateway is marked by the beauty of Two Bridges (top) and the four large boulders, swept into the Passaic River about 15,000 years ago by the Wisconsin glacier that may have once served as the base for an ancient rope bridge.

This work is and has always been intended to be a history, not an art book. No conscious effort was made to capture the images of the beauty of the Township. With but a few exceptions, the present day photographs displayed throughout the body of this book were taken with an inexpensive camera by the author, the antithesis of a skilled photographer. However, in conducting research for The History of Wayne one could not ignore The Beauty of Wayne. In reviewing the snapshots that were considered for publication to help tell the story of the roots of the Township, the following are the author's personal choices as the best examples of what a truly beautiful place Wayne is.

The serenity of a few head of waterfowl enjoying the Ramapo River (top) just behind the Schuyler-Colfax house, belies the historic past of the same site during most of the 19th century when it was teeming with activity as part of the Pompton Feeder Canal. Below, the George Kuehm farm, in the family since 1894, is one of the last vestiges of Wayne's agrarian past. At harvest time, it is a true picture of quintessential Americana farm life.

The Morris Canal and the Pompton Feeder Canal framed the western and southern portions of the Township for a century. Abandoned and drained by the first quarter of the 20th century, what remains is a bucolic trail where Wayne residents can enjoy the present and fantasize about the BEING IN past. Top photo is along the Feeder Canal path south of Pompton Plains Cross Road. Below the awe-inspiring waterfalls of the feeder dam just above the same cross road is one of Wayne's best kept secret jewels.

Perhaps not as obviously majestic as a sweeping panorama of the fall-colored mountains or the raw beauty of the swan filled rivers and lakes, the Schuyler-Colfax house (top) possesses an inner beauty along with its outward beauty that is hard to match. Factoring in the three century past of this placid historical relic it may be unmatched in charismatic charm. Likewise, the Van Riper-Hopper house and Wayne Museum complex offers both a gorgeous lakefront setting and nostalgic elegance.

Wayne From The Air, 1961

WAYNE
TOWNSHIP, N.J.

12-3-61

Map of Wayne

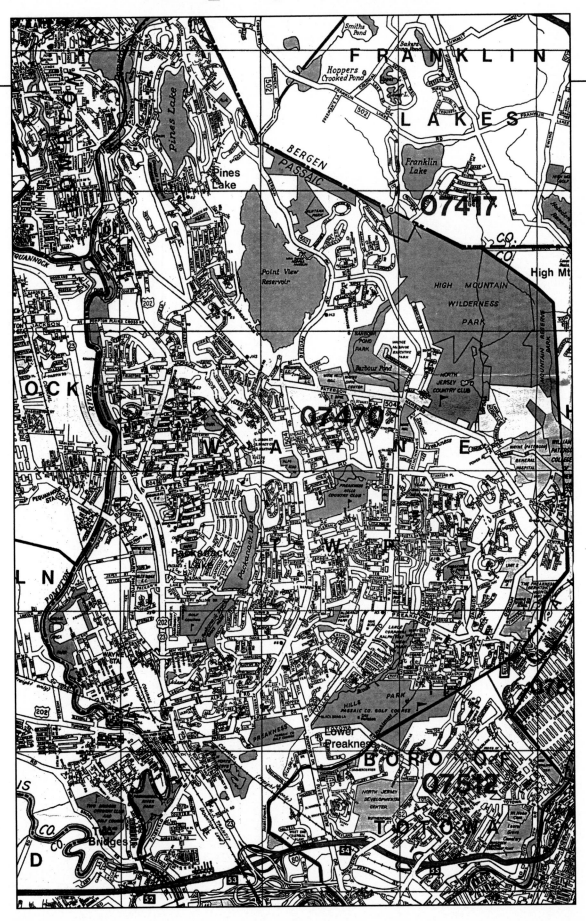

About the Author

Richard K. Cacioppo in 1998 at the site where the Morris Canal and Meads Basin once were located.

Richard K. Cacioppo has never lived nor worked in Wayne (with the one big exception noted here). Yet over the last year he has arguably spent more time in the Township than many actual residents and workers.

Born in Manhattan, raised on Long Island, Cacioppo spent a considerable portion of his adult life in Southern California where he was a criminal trial lawyer. He was the Founder, first President and first Chairman of the Board of the National Italian-American Bar Association. One of his passions early on has been local history. He authored several books on the subject in California, and after moving to New Jersey in 1994, he almost immediately wrote and published *The Glory of Montclair, Past and Present,* only months after becoming a resident of that community. The move from the West Coast followed destruction of his home by the 1994 Northridge earthquake.

In researching his book on Montclair and another on the Montclair Railway, he spent a great deal of time in Wayne exploring the Morris Canal and path of the railroad. Little by little he learned what few knew-- Wayne had a fascinating history--and there had never been a comprehensive book written about it. After deciding to right (write) that wrong, he approached the subject with much the same seriousness and thoroughness he did in preparing for a major trial as a lawyer. Along with working with all the logical local sources, historical societies, libraries, newspapers, etc., he spent time conducting his research at the Library of Congress and National Archives in Washington, D.C., along with the state archives in Trenton. As shown in the Acknowledgements section above, few, if any, stones were left unturned. In fact, he literally turned stones. Cacioppo likes to refer to himself as *The Historical Detective.* What separates his research from that conducted by many other local history authors is that he physically visits every potential site that has even a hint of some historical significance. In researching this book, he probably spent as much time in the woods as he did at the computer and in the scores of research facilities he visited. Every mile of the canals, railroads, new and old highways were covered many times over. Virtually every street in the vast Township was scouted for "remnants of the past." The result is what the author hopes will be a work all readers will find enjoyable and thought-provoking.

Cacioppo has been married for twenty three years to the former Sandra Baci who works as a store decoration and cooking studio consultant and teacher for Kings Supermarkets. The couple have one son, Richard, Jr., a Senior honors student at Regis High School in Manhattan. This past summer, Richard, Jr. served as the Speaker's Page for the Speaker of the U.S. House of Representatives in Washington, D.C.

Supporting Sponsors

The author, publisher and the Wayne Lions Club wish to thank each and every Supporting Sponsor of this publication whose messages and ads are distributed throughout this work. These businesses and local families put their money where their mouths were. Virtually every local business was invited to co-sponsor the book. Only those listed did so, thus they deserve the admiration and appreciation of every reader who enjoys *Scenic Crossroads, The History of Wayne* for years to come. The best way the favor can be returned is for readers to thank those families and patronize those businesses.

A Special Message From The Wayne Day Committee

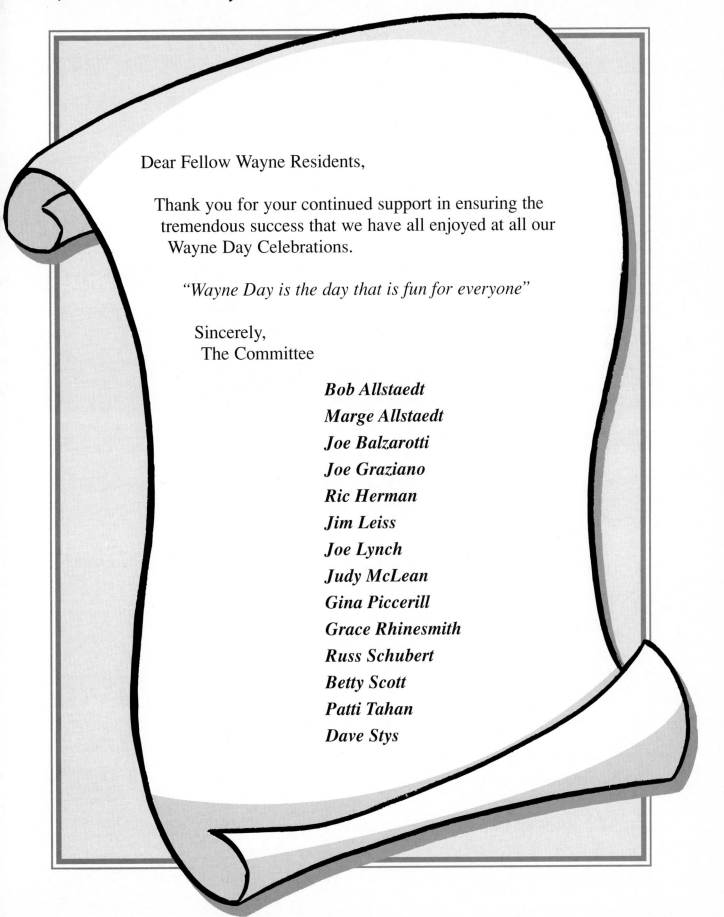

Dear Fellow Wayne Residents,

Thank you for your continued support in ensuring the tremendous success that we have all enjoyed at all our Wayne Day Celebrations.

"Wayne Day is the day that is fun for everyone"

Sincerely,
The Committee

Bob Allstaedt

Marge Allstaedt

Joe Balzarotti

Joe Graziano

Ric Herman

Jim Leiss

Joe Lynch

Judy McLean

Gina Piccerill

Grace Rhinesmith

Russ Schubert

Betty Scott

Patti Tahan

Dave Stys

Chronology
A Timeline of Historic Wayne

300 Million-200 Million B.C. -- Mountains and Valleys formed.

190 Million-136 Million B.C. -- Earthquakes and Volcanic activity creates rich, mineral-filled basin.

13,000 B.C.-- Wisconsin Glacier concludes last Ice Age.

11,000 B.C.-- Glacier melts and recedes forming Lake Passaic.

11,000-8,000 B.C.--Reforestation begins.

10,000 B.C.-- Lake Passaic drains into the Passaic River at Wayne-Little Falls border.

8,000-6,000 B.C.-- The *Original People* first visit area.

1682 A.D. -- Essex County created.

1692 -- Arent Schuyler first visits his *Wondrously Beautiful Valley.*

1695 -- Schuyler-Brockholst syndicate buys land from Indians and is later issued patent from East New Jersey
     Proprietors; Schuyler digs Pines Lake area iron mine.

1696 -- Schuyler begins construction of Schuyler-Colfax house.

1698 -- Schuyler registers as first official settler.

1707 -- Black Oak Ridge Road cut through.

1710 -- Essex County cedes Wayne area to Bergen County, for next 127 area is part of Saddle River Township.

1714 -- Thomas Hart purchases Preakness Valley from Indians.

1726 -- Pompton Ironworks formed.

1736 -- First church built along east bank of Pompton River.

1740 -- Dey Mansion built.

1780 -- American army headquarters at Dey Mansion and encamps in lower Preakness Valley and area.

1783 -- William Colfax marries Hester Schuyler.

1786 -- Van Riper-Hopper house built in Pancake Hollow area.

1798 -- First Preakness Reformed Church built.

1803 -- First stagecoach route passes through.

1806 -- Paterson and Hamburg and Newark and Pompton Turnpikes chartered.

1812 -- Mountain View School built and opens.

1824 -- Morris Canal chartered.

1837 -- Passaic County and Manchester town formed.

1838 -- General William Colfax funeral.

1847 -- Wayne Township incorporated.

1863 -- Steelworks opens at Pompton Falls.

1865 -- Morris & Essex railroad reaches Wayne and builds station at Meads Basin.

1870 -- Turnpike toll gates removed and roads become free public highways;
     Preakness wins first major thoroughbred stakes race at Pimlico Race Track in Baltimore.

1871 -- Meads Basin renamed "Mountain View."

1872 -- Montclair Railroad reaches Wayne and builds station at Mountain View.

1873 -- Laflin & Rand and Renrocks Powderworks open.

1879 -- Mountain View Brick Manufacturing Company becomes first brickyards in Wayne.

1903 -- Great flood on Ramapo River devastates iron/steel works area.

1909 -- Hixon's Mountain View Hotel (now Gabriel's) opens.

1914 -- LeGrand Parish moves to Mountain View.

1919 -- Murchio's Flying Field opens on Hamburg Turnpike and Church Lane.

1924 -- Morris Canal dechartered; main canal and Pompton Feeder drained.

1925 -- Packanack Lake created; Last powder works closes.

1927 -- Pines Lake created.

1936 -- Horrific flood inundates Mountain View.

1942 -- Albert Payson Terhune dies.

1951 -- New Jersey State Teacher's College at Paterson (now William Paterson University) moves to Wayne.

1956 -- Murchio's Flying Field closes.

1964 -- Interstate 80 reaches Wayne.

1966 -- Passenger railroad services above Mountain View permanently suspended.

1969 -- Willowbrook Mall built.

1970 -- Wayne kids win Little League World Series.

1984 -- Lake Passaic virtually recreated in part as Pompton River overflows.

1996 -- Blizzard of '96 covers Wayne with "blanket of white."

Historical Spotter's Guide

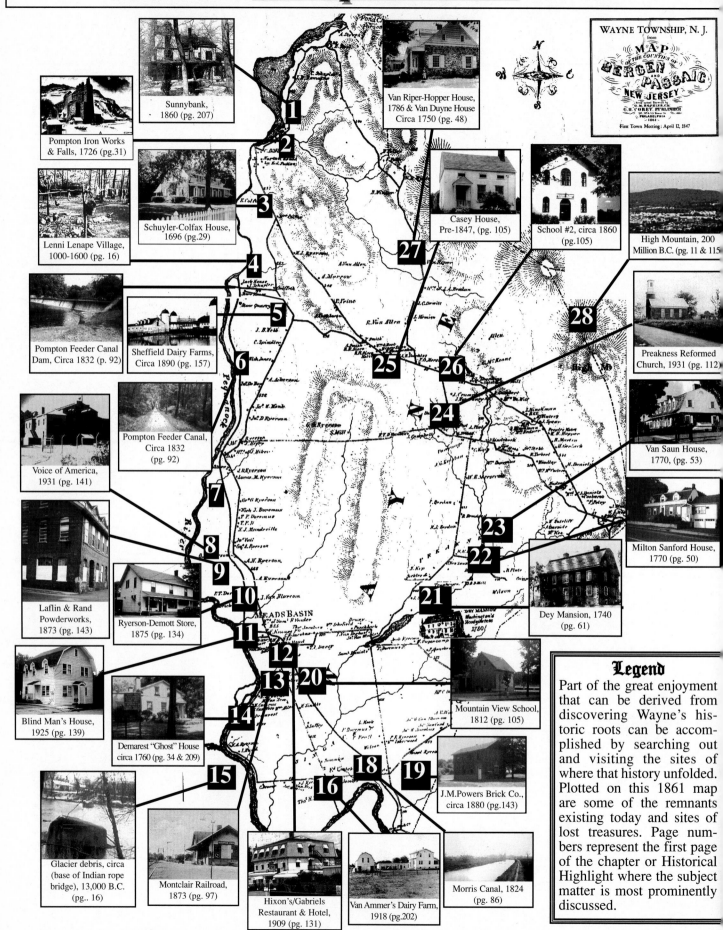

Sunnybank, 1860 (pg. 207)

Van Riper-Hopper House, 1786 & Van Duyne House Circa 1750 (pg. 48)

WAYNE TOWNSHIP, N. J. from MAP OF THE COUNTIES OF BERGEN AND PASSAIC NEW JERSEY
G. H. COREY, PUBLISHER
PHILADELPHIA 1861
First Town Meeting: April 12, 1847

Pompton Iron Works & Falls, 1726 (pg.31)

Lenni Lenape Village, 1000-1600 (pg. 16)

Schuyler-Colfax House, 1696 (pg.29)

Casey House, Pre-1847, (pg. 105)

School #2, circa 1860 (pg.105)

High Mountain, 200 Million B.C. (pg. 11 & 115

Pompton Feeder Canal Dam, Circa 1832 (p. 92)

Sheffield Dairy Farms, Circa 1890 (pg. 157)

Preakness Reformed Church, 1931 (pg. 112)

Voice of America, 1931 (pg. 141)

Pompton Feeder Canal, Circa 1832 (pg. 92)

Van Saun House, 1770, (pg. 53)

Laflin & Rand Powderworks, 1873 (pg. 143)

Ryerson-Demott Store, 1875 (pg. 134)

Milton Sanford House, 1770 (pg. 50)

Dey Mansion, 1740 (pg. 61)

Blind Man's House, 1925 (pg. 139)

Demarest "Ghost" House circa 1760 (pg. 34 & 209)

Mountain View School, 1812 (pg. 105)

Glacier debris, circa (base of Indian rope bridge), 13,000 B.C. (pg.. 16)

Montclair Railroad, 1873 (pg. 97)

J.M.Powers Brick Co., circa 1880 (pg.143)

Hixon's/Gabriels Restaurant & Hotel, 1909 (pg. 131)

Van Ammer's Dairy Farm, 1918 (pg.202)

Morris Canal, 1824 (pg. 86)

Legend

Part of the great enjoyment that can be derived from discovering Wayne's historic roots can be accomplished by searching out and visiting the sites of where that history unfolded. Plotted on this 1861 map are some of the remnants existing today and sites of lost treasures. Page numbers represent the first page of the chapter or Historical Highlight where the subject matter is most prominently discussed.